The Headscarf Controversy

RELIGION AND GLOBAL POLITICS

SERIES EDITOR
John L. Esposito
University Professor and Director
Prince Alwaleed Bin Talal Center for Muslim-Christian Understanding
Georgetown University

The Headscarf Controversy

Secularism and Freedom of Religion

HILAL ELVER

OXFORD
UNIVERSITY PRESS

OXFORD
UNIVERSITY PRESS

Oxford University Press is a department of the University of Oxford.
It furthers the University's objective of excellence in research, scholarship,
and education by publishing worldwide.

Oxford   New York
Auckland   Cape Town   Dar es Salaam   Hong Kong   Karachi
Kuala Lumpur   Madrid   Melbourne   Mexico City   Nairobi
New Delhi   Shanghai   Taipei   Toronto

With offices in
Argentina   Austria   Brazil   Chile   Czech Republic   France   Greece
Guatemala   Hungary   Italy   Japan   Poland   Portugal   Singapore
South Korea   Switzerland   Thailand   Turkey   Ukraine   Vietnam

Oxford is a registered trade mark of Oxford University Press
in the UK and certain other countries.

Published in the United States of America by
Oxford University Press
198 Madison Avenue, New York, NY 10016

© Oxford University Press 2012

First issued as an Oxford University Press paperback, 2014.

Library of Congress Cataloging-in-Publication Data
Elver, Hilal.
The headscarf controversy : secularism and freedom of religion / Hilal Elver.
p. cm.—(Religion and global politics series)
Includes bibliographical references and index.
ISBN 978-0-19-976929-2 (hardcover : alk. paper)—ISBN 978-0-19-977305-3 (ebook : alk. paper)
ISBN 978-0-19-936793-1 (paperback : alk. paper)
1. Hijab (Islamic clothing)   2. Veils—Social aspects.   3. Islam and secularism.   I. Title.   II. Series.
BP190.5.H44E48 2012
297.5'76—dc23
2011023532

1 3 5 7 9 8 6 4 2

Printed in the United States of America
on acid-free paper

To my mother Ayten Elver and my daughter Zeynep Zileli Rabanea,
with much love
affirming your choices

Contents

Acknowledgments

This book is a product of longtime firsthand observation of the headscarf debate in my personal and professional life in Turkey and abroad. For a long time, I was hesitant to write a scholarly book about the headscarf controversy as I thought wearing a headscarf would soon be normalized and disappear as a public concern. I was wrong. Not only has the headscarf controversy in Turkey persisted, in recent years the issue has generated a global debate and the headscarf is increasingly treated in parts of the West as an unwelcome symbol of Islam.

I have childhood memories of my mother's headscarf excluding her from taking part in official events in Turkey. Then during 1990s I witnessed female students being expelled from the University of Ankara Faculty of Law for wearing headscarves. In my American life I now encounter the frequent preoccupation of Muslims studying in North American universities as to whether they should take off their headscarves or, conversely, start to wear them. It is an enigma that Muslim women should be challenged in this manner early in the twenty-first century.

During the process of thinking about, researching, and writing this book I received many valuable ideas from friends and colleagues. Many of my secular friends in Turkey shared their thoughts on why headscarves should not be allowed in higher-education institutions and, even if they are allowed in Turkish universities in the future, they should still be banned in middle schools and high schools, as well as in government offices. Among many, I would single out my dear friends Ceylan Orhon, Gila Benmayor, Oren Altmisyedioglu, Turgut Tarhanli, and Gulen Guler; and my colleagues and close friends at the University of Ankara, Faculty of Law, Gulnihal Bozkurt and Bilgin Tiryakioglu. All shared their wisdom, knowledge, and profound experiences, which particularly provided me with an understanding of first-hand participants in the headscarf debate.

I am most grateful to my devout Muslim friends for opening their homes and hearths, sharing their feelings, and providing their side of the argument without any signs of bitterness associated with their own victimization. They exhibited their limitless resolve to rescue future generations, especially their daughters, from exclusions in the pursuit of professional careers that they had endured. My dear friend Dr. Sare Davutoglu helped me to access a circle of talented women. These scholars, writers, activists, and mothers included Ayla Kerimoglu, Nazife Sisman, and Yildiz Ramazanoglu. All of these women, through their own publications and institutional affiliations, work tirelessly to be heard and understood. Through Ayla Kerimoglu, I got to know several engaged Muslim women by attending meetings organized under the auspices of the Hazar Foundation. I also have learned from the younger generation of Turkish women who are still in the process of completing their graduate studies, some while wearing their headscarves, others not. My two cousins Ayse Tek Basaran and Seda Tek are examples, as are several daughters of my friends, Meymune Davutoglu, Sefure Ozokur, and Esra Albayrak. These dynamic young people helped me to understand the difficulties amid their hopes for the future, and also their privileged positions that many headscarf wearers do not have. Turkish publications were also very useful in conveying this range of experiences relating to the headscarf controversy.

Besides my personal experiences, this book is also a deferred outcome of the UCLA Law School doctorate of Juridicial Science program where some years ago I discovered critical race theory and became familiar with the American legal system. Professor Devon Carbado's and Professor Cheryl Harris's lectures were eye opening for me as to the ways in which racial discrimination in the United States was affected by court decisions and the legal system. I benefited from the study of critical race theory in the course of my efforts to conceptualize discrimination against headscarf wearers through the interpretation of court decisions in various countries. I am also very fortunate to have had Howard Winant as a friend and mentor on matters of race and the relationship between racial and religious discrimination. I consider Howie to be among the most influential and respected scholars conceptualizing critical race theory in the United States.

Professor Richard Abel of UCLA Law School was the main supporter of this project at the very early stage. He was always very generous with his time and comments, and his belief in me. I was privileged to receive comments from renowned constitutional law professor Kenneth L. Karst. I learned from him that the American legal system's approach to the freedom of religion is more complex than we might imagine and it is very fluid, reflecting changing political winds. Professor Stephen Gardbaum's comparative constitutional law scholarship was very helpful to me as I interpreted principles of freedom of religion and secularism in various countries. I shared many of experiences and developed ideas by discussing current developments about Turkish politics with my friend and honorary sister Asli Bali, from UCLA Law School.

Finally, the Global and International Studies Program at University of California, Santa Barbara (UCSB), provided a great place to work, teach, and explore issues close to my heart, including those discussed in this book. Formal and informal discussions in Global Studies with Giles Gunn, Mark Juergensmeyer, Eve Darian Smith, Rich Appelbaum, Esther Lezra and Paul Amar were invaluable, especially in reminding to view the headscarf debate in its global setting. This group's knowledge of secularism, human rights, and global politics helped orient my inquiry. The courses that I taught gave me a deeper understanding of Islam's cultural presence in American academia. My students from diverse backgrounds presented a positive model of American multiculturalism and of respect for the dignity of others. I am grateful to the Global Studies department at Santa Barbara for this positive and enjoyable experience.

My close friends at UCSB have also been very helpful throughout the process of writing. Winddance France Twine's colorful personality and feminist ideology, and Lisa Hajjar's generous friendship encouraged me to work on women's human rights, and gave me confidence in the value of what I was doing. I also was invited to contribute short pieces about Turkish politics to the Middle East Research Project by Lisa and the chief editor, Chris Toensing. I am particularly grateful to my dear friend Avery Gordon, who knows almost as much as I do about this subject matter, and what its message should be. Avery's critical points and careful reading of the manuscript from its earliest stage proved to be absolutely vital. She was a tough critic, but always in a supportive spirit. I would not have been able to develop the book as it is without her inspiration and assistance.

Throughout the process several people helped me to transform an unruly manuscript into a publishable book. First of all, I am indebted to Professor John Esposito for bringing the manuscript to the attention of Oxford University Press, and having it included in a series under his direction. Cynthia Read was the major force during the entire review process, helping me to shape the manuscript. Finally, at the very last stage, Julie Goodman worked with me as a professional editor with great skill and insight. I also would like to express my appreciation to Abdullah Yavuz Altun, opinion page editor of the Zaman daily newspaper, who assisted me in finding pictures for the cover of the book.

I consider myself very lucky to find a second home in Santa Barbara after I left my city of Istanbul. Santa Barbara is home for me because of my dear friends with whom I can share my frustration, despair, and disappointments along with my happiness and pleasures. I thank you my dear friends Debbie Rogow, Victoria Riskin, David Rintels, Ann Jaqua, David Griffin, Nora Gallagher, Vincent Stanley, Imaging and Gerry Spence, Carolee and David Krieger, Elisabeth and Mark Saatjian, and Karen Shapiro for listening to me and encouraging me, and more importantly, helping me to see that this book might be a small step toward better cross cultural understanding. Each has made a unique and invaluable contribution to my life.

Finally, I am grateful to my family. Emotionally and physically my two brothers Haluk and Aydin Elver and my niece Deniz Elver Dalton were always with me when I needed help. My late father would have been the happiest person in the world if he had lived to see this book. My mother and my daughter Zeynep, to whom I dedicate this book, are the two most important women in my life. They have shaped the person I am in very different ways. The three of us are now living on different continents, with different lives, and with different preoccupations. Yet love connects us continuously. My mother dedicated her life to her children and let go of her professional life. A true believer of her faith, she taught me how important it is to be an independent and to pursue a professional life. I am grateful to her for accepting her children and grandchildren for ourselves and respecting our life decisions without questioning. She believes that religious devotion is a private matter with no single path being the only right one.

Last, but not least, I want to acknowledge my husband Richard Falk. He is a true believer in the freedom of Muslim women who wear headscarves and strongly criticizes hypocritical implementations of human rights principles by courts and by governments. His tireless criticism of the established order, and his gracious sympathy for the aggrieved and the dispossessed have inspired and encouraged me to see controversial realities from the perspective of others. It's hard to imagine how I could have written this book without him challenging me to think beyond my limits, without his unwavering support for me and for the issue, and without his example. More importantly, his unconditional love is a precious gift for life. I thank him with all my heart.

Despite all help that I received, I am sure that I have overlooked some important issues and made some mistakes. All in all, my intention is to provide an entry point for readers who are interested in this issue and to encourage them to learn more about it.

Montreal
October 2011

The Headscarf Controversy

I

Introduction

Out beyond ideas of wrongdoing and rightdoing, there
is a field. I will meet you there.

JALAL AD-DIN RUMI

Religious pluralism is one of the essential principles of constitutional
democracies. Yet the ways in which Western democracies deal with Islamic
practices raise a variety of issues that appear to erode religious pluralism. In
recent years, there have been major public debates in several European countries about the acceptability of Islamic practices; specifically, the wearing of a
headscarf, or *hijab*, by women and girls.

In the midst of a resurgence of religion, the challenge to accommodate
Muslim practices seems greater and more urgent than ever before. It pervades
virtually every aspect of modern life, from culture to civil society, from politics to identity, from security to conflict and discrimination. These issues are
now being discussed with particular intensity in the United States, Europe,
and almost all liberal societies.

The emphasis is on determining how to accept, accommodate, and tolerate Muslim religious observances in countries where secularism (or in
France and Turkey *laïcité*) and civil liberties are held to be as important as
religious freedom. Devout Muslim women are subjected to serious restrictions, including the exclusion of some rights, not only in Western countries,
where Islam is a minority religion, but also in Muslim countries, particularly in Turkey, and to a lesser extent in Azerbaijan, Tunisia, and Albania.
In this book, legal, political, and social aspects of the headscarf controversy in constitutional democracies will be discussed from a comparative
perspective.

Upholding freedom of religion or belief involves the complex task of protecting religion and its impact on public and private life, while establishing certain restrictions to avoid religion's potential for negative impact. Such balancing necessarily bridges the universal and the particular, the public and the private, and explores the relationship between secularism and religiosity. Any adequate implementation of the freedom of religion or belief needs to consider these polarities. Added to these challenges is the safeguarding of freedom of religion in the context of gender claims and Islamic political culture. Therefore, the articulation of this specific problem in relation to Muslim women needs to address highly complex arguments about the supposed incompatibility between women's rights and Islam.

Following the 9/11 attacks on the United States, the stereotyping of Islamic societies became widespread, and the fear of political Islam became a preoccupying concern in mainstream, and especially right-wing, American and European public opinion. Discussions about whether the liberal Western democratic model is compatible with Muslim societies and whether such societies are inadequate with respect to women's rights gained much attention.[1] The significant differences among Islamic societies regarding democracy, human rights, and the rule of law are well known. Moreover, many Islamic countries in one way or another follow the principles of *Sharia*, the laws of Islam, in their legal systems and do not incorporate the Western version of secularism in their constitutions. Whether the principles of Sharia law and Islam are compatible with universally accepted principles of human rights, with secularism, and with Western-style democracy, is a highly complex question whose answer requires sophisticated theological knowledge about Islam, its relation to various cultures, and the character of Islamic thought ranging from fundamentalist to moderate and/or reformist. The evaluation of Islam vis-à-vis democracy, secularism, and human rights lies beyond the scope of this book, other than when societal and/or cultural Islam is at stake.

In this book, the position of women in Islam and the issues of Islam and democracy will not be discussed, except when these issues relate directly to the headscarf controversy. Instead, religion and law will be crosscutting themes and will provide the framework for a comparative approach to secularism and human rights in the headscarf controversy as it is manifested in several constitutional democracies. The core disagreement in the headscarf battle occupies the contested terrain of secularism and freedom of religion. At first glance, secularism and human rights seem to be the compatible and necessary elements of constitutional democracies. Nevertheless, it is never easy to balance the concepts of secularism and human rights, especially religious freedom and freedom of speech, without sacrificing one to the other. In the headscarf controversy, where these concepts travel cross-culturally, it is not surprising that contradictory results are encountered. This book does not claim to answer this fundamental question of our time; rather, it intends more modestly to offer analytical case studies of this complex phenomenon. Whenever basic legal principles encroach on social and cultural values and try to change or impose them, success and failure may be highly volatile and subject to divergent interpretations, and results may vary dramatically in different settings.

There are a wide range of policy outcomes and various degrees of tolerance toward and/or discrimination against Muslim women because of disparate domestic political settings, cultural differences, and diverse constitutional orders in assorted countries. We need to articulate these differences and similarities among countries when discussing freedom of religion in relation to the integrity of a constitutional order. They are also relevant when evaluating the extent of the country's commitment to religious diversity and international human rights principles. In examining headscarf controversies in many countries, I have come to the conclusion that the uneasy relationship between religiosity and modernity has unintended adverse consequences for Muslim women. These include forms of social and legal segregation in modern societies that are responsible for serious human rights abuses. Domestic constitutional order and international human rights remedies are not being adequately implemented to protect Muslim women who wear headscarves from the abuses they experience in many countries. There are several reasons for this failure to implement universal standards to protect Muslim women's right to manifest their religious identity, including a lack of sufficient understanding, tolerance, and acceptance; the interpretation or misinterpretation of religious and cultural motives; and the overwhelming forces of political resentment and hostility. To protect the rights at stake, it is important to diagnose the problems accurately and act effectively before tensions on both sides produce a chronic disorder that can produce profound societal tension. This is what happened, unfortunately, in Turkey.

In this book, I analyze current headscarf debates from different angles—secularism, human rights, Islamophobia, gender and religious discrimination, and legal issues—to identify policy failures and show how such failures produced outcries from both sides of these debates.

Secularism

When religious symbols are at stake, secularism is one of the most important concepts to explore. An important consequence of enlightenment and modernization in Western societies, secularism has somewhat different meanings and consequences depending on the differing history, culture, politics, and religion of specific countries. As seen in Turkey, France, and other European countries, the banning of headscarves assumes a different form depending on how the principle of secularism is interpreted and on whether Islam is a minority or majority religion.[2] An evaluation of various systems and legal principles reinforces the view that each country has its own understandings of concepts such as secularism, freedom of religion, religious practices, the relationship between church and state, and, finally, the limits on each country's ability to produce differing balances between secularism and religious freedom.[3]

I will predominantly consider Turkey, and to some extent France, as the leading examples of *laïcité*: a strict implementation of secularism. These countries are major battlegrounds in the headscarf controversy. Turkey is a unique example from the perspective of secularism and religiosity because it is a country in which the overwhelming majority of the population adheres to what I call "societal Islam" despite the fact that its existing constitutional structure is "strictly secular."[4] Although Turkey has been governed by a socially conservative political party since 2002, the strictly secular (or, more precisely, laic) structure of the Turkish state, as embedded in institutions such as the judiciary, military, and bureaucracy, has managed to prevent all efforts to alter this laic order. The most recent phase of the headscarf controversy in Turkey is illustrative of the extreme conflict that can arise between a religion-friendly elected government and a religion-unfriendly bureaucracy. Tensions over the headscarf ban in Turkish universities have been so intense as to bring the country to the brink of political collapse on several occasions.

The political and historical backgrounds of France and Turkey suggest some parallel developments. Both countries' court decisions on the headscarf ban are preoccupied with interpretation and implementation of laïcité and the incompatibility between modern life and Islamic practices in general and the headscarf specifically. Yet, the religious sensibility of the two societies, with respect to the impact of Islam on Turkey and Catholicism on France on legal issues and social lives is very different. While Turkey had been using the shield of secularism to reject devout Muslim women, France first was reluctant to rely on the laïcité principle as its main justification for imposing the headscarf ban, at least until the *Stasi Report* encouraged reliance on laïcité for banning religious symbols. More important, in France, the recent headscarf controversy involving Muslim immigrants has led to a public discussion of the principle of laïcité that extends beyond Islam.[5] Careful evaluation of these social and legal responses to the headscarf controversy in both countries leads me to conclude that the current headscarf deadlock in Turkey should be considered as a power struggle between new and old political elites, rather than, as often presented, as a challenge to strict secularism. In contrast, the same controversy in France is better understood as a breakdown of multiculturalism, which manifests itself as intolerance toward "others,"[6] instead of as an effort to implement laïcité.

Therefore, secularism should not be used as an excuse to punish expressions of religious belief and observance, especially if these manifestations of religiosity are the basis for the denial of further human rights to individuals. On the contrary, secularism should be implemented and interpreted as a principle that supports the exercise of religious freedom in order to protect other, related human rights, such as the rights to education and gender equality.

Human Rights

This argument leads to the second major focus of the book: an evaluation of principles of international human rights in relation to freedom of religion. At the normative level, it has been clear from the beginning of the modern human rights era that freedom of religion or belief is a fundamental right, and indeed a preeminent one, being categorized as nonderogable.[7] But despite well-established norms and a strong argument in favor of treating these universal principles as part of customary international law, violations are common. One question is whether freedom of religion can or should be limited in order to protect religious minorities or nonreligious members of society in democratic states. In recent years an opposite tendency has been observed toward members of certain religions. It is a known phenomenon that religion is prone to manipulation in the political sphere, leading to widespread stereotyping of certain religiously observant groups. For instance, the actuality of Islamophobia and anti-Semitism as well as antiterrorism measures and national security laws have been used to suppress, not protect, religious minorities in the West.[8] Core values protected under the banner of freedom of religion or belief allow different states to choose from a broad range of policy options. However, a core set of universal values must constitute the minimum requirements for a democratic society that upholds freedom of religion and belief, and should be protected in all circumstances. With human rights in mind, I will critically evaluate the implementation of freedom of religion in international and domestic courts in relation to a range of headscarf controversies.

Racialization of Islam and Islamophobia

The third angle of interpretation considers headscarf issues from the perspective of racial and religious discrimination. The headscarf controversy in the West is one of the elements that eventually gave rise to the racialization of Muslims, by way of the construction of "Muslim women's identity." In addition to the significant influence of long historical experience and the current version of Orientalism in Europe and the United States, the 9/11 terrorist attacks disclosed how liberal constitutionalism and religious freedom could be quickly eroded in an inflamed political climate of fear and anger that fueled intense opposition to political Islam. "Islam" has been used as a common denominator to establish a new de facto racial category. Critical race theorists and legal scholars generally agree that, in the United States, the 9/11 terrorist attacks facilitated the consolidation of a new identity category applicable to persons who appear "Middle Eastern, Arab or Muslim." This emergent category relies on religious identification as a racial signifier.[9] The resurgence of political Islam on the global level and Islam's association with several prominent terror incidents erect further obstacles to a vigorous protection of Muslim women's rights. There is no clearer sign for a woman to be identified as Muslim than the wearing of a headscarf, and Muslim women who wear headscarves are victimized because of its being an undeniable symbol of Islam. Since 9/11, the general public in the United States and Europe has engaged in racial profiling, which has produced incidents of violence, including individuals attacking women wearing headscarves.[10] Judicial cases provide strong evidence that emerging Islamophobia in the West and elsewhere negatively affects Muslim women's daily lives, education, and participation in working environments.[11] Therefore, instead of the protection of religious freedom, the reverse protection—protection from a woman's religion—receives more attention and sympathy. Especially in the West, this reverse side is justified as the protection of women from the coercive and abusive aspects of Islam, rather than protection of those who are devoted to Islam. This stereotyping of Islam, and more specifically women's questionable and complex position in relation to Islam, is one of the major reasons that international human rights principles have generally failed to protect pious women.

Contrary to general belief, Islamophobia is not only experienced in non-Muslim countries. We are also witnessing types of Islamophobia arising in

Muslim secular societies including Turkey, Tunisia, Albania, Azerbaijan, and other Central Asian societies. The Turkish secular establishment, including the military, judiciary, and specifically the Turkish Constitutional Court, exhibits significant discriminatory attitudes toward Muslim women. Observant Muslim women are regarded as a symbol of backwardness, and religiosity is seen as an antimodern institution that interferes with Turkish efforts to endorse modernization and to become part of Western civilization. Court decisions and political maneuvers also offer us provocative instances of self-Orientalism.

Gender Discrimination

The headscarf controversy is strongly gendered in several respects. For instance, in Turkey, while strict secularism, in principle, rejects any religious activity or manifestation in public spaces, in fact, women are the sole victims of such rules. Despite the seeming gender equality of Turkish legal language, in practice action is seldom taken against religiously devout men. Religiously devout Muslim men are not excluded from educational institutions or public employment. While there is an opportunity for Muslim men to "pass" as secular, religiously devout Muslim women are unable to do so without sacrificing their religious beliefs and departing from prescribed religious tradition.

Unfortunately, this dynamic of discrimination is also present among many Western-oriented feminists. In Turkey and France, the headscarf ban was supported because the wearing of a headscarf was seen as an important symbol of male domination and suppression of Muslim girls. Some feminists ask these girls: "Why do you not want to be liberated?" It is well documented that the majority of Western-oriented feminists do not approve of what is going on in the Islamic world but also lack much understanding of the position of women in these societies. They criticize the subordination of women in the Islamic world in matters that range from female genital mutilation to domestic violence and honor killing. All of these issues certainly deserve serious attention, but need to be approached in a more sensitive manner that realizes such objectionable practices are often more connected with local culture and entrenched patriarchy than with religion.

An unintended consequence of these modern expressions of feminism was to give birth to a Muslim feminist movement. Muslim women organizations in Turkey and Europe have played and continue to play an important role in bringing the headscarf controversy to the public arena and making Muslim women's voices and faces authentically heard and seen on both national and international levels. Nevertheless, despite this effort by Muslim feminists to call attention to these concerns, the agency of Muslim women is significantly constrained. Muslim feminists and headscarf wearers in Europe and elsewhere are merely invited to take part in public debate on these issues. This is one of the failures of the overall contemporary feminist movement.

Legal Front

The headscarf controversy has become a major legal battleground in courtrooms around the world. Several prominent cases illustrate the extension of the headscarf controversy from the domestic level to the supranational level via the European Court of Human Rights (ECHR). One of the most salient cases is the 2005 decision by the ECHR's Grand Chamber that upheld the Turkish headscarf ban in universities;[12] a prime example of the way a seemingly domestic headscarf debate became a transnational issue through judicial action. As a result of a comprehensive evaluation of various court decisions, I argue that national and supranational courts have been adversely influenced by the internal politics of the judicial venues, by international political events, and by their own rigid adherence to a "strict interpretation" of the principle of secularism. The consequences have been several unfortunate judicial failures to uphold freedom of religion. An additional undesirable effect has been to deny women who wear headscarves access to public spaces and protection under the equality principle.

Based on the evaluation and interpretation of several domestic and international judicial decisions, I conclude that in cases related to social and cultural controversies, the role of judges as interpreters of human rights principles and constitutional order is crucial. An ongoing debate exists concerning the extent to which the judiciary is either legitimate or competent to play such a role, especially in the current European setting and in Turkey.[13] Many influential human rights scholars have criticized the ECHR's general jurisprudence on religious freedom and belief as "incoherent and inconsistent."[14] Although many scholars consider the 2005 decision of the ECHR against Turkey upholding the headscarf ban to be a benchmark case, this ruling seems even more problematic than the court's earlier judgments that had been criticized widely, among other reasons, because of the ECHR's reliance in reaching its decision on a dubious application of the "margin of appreciation." Aside from legal inconsistencies, the court's attitude on these specific headscarf cases is indicative of a range of related considerations: the image of Turkey and Islam as it currently exists in European public opinion, the ongoing controversy surrounding Turkey's application for membership in the European Union, and, more importantly, the threat of Islamic terror in Europe. It is my contention that these judicially unacknowledged factors have had a significant impact on headscarf ban decisions.

Finally, the actualities in each case of headscarf banning discussed in this book are different. For example, some cases concern kindergarten or elementary schoolteachers, others are about university students or high school students. Yet, despite these significant differences, a consistent discursive pattern of repetition is evident, which emerges when stating the legal argument against the headscarf. Consistency across cases and boundaries is considered a form of legal networking in Europe and elsewhere, connecting outcomes in domestic and supranational courts. This network of anti-headscarf decisions has a long lasting and extended negative transboundary impact upon Muslim women's rights in various settings. It is possible that in the future this impact will reach beyond the limits of Europe and beyond the confines of public schools. Such an atmosphere might lead to a ban on headscarf use in public spaces and elsewhere. This has already happened in Turkey. The Turkish Constitutional Court has led the way on this particular issue, having exerted a remarkable influence on the European legal environment in a manner that has rarely, if ever, occurred previously.

* * *

This book is divided into two parts offering analytical perspectives on the headscarf controversy in Turkey and the West. Part 1 is devoted to the Turkish experience, which has a longer history and deeper, more complex meanings. I begin with a discussion, in chapter 2, of the modern headscarf debate from the 1980s to the present and its political ramifications in Turkey, including the power struggle between secular and religious political parties; the roles of the military and the judiciary; an emerging Turkish elite sympathetic to the wearing of headscarves, and its societal and political confrontation with the secular establishment.

Chapter 3 explores the historical roots of the current political crises associated with the headscarf controversy, focusing on the transformation of the Ottoman Empire into the Turkish Republic in the early twentieth century and the accompanying legal, cultural, and political reforms that changed Turkish society. A critical evaluation of the Turkish modernity project examines its stigmatization of part of Turkish society while privileging the other as modern, as well as the connection between the modernization project and the current headscarf controversy. An important consequence of the modernization project was to create a strong, secular country through the deliberate abandonment of Turkey's Islamic past. Finally, the chapter offers an analysis of the historical, political, and legal background of the principle of secularism that provides the fundamental rationale for prohibiting headscarf use in Turkey and of the secularization process in the West as a natural continuation of the Turkish experience. Chapter 4 carries the headscarf controversy from national to supranational courts, presenting the major decisions of the European Court of Human Rights on headscarf bans.

Part 2 offers a global perspective, as the headscarf controversy became one of the hotly debated issues in Europe and the United States. Chapter 5 discusses the general anti-Islamic discourse that emerged in a post-9/11 political atmosphere that stressed security concerns in relation to political Islam. This process of moving from multiculturalism toward Islamophobia, by way of the mainstream media, has fueled a huge outcry against "problematic" Muslim veiling practices, from headscarves to the *burqa*.

Chapters 6, 7, and 8 examine legal developments in three countries touched by the headscarf controversy and their social and political backgrounds in relation to Islam: France, Germany, and the United States. The three offer different insights. Among them, only France has a general statute that addresses the display of religious signs. Before the enactment of the French law, the headscarf controversy was subject to adjudication as early as the 1990s. The German experience has to date received much less attention than the French, yet the consequences of a landmark decision by the German Constitutional Court is likely to have a much greater impact on headscarf-wearing teachers and civil servants in Germany; the French restriction is limited to high school students.

Chapter 8 evaluates freedom of religion and its restriction in the U.S. legal system, using a hypothetical headscarf case. The headscarf controversy in the United States has not yet reached the higher courts, and political debate on this issue is not as pivotal as in Europe. So far, and increasingly, the American debate focuses on opposition to mosques and community centers, without much public attention to the propriety of the headscarf. Relevant cases on other aspects of religious dress and on the freedom of religious expression provide hints to the likely outcome of future decisions in U.S. courts concerning Muslim practices. However, emerging Islamophopia and the racialization of Islam are reaching alarming proportions in the United States that, in the future, are likely to have a negative impact on the acceptability of headscarf use in general.

The concluding chapter 9 presents a comparative overview of the outcomes of the political and social arguments and court decisions in relation to wearing the headscarf. Several issues emerge. First, the headscarf controversy extends beyond an individual's freedom of religion. It reveals the sociopolitical consequences of being "other," of belonging to a minority population in Europe and in the United States. In Turkey, the debate is embedded in its distinctive history and the struggle between a strictly secular bureaucracy and legal system and an essentially religious society and its elected representatives. Keeping the country secular is compatible with the authoritarian features of the Turkish nation-state in the twentieth century. But society and culture are constantly changing phenomena, and the headscarf controversy is also evolving and creating new meanings. Moreover, the continuing development of Turkish democracy, partly as a result of the process of its accession to the European Union, is leading to greater tolerance of differences and heterogeneous elements of society than was the case just a decade ago.

The headscarf debate is strongly gendered. This aspect of the broader controversy is often obscured. The acute discrimination suffered by women who choose to wear a headscarf has not as yet produced much concern in liberal democracies. Unfortunately, international law in general and international human right courts in particular have failed to protect the individual rights of Muslim women, causing grief to many of them. This book attempts a thorough interpretation of the tensions between headscarf bans and the rights of religiously devoted Muslim women, trying its best to present both sides fairly.

PART ONE

Turkey

2

The Nature of the Headscarf Controversy in Turkey

POPULAR DISCOURSE

> We humans have more potential for hatred when the
> object of our hatred is part of our own identity.
>
> ANDRES STADLER, May 2009[1]

Turkey is the only country where students who wear headscarves are not
allowed to attend universities. The headscarf debate has broad implications
for Turkey, dating back to the Islamic Ottoman Empire, when the state
heavily regulated the clothing of citizens as a sign of ethnic and professional
identity. In Turkey, clothing has always been a political tool that expresses
power relations and has important social, economic, and legal consequences.
The new post–Ottoman Turkish Republic inherited this preoccupation as
it transformed itself into a nation-state with a secular "Kemalist" ideology,
named after Kemal Ataturk, the inspirational founder of the modern Turkish
state. Ataturk's reforms in the 1920s represented a historically unique and significant attempt to make Turkey modern, European, and Western as quickly
as possible. Moreover, before, during, and after the transformation period
women became a barometer of modernity. In this sense, women became more
important than men as a representation of the state and society. This importance became a visible obligation for women as soon as the Turkish state
declared itself to be a Western-oriented modern, secular society.

The historical background is an important part of understanding the
Turkish state and its relation to the complex, current headscarf controversy.
The battle over the headscarf, unfolding over the course of almost a half
century, provides a symbolic battleground and illustrative case for assessing

modernity, secularism, religious freedom, and the struggles over political power, democracy, gender, equality, and women's identity in Turkish society.

1. Tolerance for the Headscarf Diminishes to Zero

Although the regulation of citizens' clothing goes back to the Ottoman period in Turkey, no major problem was associated with the wearing of headscarves until the 1980s. During the transformation of the Ottoman Empire into a modern state—the secular Turkish Republic, established in 1923—women of the urban elite were encouraged not to wear headscarves in public spaces, but there was no regulatory ban. Beginning in the 1950s, due to Turkey's essential commitment to its modernization project, participation by women in public life increased, as did the number of female students enrolled in universities, but only a few students wore the headscarf. The first important headscarf case, in 1967, involved the expulsion of a student in the University of Ankara's School of Theology. At the time, this case was considered an isolated incident.

In the 1980s, following the Iranian Revolution, political Islam gained influence in the Middle East, and Turkey experienced a growing, transnational Islamic movement. Religion joined the competing ideologies that mobilized Turkish citizens in the latter stages of the Cold War era. During this period, the social and economic conditions in the country triggered internal and external migration from villages and small Anatolian towns to urban centers. Combined with the surging transnational Islamic movement, the presence of these newly urban students wearing traditional, modest Anatolian dress, which included the headscarf for females, made their style of dress a visible symbol of adherence to the Islamic movement. The Turkish woman quickly became a symbol and a victim of an image war between Islamists and secularists that centered on the issue of the headscarf. Worse was yet to come.

Universities Become the Focus of Political Unrest

In the 1980s, the Turkish political environment was heavily affected by Cold War ideological clashes. Social and political unrest was widespread, and universities became the loci of struggle for various ideological groups. Violent demonstrations and clashes were part of daily life on campus. In response to the violent conflicts between right-wing and left-wing student organizations, the military overthrew the democratically elected government on September 12, 1980. The motive of the coup was to eliminate communist ideology from the universities and other organizations in civil society, to limit civil rights, and to establish a public order in which the military would exert control over future civilian governments. It was a dark moment in Turkish political history.

Although it was not Turkey's first military coup, it had a longer lasting, more damaging impact on Turkish politics than earlier military interventions. The transitional military government adopted the problematic Turkish constitution of 1982 in this atmosphere. One enduring institutional innovation was the establishment of a central administrative body, the Higher Education Council (known in Turkish by the acronym YOK) to control universities, academically and administratively. In this capacity, YOK took charge of headscarf policy, issuing a confusing series of inconsistent administrative decrees. The military is traditionally the most secular institution in Turkey, operating as the self-proclaimed guardian of Kemalist ideology, and in its efforts to satisfy the Cold War anticommunist mentality, it became difficult for the new rulers to allow any Muslim presence in the universities. But Muslim students, especially females, were not considered nearly as much of a threat to the Turkish state as left-wing student organizations, and universities were very relaxed about women wearing headscarves. The new government's early plan was to loosen regulations in universities but to institute a dress code and ban the headscarf in elementary, middle, and high schools, and for civil servants.[2]

A new word "turban" was invented that allowed university students to wear headscarves, based on the delusion that the headscarf was a fashion rather than an objectionable political or religious symbol. But by the 1990s, the word "turban" had lost its neutral meaning and became a negative buzzword, signifying political Islam to the secularists as increasing numbers of female university students chose to cover their heads. At the same time, the word "headscarf" became a less provocative signifier of the traditional head covering that is worn by more than 60 percent of Turkish women.[3] This distinction gradually gained ideological meaning in the headscarf battle. In the debate between Islamists and secularists, each side used their preferred word. The term "turban" is used by seculars, while the term "headscarf" is used by the religion friendly to validate headscarf use as a religious duty. Thus, the terminology of "turban" versus "headscarf" has important ideological implications.

The Pendulum Swings

In the second half of the 1980s, as the numbers of headscarf-wearing students at universities increased, there was uncertainty about the status of wearing a headscarf. It was neither legally banned nor was it socially accepted. The government was rather reluctant to issue a law banning headscarf use in universities, worried that this would create a political backlash and influence electoral outcomes. The judiciary, with no fear of political gain or loss, was secular and opposed the wearing of headscarves, and court decisions increasingly challenged headscarf use. In this atmosphere, the government issued several inconsistent regulations. The policy pendulum swung back and forth, either to allow the wearing of headscarves or to ban it in universities. In 1988, when the leader of the 1982 coup and former military chief of staff, Kenan Evren, was president of the first civilian government, the new Parliament adopted a permissive legal formulation.[4] The law declared that "it is acceptable to cover the head and neck because of religious belief." Notoriously, the secular Constitutional Court took advantage of the sloppy language and annulled the statute.[5] The decision of the Constitutional Court argued that the principle of secularism has a unique history in Turkey. In such a secular state, the legislative body cannot introduce a legal measure that takes into account openly religious convictions.[6] The decision was more political than legal. The Constitutional Court emphasized the primacy of the principle of secularism in relation to other democratic principles in the constitution and made no effort to protect the right of freedom of religion or the right to an education for the individual who wears a headscarf. Rather, the Court strongly emphasized protecting students who did not wear the headscarf from experiencing social pressure to adopt it. As the first comprehensive decision by the Constitutional Court against headscarf use, it became an important legal precedent for future cases in Turkey and, eventually, abroad.[7]

But in 1989 the Turkish Parliament passed a new, more carefully drafted law in favor of the headscarf. Avoiding any religious connotations, it stated that "dress is not subject to any prohibition in higher education, provided that it is not forbidden by law."[8] When the secular political parties immediately appealed to the Constitutional Court, the Court refused to take the case, interpreting the statute from a secularist perspective: "Freedom of clothing cannot include the wearing of a headscarf."[9] Since then no new law has been issued in favor or against the headscarf by the Turkish Parliament.

The Guardians of Secularism

From 1989 until 1998, more and more university students wearing headscarves took advantage of their legal status as religion-friendly political parties gained power. But gradually increasing social and political pressure from the secular establishment strengthened the opposition to the emerging political power of the religious party and headscarf use. Finally, on February 28, 1997, the military, in its role as self-appointed guardian of secularism, declared in its website that the founder of the Welfare Party (*Refah*), one of the two coalition partners of the government, and statements by Deputy Prime Minister Necmettin Erbakan threatened secularism. One catalyst of this "electronic ultimatum" was the announced intention of Erbakan and his political allies to enact a law in support of the wearing of headscarves in universities. The military chief of staff demanded Erbakan's resignation, and, despite the military's lack of formal authority over the democratically elected civilian government, the ultimatum, a so-called post-modern coup, was enough to dismantle the government.[10] Unlike the military coups in 1960 and 1980, in 1997 the military was able to interfere in the political process without physically taking over the government.

The February 28 ultimatum opened a new page in the headscarf controversy in Turkey. The National Security Council organized meetings to brief universities and judiciaries about the alleged approaching danger of religious fundamentalism. It was claimed that one visible sign of this danger was headscarf use in universities and public institutions. The military urged the Turkish leadership to take headscarf use seriously. Turkey was losing its "modern outlook" due to rising headscarf use, and therefore strict implementation of a ban should begin as soon as possible.[11]

In 1998, the Constitutional Court reviewed the constitutionality of the Welfare Party and abolished it. The party's support of the freedom to wear a headscarf was among the reasons for the ban.[12] Ironically, the decision concluded that, although there was no specific law against it, the wearing of a turban was unconstitutional. Following the decision, the military held high-level meetings with university presidents and judges to urge a headscarf ban, the YOK issued a declaration and universities started to implement the headscarf ban. The declaration also prohibited male students from having beards, but after many complaints, universities stopped enforcing the ban. The strange conclusion seemed that only women posed a danger to the secular state.

Turning to Politicized Courts

Headscarf-wearing students appealed to Turkey's administrative courts, claiming that there was no law banning the headscarf in universities beyond the university presidents' administrative order. Local courts initially deemed this argument to be legally persuasive, declaring that an administrative declaration is insufficient reason to expel students from universities. The university administration appealed to the Higher Administrative Court, which ruled that the presidents' declaration was binding and obligatory, and that students wearing headscarves should not be allowed on campuses: "The aim of universities must be to educate people to respect the ideology of modernity and to respect national values; therefore the declaration should be considered lawful."[13]

After the February 28 ultimatum, continual interference in judicial institutions seriously damaged the integrity of the Turkish judiciary. Judges were pressured to rule against headscarf-wearing students, briefed about the danger of the fundamentalist Islamic movement, or removed from their posts and assigned to remote outposts if they did not uphold the ban.

In 1999 Merve Kavakci, a newly elected member of the Turkish Parliament from Virtue, the new party that replaced the banned Welfare Party, forced a confrontation when she tried to enter Parliament wearing a headscarf. At the time, no specific law banned the wearing of a headscarf in Parliament. Members of opposition parties accused her of mounting a political attack on secularism and Turkish democracy. The incident received international media attention and triggered a move to abolish the Virtue Party by recourse to the Constitutional Court. Again, the Turkish justice system relied on highly creative legalistic innovations to reach their intended political results. Kavakci lost her Turkish citizenship due to a technical violation of the Turkish Citizenship Law and left the country. The headscarf became a political and legal tool used by the Constitutional Court to expel two democratically elected Islamic parties, and the impact on headscarf-wearing women has been lasting. The message was clear: such women cannot be elected to Parliament unless they are willing to give up wearing a headscarf.

During the last decade the number of students wearing headscarves continued to increase in universities. The legal ambiguity and difficulty of implementing such rules left the decision whether to allow students to wear headscarves to the discretion of each university administration, and some were more tolerant than others. Students and administrators both tried to find creative solutions. While many students made use of various loopholes, others decided to abandon their educations. In the 2000s, more than one hundred thousand students, one thousand civil servants, and three hundred primary and secondary school teachers were forced to leave their positions because the Turkish government implemented the ban—a policy proclaimed as "zero tolerance for the headscarf."[14] The minister of education declared: "This is a crime, the punishment is dismissal from the civil service. Everybody must comply with this rule. If they don't, they have no place among us."[15]

Appeals to the European Human Rights Commission and the ECHR

In the early 1990s, the headscarf dispute reached the European Human Rights Commission. In 1993, two female students applied to the commission as a last resort, claiming violations of the right to an education and of the equality principle by a Turkish university that had refused to grant diplomas to female students who wore headscarves. The commission ruled that the case was not admissible, deferring to the 1989 decision of the Turkish Constitutional Court, which held that a secular state has the right to restrict religious practices if doing so is consistent with a citizen's right to equal treatment and religious freedom. The commission failed to deal correctly with existing laws and political complexity, and, more important, ignored the gender implications of the headscarf ban. There was no consideration given in the decision about the unequal treatment of male and female students.[16] The outcome was a disappointment for both the few liberal feminists and the many headscarf wearers in Turkey. The more ideological secular Turkish courts clearly were not giving any mercy to headscarf wearers. In contrast, it had been hoped that the commission, a supranational human rights actor, should have offered a venue to protect such rights against abusive government policies. But it did not. The decision, however, was consistent with the commission's earlier, less-known decisions relating to the headscarf controversy in Turkey.[17]

When a full-time European Court of Human Rights (ECHR) superseded the European Commission of Human Rights, many victims of the headscarf ban sought relief from the new court, including the wife of Abdullah Gul, the current Turkish president. But the ECHR has been consistent in affirming Turkish judicial decisions on headscarf cases and even rejected the Welfare Party's challenge to the Turkish Constitutional Court's decision to shut the party down. The Virtue Party, also dismantled a few years later by the Constitutional Court, discouraged by the earlier decision of the Court, withdrew its similar application to the ECHR. The ECHR's first and most influential headscarf decision, delivered in 2005 by its Grand Chamber, was *Leyla Sahin v. Turkey,* in which the court ruled that the obstruction of medical school student Leyla Sahin's education because of the headscarf ban in Turkish universities was a permissible restriction in a democratic society.[18] The court's basic argument was that the headscarf ban at Turkish universities does not necessarily violate freedom of religion; such a ban was regarded as legally acceptable given the prevailing conditions associated with secularism in Turkey. The decision came as a surprise to many liberal legal scholars and human rights organizations in Turkey, Europe, and the United States, but it was celebrated in Turkish secular circles as a final victory in the legal debate.

These developments convinced much of the Turkish public that the European court, ECHR, was biased against Islamic values and that it had acted politically. In many other cases, however, especially on minority rights and due-process principles, the EHRC has adopted strong positions in favor of the protection of human rights and ruled against the Turkish government. This suggests that when Islamic values are on the agenda, otherwise universally held values and understandings of justice will be suspended. Fear, suspicion, and prejudice take over and appear to shape the judicial process. The ECHR did not hesitate to acknowledge concerns about Islamic extremism, although no evidence existed that Ms. Sahin belonged to any political movement,[19] and the court accepted her contention that she wore a headscarf only because of her religious beliefs.

2. A Changing Political Climate

In the 2002 election, an important development altered the Turkish political scene. For the first time in Turkey's republican history, a religious-friendly, self-proclaimed conservative democrat party, the Justice and Development Party (the AKP), won the election and became the sole governing party.[20] At first, AKP followers held the legitimate expectation that the headscarf ban would be lifted at universities. But, ignoring the strong demand and expectation of its own constituency, the government was careful not to challenge the headscarf ban before the wider political and social climate seemed supportive, despite the fact that strong support by women voters was one reason for the AKP's landslide victory. To their constituency's disappointment, and to the surprise of the secular opposition, the leadership of the party did not make any special effort to end the headscarf ban in universities during its first five years in power. Experience had taught the founders of the AKP to be very cautious about taking initiatives that were sure to be opposed by strictly secular and military forces and by the Constitutional Court. They feared that the military would intervene or the Constitutional Court would try to close down the party for its allegedly antisecular activity, as had happened in the cases of the Islamic-oriented Welfare and Virtue parties.

The Headscarf of Mrs. Gul

In April 2007, just before the general election for the Turkish Parliament, the presidential election took place in an atmosphere of legal and political chaos that brought Turkey to a dangerous impasse. According to the Turkish constitution, the prime minister presents his or her presidential candidate to Parliament for a vote. When the prime minister chose then Foreign Minister Abdullah Gul, a devout Muslim, as his candidate, it immediately caused a national furor. The military used threatening language against the government, insisting that any action that might jeopardize Turkey's secular outlook—a slightly disguised reference to Mr. Gul's wife wearing a headscarf—would not be tolerated. They contended that it was unacceptable for the Turkish state to be represented by a leader whose "first lady has a headscarf." It may seem surprising to outsiders that the opposition to Abdullah Gul's presidency focused on Mrs. Gul's headscarf instead of on his own personality, credentials, capabilities, and religiosity. Day after day, pictures of Mrs. Gul wearing a headscarf were published in the leading secular newspapers. Some fashion designers even suggested a "fashionable headscarf" for her. The debate centered on the official image of Turkey and the representation of Turkish society. The attacks on the proposed nomination of Mr. Gul focused on a single question: how dare the first lady of Turkey wear a headscarf, a symbol of Islam? Or more crudely, how dare someone supporting this purported symbol of backwardness be allowed to enter the Cankaya (the Presidential Palace)?

Turkish citizens, including those who considered themselves to be apolitical, took sides in this sharply polarized debate. They either defended the freedom to wear a headscarf or insisted on maintaining the ban, leaving almost no political space for compromise between the two camps. Street demonstrations, meetings, TV advertisements, art exhibitions, and dance and music performances were organized by secularists to demonstrate how Turkish women would be suppressed, imprisoned, and victimized if the headscarf ban were lifted. They ardently claimed that the headscarf ban in universities sought only to protect secularism, one of the most important founding principles of the Republic of Turkey, with no ulterior purpose. Secularists believe and fear that the freedom to wear a headscarf in the universities will be the first step backward, inevitably leading to the downfall of secular Turkey and a return to Ottoman times. More bluntly, condescending secular Turks privately claim that they have no problem with their grandmothers' headscarves nor with those of the peasant women from Anatolia who do the urban elite's housework, but they cannot accept a first lady wearing a headscarf. Underlying the intensity of the opposition was the fear of losing political power; the uneasiness of the so-called "White Turks" of the urban, secular elites centers on the unwelcome prospect of sharing public space with an emerging Anatolian middle class that is moving into their business and political spheres of influence.

Secular newspapers bluntly supported the idea that Turkey was becoming an Islamic state, similar to Malaysia or Iran.

Agitation by the Secular Media

The secular sectors of Turkish society had been influenced by media images of headscarf-wearing women coupled with dire political scenarios depicting Turkey's future as an Islamic state. These portrayals were accompanied by the rise of strong anti-American sentiments and the increasing popularity of various conspiratorial theories. Anti-AKP columnists claimed that the government was seeking to change the concept of secularism in Turkey, which is modeled after French *laïcité*, and to replace it with religion-friendly American secularism, which, they argued, would be very dangerous for Turkey. Indeed, the secular Turkish media's representation of women with headscarves is not very different from Europe's xenophobic caricatures. Depicting Muslim women as subject to polygamy, four women with headscarves are often pictured walking silently behind one husband. Women with headscarves are drawn as pigs—an animal considered unacceptable in Muslim culture. Ironically, the same media did not hesitate to harshly criticize the famous Danish cartoons that satirized the prophet Muhammad. These media sometimes justify the invasion of Afghanistan as a civilizing mission, claiming that Afghan girls in headscarves will be able to attend school following the American intervention—overlooking the irony that girls wearing headscarves cannot go to school in Turkey! These paradoxes show that the headscarf has become the subject of contradictory narratives of human rights in Turkey and internationally.

As the headscarf controversy turned bitter in 2007, the secular media relentlessly published pictures of wives—of ministers, of the newly elected president of the Constitutional Court, and of high-level civil servants—with covered heads. Secular newspapers and TV channels (owned and run by a single family in Turkey) continuously attacked the new government and published stories about the wives of the AKP leaders. It was rather difficult to explain why wives of the president, the prime minister, and other ministers, with their glamorous headscarves, were seen to dominate the official scene, while Turkey's headscarf-wearing university students, often simple, apolitical young women and girls, were not allowed to enter educational institutions and public buildings.[21] The media stirred intense agitation in the political environment, where some insisted that without a solution to the headscarf controversy there would be no restful future for Turkey. The main opposition, Republican People's Party

(CHP), which traditionally claims to represent the legacy of Ataturk, failed to offer legitimate, responsible criticism of AKP policies and governmental leadership. Instead of creating healthy and constructive opposition, the CHP focused all of its political energy on the headscarves of the wives.

Women's organizations also played an enormous role in the anti-AKP campaign. In many urban centers, in the spring of 2007, acting in solidarity with the opposition CHP and the military leadership, huge public demonstrations were organized called "Republic Protests" in support of the Kemalist ideal of state secularism, said to be threatened by the AKP program.[22]

In contrast, for the first time in modern Turkish history, socially conservative, religiously devout Turks have become politically powerful, visible, and, perhaps most significantly, economically formidable. They are raising their voices, demanding to be equal participants in the public arena of their own society, yet they remained largely silent in the face of the secular demonstrations, careful not to behave in a way that might have a significant negative impact.[23]

In the end, the political-legal struggle, between the AKP on one side and the secularists, opposition party, military and judicial elite on the other, seemed to help the AKP in the elections of July 2007. In one of the most decisive victories of any party in the history of the multiparty system in Turkey, the AKP, with the success of its new image and EU-friendly policies, solidified its hold on power, receiving 47 percent of the overall vote and adding significantly to its numbers in Parliament.

3. The Headscarf as Political Suicide

When the AKP began its second term in the summer of 2007, one of its first undertakings was to keep its election campaign promise to the Turkish citizenry to work for the long-overdue adoption of a "civilian constitution." The country's present, problematic constitution, promulgated in 1982 by the military following its displacement of a democratically elected government, contains many limitations on human rights and has been a major stumbling block in Turkey's prolonged accession talks with the European Union. Since taking control of Parliament in 2002, the AKP has made greater strides toward meeting the EU's "Copenhagen criteria" for accession talks than any of its secular predecessors. The constitution had been amended several times, yet it contains major deficiencies, especially in relation to minority rights and freedom of expression and speech. It seemed a rare and happy moment in Turkish politics when a democratically elected government embarked on the project of a human rights friendly, non-militaristic constitution for the country.

However, as soon as a draft of the document was prepared by a group of constitutional law scholars, furious criticism of the whole undertaking dominated the political atmosphere. New formulations concerning secularism, freedom of religion, religious education, and a permissive dress code for university students prompted the secular establishment to articulate their fear that the AKP intended to curtail secularism, beginning the process with the lifting of the headscarf ban. A focus of the opposition was the fear that the AKP government's "hidden agenda" was to "Islamize" Turkey and loosen the strict secularism established by Kemal Ataturk.[24] In reality, the proposed new constitution was a moderately liberal document, following closely the principles of the European Human Rights Convention, to which Turkey has been a party since 1954. Despite the importance of other elements of the reform package, the headscarf controversy brought the whole civilian constitution project to a standstill, and public debate was preempted. Long-anticipated reforms in the proposed constitution, now on indefinite hold, were crucial matters such as comprehensive cultural rights for Kurdish citizens and a more robust concept of freedom of speech. These vital concerns, as well as important shortcomings in the draft document, went almost unnoticed, drowned out by the secularist obsession with covered female heads.

So why has this outcry taken place? Is Turkish society not ready for genuine liberal democracy, greater freedom, and civilian democratic governance? Is secularism more important than achieving a liberal civilian constitution? Why are so many Turkish citizens ready to sacrifice freedoms and the principles of liberal democracy to maintain a strict, Kemalist version of secularism? More important, why should one part of Turkish society object so forcefully to the wearing of headscarves when the majority of Turkish women wear them? Since the founding of the Turkish state, Turkish governments have always controlled religious affairs, promoting a particular version of Sunni Islam (the Hanefi school), while ignoring other Islamic traditions.[25] Would the AKP choose to weaken governmental power over religious institutions and provoke a distracting controversy just for the sake of headscarf freedom? Deeply puzzling to outsiders, these questions can only be answered by gaining an understanding of Turkish historical, political, and cultural conditions, which in many respects are *sui generis*.

Wearfare and Lawfare

Successful efforts by opposition forces put an end to drafting a new constitution, to the profound disappointment of headscarf-wearing students and their families. In this environment, the second opposition National Action Party (MHP, a far-right nationalist party, announced its willingness to join the governing AKP in amending the constitution to lift the headscarf ban from universities as an incentive for enacting a new constitution.[26] Together, the two parties commanded a supermajority in Parliament. The government prepared a constitutional amendment, but the hasty initiative was not properly articulated, and neither side was happy with it. Instead of solving the ongoing problem, the constitutional amendment created a huge outcry and much confusion in the politically diverse universities, where a few administrators implemented it. The president of the YOK declared that headscarf-wearing students should now be allowed on campus.[27] Most academic administrators refused, however, expecting that the Constitutional Court would soon strike the amendment down, as had happened to numerous similar laws since the 1980s.

Turkey has been waging "lawfare" for a long time, appealing to the Constitutional Court and the administrative courts and recycling the endless headscarf arguments.[28] Opponents of the headscarf have historically relied on the courts to invalidate periodic efforts to lift the ban. Following the introduction of the constitutional amendment, both sides waged "lawfare" with unprecedented vigor, bombarding not just the Constitutional Court but also a host of lower courts, bringing claims and counterclaims in administrative and penal courts. Unsurprisingly, the secular opposition party CHP was unwilling to accede to the 411–103 parliamentary vote in favor of the amendment and appealed to the Constitutional Court to annul it.[29] Despite the clear constitutional limitations to the Court's authority to review constitutional amendments, the Constitutional Court accepted the case for review.

The Battle Heats Up

While everyone was waiting for the outcome of the constitutional amendment, an unexpected development happened in March 2008. The chief prosecutor of Turkey, a staunch secular Kemalist, filed suit against the AKP, asking the Constitutional Court to take the extreme measures of closing down the AKP and banning Prime Minister Erdogan and his top sixty-nine colleagues, including President Abdullah Gul, from politics because of their "anti-secular activities." The Court agreed to hear the case. Turkey is familiar with military coups, having witnessed no less than four during the republican period that led, on one occasion, to the executions of a deposed prime minister and hundreds of imprisoned politicians, and the torture of thousands of intellectuals and activists. But this time, according to a Turkish journalist, "the bureaucratic legal empire in Ankara attacks representatives of the people with court decisions, not armed battalions."[30] Many commentators in Turkey treated the Court's decision to hear the case as amounting to a "judicial coup," which would take place without the army's direct involvement and would attempt to depose a party that recently had been reelected by a significant margin.

Like military coups, closures of political parties are common in Turkey. Following each closure, new parties come into being under new names, comprised of the same politicians, with the exception of leaders who have been banned from politics. Nevertheless, the prosecutorial initiative was an unexpected attack on the governing party that placed the fate of the AKP and the newly elected government, as well as the future of Turkish democracy, in an unstable, suspended state. While waiting for a decision that would not be delivered soon enough, the Turkish economy declined, the EU accession talks were adversely affected, and progressive tendencies in Turkey were stymied because of the lawfare campaign against headscarves.

In the meantime, the Constitutional Court quickly issued an injunction, not backed by any reasoning, concluding that the headscarf amendment was unconstitutional and should not be implemented by educational institutions. Overshadowed by the issue of closure of the AKP, the judicial action did not receive significant attention from the public. In July the Court handed down its historic decision. By the narrowest of margins, the AKP escaped closure but received a substantial monetary fine because leading party members were held to have made "anti-laic" statements.[31]

The decision was interpreted by many, including the international media, as a very serious warning to the AKP that threatened its future viability by keeping it on a short leash.[32] Despite the legal authority of the Constitutional Court, both the injunction and the final decision remain controversial. While the party closure case was technically within the proper scope of the Court's authority, the Court seemed to go beyond its jurisdictional authority in its decision about the constitutional amendment on the headscarf ban. And, in this latest case, the Constitutional Court articulated its jurisprudence carefully: to close all doors to future legislative attempts to amend the constitution as a prelude to lifting the headscarf ban and even to prevent the Parliament from enacting a new constitution in the future.[33] The Court reflected the fear that the AKP-dominated Parliament would eventually transform the structure, spirit, and language of the constitution and erode the secularism principle so carefully embedded in it.[34] An unelected institution, the Court implicitly designated itself as the sole arbiter of its own authority.

The Turkish experience may be the perfect example of antidemocratic judicial activism, and, as such, a contribution to the literature of constitutional law. It seems no exaggeration to interpret the Constitutional Court's decision as depriving the democratically elected legislative body in Turkey of its essential lawmaking authority.

The Explosive Ergenekon Affair

Turkey's internal politics were shaken again in 2009 by the discovery of a failed attempt to topple the government through a planned series of clandestine operations by the secular elites and the military establishment. The Turkish political scene had long been subject to the invisible control of antidemocratic forces, the so-called deep state that has its roots in the Ottoman period. In the republican period, military leaders have exerted enormous influence on and power over democratically elected Turkish governments and have not hesitated to interfere in the democratic process while claiming to protect the secular Turkish Republic and the principles of Kemalism against internal danger. After the AKP became a governing power, this clandestine network named itself *Ergenekon* and tried to provoke domestic chaos by planning assassinations of public figures and by bombing public places, thus paving the way for a military coup to defeat the government's alleged plot to transform Turkey into an Islamic state.

The case has brought into relief the larger strains in Turkey between a secular elite seeking to hold onto its waning influence and a growing, increasingly assertive population of observant Muslims. Hundreds of retired high-ranking generals, professors, lawyers, and journalists were accused by prosecutors of planning criminal activities against the state. These activities were by no means a novelty in recent Turkish political life, but what *was* new was the government's attempt to make the powerful secular coalition accountable to Turkey's criminal justice system. This legal process has become one of the most explosive in the nation's history, exposing shadowy activities and political secrets to public scrutiny.

Some secularists question whether the government is exaggerating the Ergenekon threat in order to wage a larger battle against the secular establishment and eliminate the opposition. They claim that the Ergenekon investigation is being used as a dragnet to sweep up suspects from across civic society and to cleanse Turkey of its major secular opponents. Proponents of the investigation argue that the trial is a long-overdue historical reckoning aimed at bringing the "deep state" to account by targeting the operatives of a murky, military-linked coalition dedicated since the Cold War to acting against the perceived enemies of the state—enemies originally identified as the Marxist left and more recently as a supposed Islamic adversary. Because of the vast amount of evidence and numerous allegations to be considered, the Ergenekon case is not likely to be resolved soon. Whatever the outcome, the judicial system is polarized by the AKP-secular conflict and contentions of bias will be sure to cloud the meaning of the results.

4. Forgotten Women

For almost four decades, two generations of religiously devout women lost educational and professional opportunities because of this ongoing power struggle. Only one life path was open to them: go home, get married, become a mother, and stay there quietly! The first generation of women expelled from universities are now grandmothers. These women were not allowed to hold positions in public offices, and women lawyers were not allowed to represent their clients before courts, facing great difficulties even to gain access to court buildings. In some instances, women defendants or litigants were asked to remove their headscarves if they sought to testify before a court.[35]

The political and social struggle that stems from the headscarf controversy has polarized, and even divided Turkish society. Although seculars generally reject the idea that intolerance exists in Turkey against conservative religious Turks. But it is easy to find tension between the two groups in schools, work-places, neighborhoods, and sometimes even in the same family among close relatives. This wall of tension between the two groups makes it almost impossible to initiate a useful dialogue. Occasional gestures are made but not in a spirit of rapprochement. In some instances, even if a dialogue starts, it goes nowhere. While seculars feel enormous fear, devout Muslims suffer the actual consequences of a strict secular regime. Young, headscarf-wearing female students, especially, are not only often socially humiliated, but also, in fact, are excluded from many places. They often cannot attend schools and cannot enter "public spaces," while no clear definition exists to distinguish between public and private places.

The Headscarf and the Status of Women in Turkey

Legitimate concerns among seculars have focused on the fear of undermining the rights of women and gender equality that had been achieved as a result of the Ataturk reforms and were based on secularism and its propensity to free society from the influence of Islam. In reality, the headscarf controversy has been cleverly used to stand in for all of the social and economic problems of Turkish women, creating the misleading impression that wearing the headscarf is the only issue of concern regarding the condition of women in Turkey. But in a recent international study on the status of women, Turkey ranked an embarrassing 105 out of 115 countries around the world.[36]

Improved access to education in rural regions and the removal of institutional and social barriers to women's participation in the workplace are of paramount importance to improving societal attitudes toward women. These substantial issues do not make it into the headlines of the secular media, nor do they find a place in the agenda of most feminist organizations. However, secular Turkish feminists regularly and publicly emphasize their concerns about the peer pressure brought to bear on women who do not wear headscarves when surrounded by the majority of women who do.[37]

Enforcing the Headscarf Ban

University administrations created infamous "persuasion rooms" used to convince students to remove their headscarves. The female students are told that Islam does not require a headscarf, that a modern lifestyle is better for them, that they just should throw their headscarves away in order to become part of the modern society that the state created for them.[38] Even more dramatically, security forces have expelled headscarved students from classrooms by force.

Rather than treat the wearing of a headscarf as a human right, state authorities regarded it as a security matter. Women who defied the ban were accused of civil disobedience and subjected to the use of force by the police. Headscarved university students were isolated and separated from the rest of the student body. During times of strict implementation of the headscarf ban, enforced by security forces, not only universities but also the *Imam Hatip* religious high schools were obliged to uphold the headscarf ban. [39] The state, using school administrations, disciplined the girls as if they were terrorists, using persuasion rooms, police barricades, and punishments. The judicial system was used against headscarf wearers, whose action was alleged to breach the public order by rejecting "a desirable identity fitting to state ideology."[40]

The inconsistent enforcement of the headscarf ban resulted in some female students eventually graduating from universities, but it sometimes took more than twenty years of resistance.[41] A few organizations sympathetic to their struggle have publicized the personal experiences of women who have been expelled from public institutions or subjected to discrimination in their schools or workplaces. The individual life stories provide a deep understanding of the impact on Turkish women, families, and society of this seemingly simple headscarf ban,[42] but seculars often disparage their testimonies as biased or exaggerated.

Secularized Public Spaces

Apart from the obvious human rights abuses taking place in institutions of higher education, the headscarf ban has been unjustly advocated and promoted using the concept of "public space," a phrase that does not derive from legal terminology.[43] Ironically, the concept of public space, developed by Jurgen Habermas, actually favors inclusion. In his view, state and public space are not overlapping concepts, and public space does not include state authority and economy.[44] In Turkey, this concept has been used and abused to exclude Muslim women, through defining almost all places as "public" and regarding all public space as shaped and determined by state authority and ideology. For a long time, the distinction between the private and public sphere was subject to furious discussion because of controversy over the nature of secularism. The concept of excluding religion from public spaces became integrated into the implementation of Turkish secularism. As it turned out, excluding Islam from public spaces in Turkey was "mission impossible," but it was possible, at least, to deny women with headscarves access to public spaces and thereby project an image of the secular Turkish state as Western and modern. One irony is that Muslim women believe that a headscarf must be worn only in public spaces and not in the private sphere, such as in her own home or when socializing with close relatives.

Many strange things have happened in Turkey that may be amusing to outsiders but are heartbreaking for those victimized. While many administrators have claimed the power to regulate public space in order to exclude women with headscarves, without any legitimate foundation, the real danger was introducing this exclusionary concept into the judicial arena. For instance, the Supreme Administrative Court (Danistay) affirmed a decision by a lower court denying entry into a public library to citizens who wear the headscarf, reasoning that if it were allowed, the Constitutional Court and other high courts would find it difficult to apply a consistent jurisprudence to regulating headscarf use in public spaces.[45]

There are endless examples of the exclusion of headscarved women from military buildings, public libraries, universities, and hospitals, including mothers celebrating their children's graduations or military ceremonies. But most women who wear headscarves testify that they use the headscarf only in public spaces to protect themselves from the unwanted gaze of others. If these places are not open to them, they find themselves completely imprisoned at home.

The headscarf ban in the public sector influences the private sector, posing a tremendous obstacle for women seeking job opportunities. Despite there being no ban on headscarf use in the private sector, women wearing headscarves face a variety of difficulties and discriminations in the job market, where positions are limited at best.[46] If they are employed, headscarf-wearing women work for unfairly low wages. In traditional Turkish families, a desirable job for a girl is to become a teacher. Because the headscarf ban was generally implemented in the educational sector, many women with a middle-class, small-town, traditional family background lost their means of livelihood. Only a few brave women were able to pursue careers as "independent intellectuals," carrying a flag of resistance to the next generation to continue the struggle against the headscarf ban.[47]

Because the headscarf ban is applied in an inconsistent manner at different times and in different forms, it is very difficult to assess its scope or verify the number of women who have been discriminated against. This pattern of inconsistent implementation has created uncertainty among headscarf users as to their degree of vulnerability in the secular section of society. It also makes it difficult for these women to form coherent political resistance. On the one hand, inconsistent authoritarian practices and tactics can be interpreted as "total war" against the headscarf; on the other hand, seculars viewed the inconsistencies as nothing more than a political game, problematic from time to time, but protecting society from Islamic tendencies in the long run. Unfortunately, even the ECHR has interpreted the ban this way.

Roadblocks to Reversing the Ban

The Turkish judicial establishment intimidates women who wear headscarves because it operates in such a dogmatically secular fashion and refuses to hear hundreds of headscarf cases. As a result, there are not as many court cases as one would expect. On the few occasions when a lower court makes a concession to headscarf wearers, the deciding judges are likely to be demoted and exiled to a remote district. Some judges have even been prosecuted because their wives wore headscarves. These incidents raise serious questions about the independence and legitimacy of the Turkish justice system.[48] According to a 2007 survey, 63.9 percent of women had lost their confidence in state institutions and 60.6 percent had lost their confidence in the judicial system.[49] This attitude among religious women poses a potential threat to politicians. The government should carefully consider how to resolve this lack of confidence among many of its citizens.

Further, it is not possible to document reliably the full extent of rights violations due to the ban. There are no reliable statistics on how many girls were expelled from universities because university administrations do not give reasons for expulsion. Approximately 90 percent of expelled female students who were not permitted to attend classes due to the ban on headscarves were expelled under the guise of absenteeism.[50] Since June 2000, an estimated 270,000 students out of the 677,000 who were expelled from institutions of higher education were casualties of the headscarf ban.[51] There have been reports that approximately 5,000 female teachers have lost their jobs.[52]

Inconsistently enforced for a period of three decades, the headscarf ban has been imposed more consistently starting in the late 1990s. It is reasonable to conclude that the number of women who have been deprived of their right to work and receive an education numbers in the hundreds of thousands, although this is a rough estimate. Some women have to give up the headscarf entirely, or wear wigs, just to be able to finish their education or to work. When a woman removes her headscarf, the major obstacle disappears, but not entirely. In one Supreme Administrative Court decision, a female teacher lost her job because of her headscarf, even though she did not wear it at school, on the grounds that "As a teacher, she is a role model for her students; therefore it is not acceptable to wear a headscarf, even in her private life."[53] This decision reveals how far courts can extend the ban from public to private spheres.

A Majority Opposes the Ban

In the late 1990s, emerging national and international interest in Turkey's headscarf ban led several research organizations to study the issue.[54] All of these research reports indicate that the majority of the Turkish public does not find the headscarf ban justifiable. According to one of the most cited studies, by the Turkish Economic and Social Studies Foundation (TESEV), 76 percent do not support the ban and 72 percent would not be unhappy if the ban were lifted.[55] It is telling, however, that almost none of this research into the impact of the headscarf ban on Turkish society focused on women who wear the headscarf, that is, on the real victims of the ban.[56] Only one public survey, conducted in 2007, asked: "What are the social, economic and psychological impacts of the headscarf ban on women who wear headscarves?"[57] Another conspicuous example is the fact that the European Parliament's 2005 report on Turkish women's social, economic, and political participation in society did not even mention the headscarf ban.[58]

The economic, social, and, more importantly, the emotional consequences of the ban on women and their families, generation after generation, will always be difficult to assess fully.[59] Paradoxically, it is acceptable for men to be religious without risking being humiliated or excluded from universities or public jobs. The one humiliation for a religious man is to have a wife who wears a headscarf! Some civil servants, especially military officers, have lost their positions because of their wife's headscarf. The military, the most secular institution in Turkey, made clear that there is no place in the armed forces for a headscarf.[60] Some cases of officers who lost jobs for this reason, as a last resort, have reached the ECHR. Some Turkish court decisions indicate that the courts accept government intrusion on the private lives of civil servants if the case involves the headscarf.[61] To punish an individual because of another person's action (in headscarf cases generally, this person is a spouse) is completely contrary to general principles of law. The headscarf ban is based on an understanding that women who wear headscarves cannot be considered independent individuals with their own ideas, beliefs, and decision-making abilities in choosing to wear a headscarf.[62] However, public surveys show that less than one percent of women wear a headscarf because of their male relatives.[63]

The lack of sympathy among the seculars for the suffering of, and discrimination against, devout Muslim women is remarkable. Even feminist organizations claiming to be the authoritative representatives of women in the public controversy, as well as the most respected civil society organizations, were inactive in mobilizing the whole of Turkish society against headscarves. The silence of Turkish liberal intellectuals, with few exceptions, is disappointing. The great majority of Turkish intellectuals do not pay attention to the negative consequences of the exclusion of women who wear headscarves.[64] An example of the general insensitivity among scholars is a recently published, comprehensive book on human rights in Turkey that does not even mention the headscarf ban as part of the human rights debate, let alone devote a chapter to the problem. This oversight is astonishing, considering that Turkey is the only country in the world where the headscarf ban is actually implemented in institutions of higher education.[65]

"Reverse Discrimination" in Anatolia

In academic circles, however, the negative impact on women who do not wear headscarves has become an important subject, especially following a public debate initiated by a prominent scholar, which led to the publication of a report on peer pressure in Turkey.[66] The report concluded that social pressure in Turkish society toward people with different identities paints a worrisome picture for the country's future. This social pressure is more serious, wider, and deeper in Anatolian cities. Along with the exclusion of women from the public sphere, discrimination against minorities and vulnerable ethnicities is long-standing and deeply rooted. Contrary to the general assumption of the report, government influence alone cannot explain the severity of the problem, which is attributable to the intense pressure to conform in communities where conservative religious and social traditions prevail.

Conservatism has a wider impact on society than just on women. Any deviant lifestyle is subject to social pressure regardless of gender, such as long hair, style of beard, or earrings for men.[67] Nevertheless, the most serious finding of the report was the existence in Anatolia of social pressure on women "beyond time and space." Women and young girls in many small towns have a much tougher time than other minorities, and their individual freedom and even their physical well-being can sometimes be threatened.[68] In the early 2000s, a series of female suicides in eastern cities was one consequence of such pressure and produced a huge public outcry.[69]

The report claims that the dominant interpretations of woman in Islam are problematic and, when coupled with the prevalent patriarchal traditions in Anatolia, result in women suffering more than their share of repression due to conservatism. There is a widespread belief among urban secular groups that the texture of life in cities has become more conservative since 1994 due to the influence of the Welfare Party and the AKP at the local level. The evidence in the report of the shift toward conservatism, however, cannot be adequately explained by reference to the political transformation in Turkey. Even if one accepts that political parties with religious sensitivities have played a role in this rise of conservatism, one must acknowledge that the AKP's approach to gender issues has also led to significant reforms in Turkey. For example, the new Penal Code adopted by the AKP-led Parliament contains heavier penalties for sexual harassment. In the case of "honor killings," the new Penal Code calls for penalties for the family members who participate in the decision to inflict death. This new law also forbids marital sexual harassment, considered a punishable offense in very few countries.[70] Despite the fact that the AKP has not accepted the quota system for female parliamentary representation that feminist organizations have demanded (and only the ethnic-oriented Democratic Society Party [DTP] implemented), it was under AKP rule that the number of female deputies in Parliament almost doubled, reaching its highest point since the founding of the Turkish Republic. However, any female parliamentarian of the AKP cannot be seated in Parliament if she dares to wear a headscarf.

Furthermore, the rise of political Islam also does not sufficiently explain the phenomenon of increasing conservatism. In Anatolian cities, it has more to do with complex processes rooted in the history, traditions, and socioeconomic conditions of village and city life.[71] Immigration from rural areas to small towns and from small towns to large urban centers such as Istanbul, Ankara, and Izmir made a vital change in peoples' lives and values. While more educated, wealthy families move from small Anatolian cities to urban centers, newcomers from villages bring their conservative values to Anatolian towns and cities. Similarly, relatively wealthier small-town families bring their conservative values to urban centers. This internal mobility due to economic status has mixed different lifestyles in Turkish cities. Urban centers have become public platforms for conservative views, leading to clashes among differing values, from conservatives versus modernizers, Islam versus secularism, and to patriarchal hierarchy versus gender equality.

A reverse mobility also brought different cultures together that for a long time had lived without much interaction. Until very recently, universities were located predominantly in urban metropolitan cities in Turkey, but, during the last decade, new universities have opened in many Anatolian cities. These bring secular urban students to traditionally conservative Anatolian towns. Interaction between locals and urbanite students resulted in a new relationship between the two groups. University campuses in Anatolia became relatively more relaxed; female students were free, to a certain extent, to wear whatever they wanted and participate in student activities together with male students. However, this freedom was granted only to students who did not wear headscarves. Under the strict headscarf ban, however, in universities in the middle of Anatolia—a region where the great majority of women and girls wear the headscarf—young women cannot be admitted to schools in their own neighborhood. Instead, girls from Istanbul gain admission because they do not wear the headscarf. These complex internal displacements in Turkey

allowed people to get to know one another better and to live together in what was viewed as an exceptional situation. This interaction created a clash that focused symbolically on an obsession with the headscarf controversy. At the same time, it must be acknowledged, the choice not to wear a headscarf was also a problem in some Anatolian towns.[72]

Testimony from the two groups of women, those who wear a headscarf and those who do not, shows that both sides are complaining about similar problems of free access to public places and individual freedom that arise from social pressures. In traditional areas, women are more comfortable with the headscarf and less comfortable without it, and the reverse is true in areas where modernity dominates the scene. We must, however, keep in mind that women without headscarves do not lose any of their constitutional rights, such as the right to an education and the right to have a job. Education and job opportunities for women who wear the headscarf would help to emancipate them from the existing rigid social structure.

Political Power of Women and Excessive Covering

In the aftermath of the political turmoil created by the Constitutional Court, the current Turkish government has shown little desire to take action on behalf of women with headscarves. It seems that these women are forgotten, at least until the next election when their political power will be needed—but only temporarily. Not only the AKP, but also other Turkish political parties have discovered the important political power of women at election time. Recently, the strong secularist opposition party CHP has accepted the membership of several women delegates who wear the *carsaf*, a more extreme religious dress than the headscarf, which covers the entire body and hair but not the face.[73] This move by the CHP is widely considered to be an opportunistic political tactic that reveals no intention to include such women in political life. But for headscarf-wearing women who seek to be part of the public sphere in Turkey, this gesture is threatening and further endangers the position of headscarved women. Some belong to a reformist feminist Islamic movement and have their own struggles with the religious community. These reformists contend that Islam is a sufficiently diverse religion that can allow different cultures to play their roles. The claim is that a woman can fulfill religious duties and still participate in Turkish modernity. In a modern world, modesty does not require wearing the *carsaf*. The headscarved women are fearful that a religious fundamentalist image will set them back in their daily lives and reformist agenda.

Despite recent public debate in Europe, especially in France, the Netherlands, and Spain, a movement to make laws banning Muslim face-covering has, apparently, never become an issue in Turkey. The various types of veiling, such as the *nikab* or the *burqa,* are based more on local traditions than on religious beliefs and are not part of Turkish Islam. In fact, Turkey is a popular destination for residents of Muslim countries with strict face-veiling traditions, and no controversy exists as to whether this form of dress should be banned in Turkey's public spaces. Syria, for instance, very recently banned the Islamic veil in its universities.[74] Obviously, this issue will not arise in Turkey. This distinction between veil and headscarf indicates that the general public in Turkey considers the headscarf to be a political symbol of a power struggle over class, gender, and race rather than simply as a matter of the religious convictions of Muslim women.

What Is the Future for Women?

As a consequence of the legal conflicts and constitutional principles that neither block nor pave the way for headscarf wearing in public, the implementation of the headscarf ban in Turkey is always subject to uncertainty, swinging between tolerance and strict bans, depending on the political climate. Following the political crises of 2008 precipitated by the Constitutional Court's actions, the AKP government and YOK have more or less abandoned the controversy over the headscarf ban. Currently, many university administrations accept students with headscarves; moreover, municipalities and the private sector are hiring female civil servants who wear headscarves, and the number of female employees in these areas is increasing significantly. Only the more visible occupations, such as law, the courts, university researchers and professors, and doctors working in public institutions are denied the right to wear a headscarf if they wish to keep their professional jobs. The growing number of headscarf-wearing employees could be falsely interpreted by the seculars as an indication of increased tolerance, backing their claim that no headscarf problem exists in Turkey today.[75] Public opinion, however, has remained unchanged over the past few years, surveys indicate, contradicting the beliefs of the secular public.

What will happen to the headscarf-wearing women who now have jobs if the AKP loses the next election and a secular government comes to power? At present, this question is not in the public consciousness, as the headscarf ban has relaxed because of the AKP's evasive approach, taking the discussion off the table to avoid clashes between the two groups and to protect itself against a potential attack in the Constitutional Court. Relying on *de facto* implementation, rather than achieving *de jure* solutions, is likely to present more serious problems in the near future.

In light of the contemporary crises of the Turkish system, the fundamental question remains: why do the most powerful institutions (the high courts, the military, universities, and bureaucracies) feel threatened by young women wearing headscarves attending universities? To assess the current conditions in Turkey in relation to the headscarf controversy, in the next chapter we will examine the complex historical context, especially the transformation of Turkish society from an Islamic emphasis to a Western-oriented public and legal order in the late nineteenth and early twentieth centuries.

3

Understanding a Complex History

Our most important question is where and how we are
going to connect with our past.

AHMET HAMDI TANPINAR, TURKISH NOVELIST

1. The Modernity Project and Turkish Legal History

One of the most important historical transformations in Turkish society was
the modernization project that unfolded in the late nineteenth and early
twentieth centuries. During this period, Turkey experienced an important
nation-building process that transformed it from an Islamic empire to a secular nation-state. The Turkish state was formed in the wake of the collapse
of the Ottoman Empire and was coupled with a dramatic cultural "revolution from above," conceived and carried out by Mustafa Kemal Ataturk and
the military leadership that had emerged victorious from the Turkish War
of Independence. Inspired by European models, the cultural revolution
became integral to the nation-building effort, transforming Turkish society
from a remnant of a failed empire to a unified and homogenized social entity.[1] The root causes of the recent debate that has divided the country sharply
between secular moderns and religious traditionals can be traced back to the
original transformation and modernization project of the Republic of Turkey.
During this period, radical cultural and legal reforms were adopted, including the codification of the entire corpus of domestic law. Such modernization
involved the coercive transformation of the social structure of the society to
resemble, as much as possible, its European model.[2]

During the transformation period, two consecutive, ideologically distinct policy approaches were offered to best implement the reform program

for rescuing Turkish society from the failed heritage of the Ottoman Empire and Islam: the Ottoman modernizers and the Turkish republican modernizers.

The Ottoman Period: Mixing East and West

From its beginnings in the fourteenth century until the second half of the nineteenth century, the Ottoman Empire was committed to the advancement and defense of the Islamic faith, despite its multiethnic posture. For more than six hundred years, Islamic law was the fabric that held the Ottoman Empire together, while at the same time it was governed by a distinctive, decentralized form of imperial rule.[3] The various ethnic and religious groups were allowed to regulate their internal affairs according to their own legal traditions. Unlike the Western European powers, which carried the law of their homelands with them to their new settlements, Ottomans did not transplant their legal system.[4] At the end of the eighteenth century, Western influence on the Ottoman Empire was strongly felt. European law was gradually introduced into the Ottoman legal system through voluntary reforms, initiated by Ottoman elites partially in response to pressure from external forces. These changes were not outright impositions but rather a mixture of imposed on and introduced from within the empire.[5] The main preoccupation during this period was the Ottoman search for ways to arrest the decline of the empire. The improvement of the legal system through Westernization and secularization was thought to be helpful in this effort. The idea was to show respect for Turkish traditions and culture while selectively adopting certain European legal principles.

From the 1839 *Tanzimat* (reorganization) reformation to the fall of the empire in 1920, there existed a mixed jurisdiction that reflected considerable French influence. Turkish military leaders and government officials also were heavily influenced by French political ideas, and many members of the government elite received training in France. Therefore, the ideology of the Turkish nation-state was quite naturally modeled on the French republican system. In this period, Sharia (Islamic) law continued to govern personal relations, but significant improvements were achieved in the area of commercial law and property law, based on the adoption of French civil law (*Code Napoléon*). Unlike the empire's earlier consensual climate of opinion, this period saw a controversial duality. The hybrid model of legal reforms in the Ottoman Empire attracted the attention of many Western observers because it offered a unique model for combining both the internal (Sharia law) and external

(European civil law) legal orders. This mixed legal system, called *Mecelle*, still survives in part and is applicable in some parts of the Middle East.[6]

In the meantime, the Ottoman Empire was experiencing political and economic decline. Emerging nationalism in various provinces posed greater challenges to the cohesion of the empire. To stop this decline, the Palace took various steps designed to revitalize the Ottoman bureaucracy in the areas of military affairs, education, and the legal system.[7] Some of these reforms were forced on the Ottomans by the European powers after military defeats. Others were genuinely initiated by the Ottoman administration on their own. Yet all were designed to introduce new ideas from the West without seriously compromising Ottoman identity and tradition. Although reform began with modernizing the military, the efforts increasingly came to mean the wholesale adoption of Western institutions and culture. By the late nineteenth and early twentieth centuries the Ottoman elite was divided about the proper course of reform. The debate between the Westernists and the Islamists revolved around the question of how and which initiatives to adopt from the West. Whereas the Islamists favored the adoption of Western technology and industry only, the Westernizers pushed for a wholesale shift to Western civilization.[8] Despite these efforts, the fate of the empire was unchanged. The end of World War I also marked the end of the Ottomans. At Versailles in 1919, the European powers divided the lands of the former empire.

Legal Reforms and European Law in the Turkish Republic of 1923

The reforms were interrupted when the Ottoman Empire was dismantled, and the debate ended in favor of the Westernizers to whom "civilization" meant the West. Repeatedly, Mustafa Kemal, the founder of the new republic, and his colleagues would insist that there was only one civilization to emulate—Western—and the Turkish Republic would find its place among "the civilized nations of the world."[9] The second period of reforms, from 1923 to 1930, initiated with the ideology of transformation and the creation of new national institutions, led to a series of changes. Major reforms were adopted in parallel with the general framework of an ongoing cultural revolution. The founders of the republic started to abandon Islamic law and launch the European legal system within a very short period of time. In 1924, the decision was made to initiate an entire indigenous system of laws rather than attempt merely to integrate some European legal norms and update the existing legal framework. More specifically, Turkey relied on a combination—predominantly Swiss, German, Italian, and French—of laws that were translated meticulously by Turkish legal experts over a period of two years and then introduced into the Turkish domestic legal system without modification. The boldness of the move to adopt foreign legal codes and use this all-out appropriation as the sole tool of legal reform amazed foreign observers. The Turkish experience was believed by a number of legal scholars to be the most extreme and important example of "legal transplant."[10] Even decades later, Perry Anderson described the Turkish case as "the triumph of Kemalism"; a rare example in history of a revolution with no social base. In other words, the Kemalist revolution was accomplished through a top-down penetration of society by powerful state institutions.[11]

Turkish reformers believed that the real basis of European political superiority was embodied in European culture. Moreover, Ottoman law was widely regarded as a strong negative force that prevented Turkish economic development. Many observers blamed the old legal system for the inability of the empire to keep pace with European nations. The Turkish comparative law scholar Esin Orucu stated that "the main purpose behind the adoptions was to tear up the foundation of the old legal system by creating completely new laws, and to regulate and legislate the…relationships of the people according to what was thought these relationships ought to be, and not according to existing customs, usages, and religious mores. This was revolutionary and radically reformist, and can be summed up as a prime example of social engineering through law."[12]

During the legal reform period, codes of various nations were adopted for different reasons. No single legal system served as a privileged model. The choice was driven in some instances by the perceived prestige of the model, in some by efficiency, and in others quite by chance. Social and political considerations also played a role in the choice of a source country to rely on for the modernization of Turkish law. The Swiss Civil Code, which codifies all family and inheritance law, was chosen because its characteristics seemed suitable for Turkey, and, more important, Switzerland was the most conservative country in Europe regarding family law. This was viewed as preferable and desirable, given the conservative and patriarchal foundations of Turkish family structure. Also, Switzerland was a neutral country, and it was deemed important that Turkey not fall under the influence of any particular Western power.

The idea of Turkish independence in relation to European powers was especially important at the birth of the Turkish Republic. Choosing a number of different models of foreign law may have given cultural legitimacy to the borrowings, because the desire to modernize and Westernize was not beholden to any one dominant national culture. Yet, the nineteenth-century French influence over the Ottoman government elite was thought to be strong and persistent, and, unsurprisingly, the new Turkish Republic was modeled after the civic-republican model of France.

Although the founders of newly independent Turkey were careful to avoid domination by any European power, they did not hesitate to adopt European culture. Many Turkish leaders even came to see themselves as European, after centuries of political and cultural interaction between the two cultures.[13] Ambivalence arose among reformers between the negative aspects of European imperialism and the positive aspects of European culture. In contemporary Turkey, this ambivalence still exists in Turkish society and is evident in conflicting attitudes toward Turkey's effort to obtain membership in the European Union.[14]

2. A Preoccupation with Western Imagery

Legal reforms were part of a wider series of reforms imposed on Turkish society designed to alter the daily lifestyle of ordinary Turkish people, including the Turkish alphabet, style of dress, the Western calendar, European numerals, the metric system, surnames, the weekly holiday, and much more. Some of the reforms were symbolically important and image based, standing as perceptible manifestations of the resolve to "look like the West."[15] A number of reform laws abolished the link between religion and dress codes. The transformation of the individual included her or his personal and political identity, with the aim of producing the idealized Turkish citizen—someone free of Ottoman-Islamic cultural baggage and ready and eager to affirm Kemalist modernization.[16] Ataturk's aim was to transform the outlook of Turkish society from its supposed "backwardness"—identified by him as anything related to Islam—to modernity, which was associated with being European.[17] An integral step in the modernizing revolution in Turkey, this cultural shift represented an uncritical embrace of Westernization, involving the Europeanization of Turkish society through law.

The dramatic shift in the new code was not only from one legal family to another but, more profoundly, from a religiously based legal system to a secularized system. In this transformation, religious schools (*medereses)* and Sharia courts were abolished and replaced by secular ones, clerics were forbidden to wear ecclesiastical dress outside religious premises, and the caliphate system of Islamic leadership was dismantled.[18] The Turkish alphabet shifted from Arabic, the language of the Quran, to Latin script. A main reason for shifting from the Arabic to the Latin alphabet, apart from the low rate of literacy in Turkish society due to the difficulty of the Arabic alphabet, was to take an important step toward breaking old religious traditions and weakening the link with the past.

In this process, secularism and the emancipation of women were the overarching objectives, to which all other goals were subordinated. To achieve Westernizing reforms not only in the public sphere and political life of the republic but also in the private sphere of its social fabric is characteristic of a cultural revolution.[19] Reform laws that addressed clothing, however, made careful distinctions between men and women. For example, a law prohibited men from wearing a fez, but women were not prohibited from wearing a headscarf; still, Ataturk ridiculed the headscarf in various speeches. The reasoning behind these reforms was to transform the Turkish nation into a secular one and specifically to "rectify" the damage that Sharia law had imposed on Turkish society, especially on women. Ataturk believed that "unless women were on an equal footing with men, The Turkish Republic would remain irremediably backward," incapable of treating women on equal terms as understood and generally practiced by the civilizations of the West.

Turkish women's development in public life during the republican period was very impressive. Nevertheless, social and political change in Turkish society had a lasting effect only on a particular layer of society, that of urban, middle-class professionals, the main beneficiaries of this approach to the modernization and Westernization process. The founders of the Turkish Republic held very strong views about the negative impacts of religion, particularly Islam, on society and blamed religion for everything that went wrong. They were unable to understand how deeply Islamic culture was embedded in Turkish society, and despite despotic measures designed to uproot elements of adherence to Islam, many Islamic social practices were not eliminated.

During the final period of Ottoman decline, the Eastern lifestyle of Turks had been criticized in European Orientalist literature and art, and the Turkish elite had been deeply influenced by Orientalist European writers.[20] The Ottoman Empire was always represented as a woman with a veil, who needed help from Europeans to be liberated. This image has had a lasting impact on the reformers. Unconsciously or consciously, the founders of the new republic thought they must change this image immediately to encourage a change in the European's perception of a Turk. European stereotypes also constituted the Turkish self-image in the late period of the Ottoman Empire and in the early phases of the new Turkish state. In many speeches delivered by the Turkish leadership to justify the extraordinary reforms of the Ataturk era, a high priority was to "free" Turkey from some of the "backward-looking institutions" of Islam.[21]

In parallel with social and cultural transformation and the wholesale adoption of laws from Europe, the degree to which a top-down, authoritarian elite imposed legal reforms on Turkish society is a revealing example of what Edward Said calls "self-Orientalism." [22] Said's critique of the West's understanding of the Orient has become influential, especially in relation to the Ottoman Empire. [23] In Turkey, the contemporary self-Orientalist secular elite, many of them unaware of this perspective, willingly distance themselves from religiously devout young Muslim students and strongly resist being associated with them. Historical images of Orientalism, most vividly in relation to Oriental women, are still very much present among the secular elite and operate as a symbolic reminder of the Ottoman past versus the modern Republic of Turkey. As we will see, these images are also very much alive and effective in contemporary Europe, contributing to the rise of anti-Islamic sentiments and practices.

3. A Critique of the Turkish Modernity Project

In the early twentieth century, Eurocentrism provided a fertile environment in which to propagate Western legal systems throughout the Muslim world while claiming their superiority over Islamic law. This process did not occur in Turkey only, but also in many Middle Eastern countries, especially in societies formerly part of the Ottoman Empire. In the early period of the Turkish Republic, the effort to achieve modernity also reflected the impact of Enlightenment thinking. [24] Yet, the uniqueness of the Turkish case is bound up with Turkey's modernizing revolution, a dramatic and rapid shift from an Eastern-Islamic legal culture to a Western secular legal system. This is considered the only example of such an abrupt process throughout the long legal history of reception. [25] Turkey is also the only country in the Muslim world that entirely gave up the Islamic law of Sharia, including family law. Another example somewhat similar to the Turkish experience is the Japanese model, which is considered a success, but it is not as dramatic as the Turkish case in terms of cultural transformation. Japanese modernity, unlike the Turkish model, did not attempt to disturb the traditional roots of society and was limited to the legal and economic spheres. [26]

Social Trauma

The fast track of legal and cultural reforms, and a slow process of democratization, arguably established a workable system for Turkey, despite the bipolarity in the society arising from clashes between the civic Islamic culture and the governing secular elite backed by the military. After eighty years of revolution, strictly from a black-letter point of view, the emergent constitutional order has been a tremendous success. Yet, we must analyze the sociolegal sphere before giving our assent to this affirmative conclusion.[27] According to a well-known Turkish legal historian, "how much the adoption of European laws affected society remains one of the most difficult questions for sociological and historical studies of the law... One hesitates, therefore, to categorically state that the reception [of European legal models] movement was beneficial or detrimental to Turkish society."[28] The deep roots of the current headscarf controversy, which have, somewhat unexpectedly, created widespread political turmoil, underlie this abrupt legal transformation. This Turkish experiment with legal reform might be considered a social trauma that Turkish society is still enduring.

Because Turkey was predominantly Muslim and the great majority lived rurally and cherished a traditional outlook, Turkey did not enjoy as smooth a transition to modernity as Kemalists claim. Only a small minority of the population lived in urban areas that became Western in outlook and mentality, and the shift was mostly confined to the middle and upper classes. Under such conditions, the implementation of a completely foreign law, based on foreign cultures, constantly needed adjustment, especially with respect to family law. The dramatic departure from Islamic law, especially as governing family relations, was not painless. A majority of citizens who live in small towns and villages in Turkish rural areas (Anatolia) have not abandoned their adherence to religious traditions and law. In some instances, they try to meet the requirements of both laws, which are sometimes in conflict. Historically, rural citizens have often refused to follow the family law rules derived from Switzerland, especially those relating to marriage, divorce, inheritance, and the legitimacy of children. Sometimes, people manipulate both laws to achieve their desired results. In family relations, women are generally more vulnerable than men. Therefore, women have suffered more, due to the state's nonrecognition of the underlying Islamic socio-legal reality, which was in tension with the militantly positivist effort to transform Turkish society in a hegemonic way.[29]

Turkey offers an important example of how an imported legal system adjusts itself in a national setting where there exists a strong traditional culture that persists in the face of social transformation conducted by reformers under the banners of Westernization and modernization. A somewhat paradoxical relationship emerged between the official legal order based on

Western principles and the majority of the population that remained under the primary influence of traditional Muslim values and lifestyle. In other words, the secular and modern elements that shape Kemalist ideology could not fill the gap created by this positivist attempt to supersede Islamic law. The Turkish state, through its secular policies and programs of Westernization, threatened the value system of Muslims without providing an alternative ideological framework with sufficient mass appeal to replace Islam. Therefore, despite all of the attempts of the state to eliminate religious content from the legal system, Islam survived, unofficially and locally, as the living law for much of society. Islam remains a pervasive force in most of the Turkish public and private life.[30]

Modernization with Authoritarian Secularization

In recent years, the modernization with secularization thesis, which assumes an evolutionary decline and dissolution of religion by the modernization process, has come under increasing attack. Religion, despite various forms of secularization, remains a constitutive basis of national identity and nationalism.[31] It has become evident that "the secularization processes do not dissolve religion, but they develop in different patterns combining religious and secular components and proceed in oscillating movements of secularization and de-secularization."[32] Recent studies on the relation between religion, nation building, and nationalism have questioned the modernist assumption that nation-state formation and modern nationalism supersede religion and religious identities, replacing them with purely secular forms of national identity.[33] In recent decades, several Muslim countries such as Algeria, Tunisia, Egypt, and Iran have been transformed from secular nation-states adhering to the European model of modernization into various models of Islamic revivalism. The contemporary global rise of nationalism and religion, in some cases blended with a form of religious nationalism, must be seen as a reaction to the previous authoritarian imposition of the Western European model of state secularism onto non-Western, predominantly religious, and often multiethnic societies.[34] In many non-Western societies, modernization, state formation, and nation building were combined with authoritarian state secularism. Thus, the continuing search and struggle for liberalization and democratization on a global scale is mostly directed against authoritarian state secularism by relying on religious and ethnic identities as sources of resistance. This is one partial explanation of the intensification of religious and ethnic nationalism all over the world.[35]

The Ottoman-Turkish case is a prime example of this type of nation building and modernity. As noted, in the early twentieth century, following the breakdown of the Ottoman Empire, the new Turkish nation-state combined Turkish ethnic nationalization with a secularist transformation of the legal and educational systems, and confined Islam to the private sphere.[36] In the context of liberal-authoritarian regimes, and following the delegitimization of socialism, the present tendency is for conservative-democratic parties to treat religion as integral to their political ideologies. Thus, with deepening participatory democracy, Turkish national identity is integrating a growing Islamic component that inevitably poses a challenge to previously hegemonic secularism.[37]

Turkish Model?

Looking back to evaluate the Turkish case after almost a century, we take note of two distinct arguments. To many scholars, the Turkish model is the most successful realization of Westernization and modernization that has so far taken place in the Islamic world.[38] These scholars believe that Turkey's apparently successful adoption of Western norms, styles, and institutions, most conspicuously in education, law, social life, women's rights, clothing, and even in music and the arts, bears witness to the viability of the project of modernity even in this overwhelmingly Muslim country. The Turkish elite has claimed that Turkey is the only successful example among its Muslim neighbors and that Turkish society has reached the level of Western modernity by escaping from the Islamic world, although without the elite ever questioning whether Western modernity is to be uncritically regarded as positive.

In the West, however, several scholars have seriously and persuasively questioned the nineteenth-century project of modernity, with special reference to the European experience of communist and fascist systems, internal abuses of human rights, and the resulting devastating warfare. This kind of criticism of the West never found a following among Turkish mainstream scholars because of their commitment to Ataturk's principles and reforms, as well as their belief in the positive impact of Westernization and modernization on Turkish society. Mainstream urban elites believe that Ataturk and his supporters succeeded in transforming what was arguably "the most fundamentalist regime" in the world into a secular and democratic republic.[39]

However, in the late 1960s and the 1970s, as the influence of Marxist perspectives grew, the celebratory tone of depictions of modernity eroded significantly, and, toward the end of the 1990s, the criticism of Turkish modernity became more visible and straightforward than earlier.[40] For some, the failure to gain acceptance by the West despite the loosening of Islamic identity is viewed as a disadvantage of the Turkish modernization project. Underpinning these criticisms of Kemalist modernization is a more general doubt about the universalistic claims and aspirations of modernization theories. Gradually, the Turkish modernity project began to be criticized on its own terms by a new generation of scholars. They were able to evaluate the sudden transformation of society through a dictatorial, nation-state–making process that had traumatic impact on the more traditional sectors of Turkish society.

There is a structural difference between Turkish modernity and European modernity. Modernity was part of a process in which Western societies experienced significant struggle and polarization, but whose results were accepted finally by all. Secularization arose in this process, prompted in European countries mainly by an effort to diminish the power of religion and replace it with rational thinking. But in non-Western societies, the struggle between premodern and modern values was never effectively negotiated. Modernity and its major result, secularism, were simply imposed by a governing elite. The major goal of Turkish modernity was to create a new nation that accorded no public role to religion. It was not an easy task, given Turkey's long history of association with Islam. From this perspective, the "right religion" must be initiated and controlled by the state, if necessary by using force to restrict its influence. While secularism was busy reinterpreting religion, it generated for itself a new type of sacred concept that became crystallized as nationalism. With this outlook, religion became something that should be a source of shame and should be publicly forgotten in the name of modernization. If traditional society could not adjust to this new order, it should not be allowed participation in public space as defined by the modernizers. In fact, the public sphere, instead of being a free place for the exchange of ideas, became a restricted area available only for various strands of secular discourse. This underscored the distinction between public and private, establishing two distinct places for two different views.[41] In recent decades, those two viewpoints eventually met and clashed. When the traditional sectors tried to take part in the modern world, the modernized seculars, with the help of the ideologies of Kemalism, nationalism, and militarism, strongly resisted. The military, on several occasions, helped modernized elites to regain control of the government, repudiating unwanted intrusions by the so-called nonmoderns. While modernized seculars were supposedly dedicated to European moral principles such as democracy, equality, and freedom, they were ready to ignore such restraints on power to maintain their positions of privilege. In actuality,

Turkish seculars never internalized European values, perhaps because the European transplant was too shallow. This assessment of Turkish modernity is, of course, quite controversial.

Islamic Modernism

The headscarf controversy has made this interpretation more plausible. The headscarf is an important symbol in relation to modernization, allegedly representing nonmodern, backward citizens who have "different" values than the modern Kemalist norms. Therefore, these adherents of tradition should not be part of a truly modern Turkish society and should not be allowed to receive public services such as education and job opportunities. According to the French sociologist Pierre Bourdieu, in order to reproduce a new society, cultural and economic norms should be defined in areas of science, art, education, economy, and management.[42] In other words, certain norms are needed to protect class privileges. Turkish modernizers defined their rules to exclude traditional cultural values. The headscarf was not part of the social norms defined by the Kemalist founders when they decided to rebuild Turkish society. Moreover, the Turkish secular elite keep class privileges only for themselves and exclude those who are different. The headscarf is a perfect tool to block the nonmoderns from participating in the class privileges that the modern state represents. However, to exclude nonmoderns by way of the headscarf ban targets women only. There is no easy tool such as the headscarf for excluding men. In other words, there might be a way to exclude a nonmodern man, but Turkish patriarchy does not allow for the exclusion of Muslim men from social, political, and economic privileges. This is a vital and often forgotten part of the headscarf argument. In reality, the principal victims of Turkish modernity are women. Men have no problem because of their religiosity. No man is excluded from educational institutions, jobs, or subject to visible humiliation, except in unusual cases where his rights are violated because his wife wears a headscarf.

It remains to be seen whether the new "conservative" government, as the democratically elected and legitimate representative of the population, will be able to give a different spin to the idea of modernity. If Islam were reconciled with secularism, the government would accept religiously devout women as fully entitled to access to public spaces, but would also accept the conservative section of society as a nonnegotiable part of the social, political. and intellectual structure of the country. The possibility of an "Islamic modernism" that may be attributed to trends developing in the Islamist movement in Turkey are conveniently categorized by seculars as belonging to the realm of the pre-modern or traditional, or are treated simply as irrelevant anomalies.[43]

Recently, the early efforts of implementing modernity in non-Western cultures, especially within Islamic societies, have been revisited, and some scholars have utilized the concept of "multiple modernities" to compre-hend and evaluate the distinctive transitions to modernity in different non-Western societies.[44] Among them, particularly, Schmuel Eisenstadt offers a comparative civilizational approach to overcoming the theoretical challenge of explaining the global rise of ethnic and religious nationalism in the con-temporary period.[45] The idea of multiple modernities assumes that traditions are not simply dissolved by modernization or globalization, but rather that religious and imperial traditions remain constitutive dimensions of mod-ern societies. These religious and imperial traditions are reconstructed and reshaped but retained, despite the evolving processes of secularization and imperial decline that created multiple programs of modernity and multiple processes of modernization.[46]

Turkey's effort can only be understood by looking at the whole picture of current social and political conditions. It cannot be evaluated by looking only at its European-induced modernity. The traditional majority seems to have absorbed modernity in a more comprehensive manner than its secular counterpart by combining traditional values with modern possibilities. The emergence of a new, socially conservative Turkish elite is an example of such hybridity. Members of this group are devout Muslims in private life, who want to display their Islamic identities in public without interference, yet, at the same time, they are committed to being intellectually and economically successful, technologically innovative, and are prepared to play an active and constructive role in society.[47] These recently ascending modern Muslims have found political identity and representation in today's governing party. Their approach contrasts with the Kemalism that is content with simply accepting what is given by top-down modernity organizers, and their dual background supports an image of Turkey as the scene of multiple modernities.

The current Islamist modernization project seeks to enable Turkish society to recover its authentic culture, previously suppressed by the Westernizing, imitative state. For Islamist modernizers, establishing liberal constitutional democracy and protecting individual human rights are considered the best ways to emancipate people who are otherwise excluded from their own soci-ety by the secular legal order. The headscarf debate is one of the most symbolic and visible examples of this battle. In the 1920s, the Turkish modernization project depicted Turkish women's traditional dress and headscarf as a symbol of the backwardness of Islam and as a strong reminder that the Ottoman era was antimodern. If the new, conservative Turkish elite achieves a successful implementation of its vision, it will be clearly demonstrated that modernity, secularism, and, more important, liberal constitutionalism are not exclusively Western and can be found in non-Western cultures. The Turkish revival of its traditional "purely indigenous and authentic" cultural setting has the potential to achieve a successful synthesis of tradition and modernity. In this context, solving the headscarf problem within the democratic system is vital, not only for Turkey, but also for countries where Islam is a minority religion and the headscarf is treated as a symbol of the antimodern or unwanted "other."

4. The Role of Secularism in Law, Religion, and Politics

When they realized that the eradication of Islam altogether was not a realistic option in Turkey, the founders of the Turkish Republic favored a certain so-called civilized approach to its containment. Instead of formally separating state and religion, as France had done in 1905, the modern Turkish state monopolized religious functions, insisted on a single official version of Sunni Islam, and enlisted religious personnel in the state bureaucracy. Turkish secularism, called *laiklik*, is derivative from the French *laïcité*, because both countries have similar historical backgrounds in relation to Islam and Catholicism. In France and Turkey, religion has stood as a symbol of counterrevolution and opposition to the new republics. However, because of the social and political differences between the two republics, Turkish *laiklik* ended up with a very different model of secularism than France.

For a long time, secularism was unconditionally defended as one of the fundamental features of the modernity project by the Turkish governing elites. Since the founding of the modern Turkish state, the military has assumed a mandate to protect secularism and the Ataturk legacy whenever the Turkish secular model was deemed to be threatened.

At the same time, Turkish secularism created serious practical problems in the social life of citizens, and the headscarf controversy is one of them. The transformation of the image of women constitutes a fundamental element of Turkish modernity and its founding ideology. Any proposal that dares to question these frozen values in the constitution is threatening and unacceptable to the strictly secular side of Turkish society. The most recent attempt to devise an alternative to the frozen state of nationalism and secularism arose on the wings of the rising popularity of the AKP. Renewed controversy over the secularism principle might be considered a sign of a tendency to assert

Islam in the public space. This helps us understand why the Turkish secular elite, followers of European identity and ideology, is strongly opposed to the liberal democratic principles embraced by the current Turkish government. Secular political culture does not allow the flexibility required for an adaptive interpretation of secularism.

The Constitutional History and the Sacrosanct Principle of Secularism

Today, Turkey is perhaps the only country in the Islamic world where the secularity principle operates as one of the basic pillars of the constitutional order.[48] As a modernizing reform, the constitution was stripped of all religious references. Beginning in the 1920s secularism, along with several other Kemalist principles, was introduced into the Turkish constitutional order in a gradual manner. From the first republican constitution of 1924, through the more liberal and democratic constitution of 1961, and, finally, to the most recent and more authoritarian constitution of 1982, the concept of secularism has emerged in stages to occupy a central role in the Turkish legal order and in political life.

From the establishment of the secular Turkish Republic until the end of World War II, Turkey remained under the political control of a one-party dictatorship, the CHP (Republican People's Party), founded by Kemal Ataturk. In 1950, a second party DP (Democratic) came to power in the republic's first free election but was removed from power by a military coup in 1960. The justification for the military intervention was that it was a reaction to "religious activism that was distracting the people from hard economic times."[49] Military rule lasted only one year, leaving behind a new constitution. Consistent with the reasons for the military takeover, the new constitution sought to prevent the use of religion as a political tool. At the same time, it offered a framework for a liberal-democratic polity with guarantees of civil and political rights. More important, the first Constitutional Court was established on the model of European constitutional courts.

Despite its military legacy, the constitution of 1961 was the most liberal constitution Turkey has ever had. It guaranteed freedom of religion and conscience—as long as the freedom was not exercised in a manner designed to reach political goals. The guarantees of freedom did not embrace religious activities, especially if these took the form of political activities inspired by Islam. The inspirational period of the 1960s also influenced the judicial elite. Against this background, the Constitutional Court has, since its inception, been one of the strongest secular institutions in the Turkish system. Even during this early period, the Constitutional Court did not hesitate to dissolve Islamic-oriented parties because of their alleged antisecular activities. The Court also issued several judicial decisions against wearing headscarves on the basis of the secularism argument.

On September 12, 1980, another military intervention dismantled this historic, liberal constitution. Shortly after the interruption of the democratic process by the second military takeover, in 1982 the new regime adopted a new Constitution of the Republic of Turkey, constructed around a reaffirmation of the Kemalist ideals of secularism and modernization. Turkey was defined as a strong, unified, and indivisible nation, with a powerful president and a semi-parliamentary system of government that adhered to a strictly secularist concept of the state, which was demanded by the politically powerful Turkish military. Two characteristics of the new constitution are that it is highly protective of state interests and is relatively restrictive, compared with European standards, containing a long list of limitations on citizens' freedoms. Unlike the earlier, relatively liberal democratic constitution of 1961, this new constitution was a setback for democratic development in Turkey. Turkish politics entered a new era that was hostile to social and political pluralism. The generals systematically militarized the state system in their favor and curtailed the power of civilian governments in order to secure amnesty and immunity for their actions.

The 1982 constitution extended the powers of the office of the president, granting executive authority over national security, defense, and foreign policy, as well as control over the appointment of higher court judges, presidents of universities, and the directorship of the Higher Education Council (YOK). The president was also granted the power to approve senior bureaucratic posts, thereby insulating these crucial positions of power from the vicissitudes of democratic politics. General Kenan Evren, the army's chief of staff who led the military coup, became president of Turkey. Because of this transition, the civilian government was to remain under the tutelage of the Turkish military for a long time.

During the 1980s, international Cold War political trends were very influential in Turkish domestic politics. Due to their fear of communism, Turkish generals were not strongly opposed to "nationalized Islam." The military, however, injected strict secularism into the core of the constitution of 1982, defining religious belief as a "feeling" and as a private matter of individual conscience. In practice, this meant that public and political life would become prohibited zones for devout Muslims. They were allowed to practice

Islam but only in private venues.[50] In addition to the key, irrevocable Article 2, which describes the republic as secular, several other articles in the constitution refer to the secularism principle.[51]

The preamble of the constitution of 1982 declares that the constitution is "in line with…the reforms and principles introduced by the founder of the Republic of Turkey, Ataturk." His reforms centered on the principle of secularism, and it is not surprising to see the principles of Ataturk carefully incorporated into a constitution authored by the military. It was surprising, however, that unlike the military coup of 1960, the coup of 1980 was not directed at Islamists, but against leftists.

The constitution of 1982 is still operative, although it has been altered by numerous amendments, especially since 2001, to meet conditions of the European Union accession process.[52] Yet, the general philosophy of the constitution is still problematic, because its fundamental structure is dictatorial and authoritarian, as well as unsupportive of human rights and the rule of law. Most of the amendments deal with matters of detail or are simply changes in language that did not produce new, more liberal realities. Therefore, the amendments, although they do constitute modest but important steps in the right direction, do not go far enough to satisfy European Union criteria or even to meet the reformist expectations of domestic public opinion.

The new constitutional amendments did not make any attempt to tone down the language of secularism, given internal political concerns. On the contrary, it added to the preamble and to Article 13 more affirming sentences about secularism.[53] Likewise, Article 14 on the "prohibition of abuse of fundamental rights and freedoms" was injected as another protection of secularism in the constitution. It states that "none of the rights and freedoms embodied in the Constitution shall be exercised with the aim of…endangering the existence of the democratic and secular order of the Turkish Republic." Moreover, to ensure the permanence of Kemalist ideology, the reform laws of the 1920s received a special constitutional status in the preamble.[54] The special status afforded to the reform laws in the constitution demonstrates the important role they continue to play in Turkish society.

Until the present, no constitutional amendment or law enacted, or even proposed by any Turkish government, has jeopardized the social order established by the reform laws. These laws that embody the secularism principle are treated as sacrosanct principles set forth by Ataturk in the 1920s to guide the Turkish Republic. The Turkish Constitutional Court also has indicated in several decisions that the secularism principle is to be protected over other principles as an essential foundation of the republic's existence.[55] According to a secular commentator, this "signifies the importance of secularism in Turkish society…both at mass and elite levels, particularly in response to the latest Islamist movements all over the Middle East, including Turkey."[56]

5. Is Turkish Secularism Compatible with Freedom of Religion?

Since the late 1990s, the fear of Islam among the secular political parties, the military, the judiciary, universities, and government bureaucracy has become almost hysterical as religious-oriented political parties have gradually gained electoral power. It is remarkable that the 2001 amendment to the constitution, which affirmed secularism, was an initiative of the AKP government— the political party that the strict secularists believed posed the greatest danger to secular order.

For the framers of the constitution, Turkey's secular republic is the most significant element of Turkish sociopolitical identity. More simply, it is a continuation of the social project of secularization that had been pursued since the founding of the Turkish Republic. Such a social project requires, in practice, the involvement of the state to guide the process of engineering that will allow the government to establish control over religious life. In the Turkish context, secularism does not mean that the state assumes a neutral position toward religious doctrine and the separation of religion and state. Instead, it implies that the state should actively control religious life and that governmental policy should always aim at modernizing society by means of secular legislation and practice.

While the secularism principle insulates the political system from the influence of religion, the other side of the coin is that of protecting freedom of religion. The Turkish constitution, due to its militaristic background and the historical and ideological concerns of the founders, limits individual freedoms. Article 24 of the constitution permits believers to carry out rites of worship and to conduct religious services and ceremonies. But it also requires that "no one shall be compelled to worship, or to participate in religious ceremonies and rites" and that "no one shall be allowed to exploit or abuse religion or religious feelings, or things held sacred by religion, in any manner whatsoever, for the purpose of personal or political influence, or even partially basing the fundamental, social, economic, political, and legal order of the state or religious tenets."

As the constitutional law scholar Erdogan stated, this provision has three main implications.[57] First, politicians and political parties are prohibited from invoking any religious conviction in the course of political activity. Even indirect references to religion in public and political discourse are considered an "abuse" or "exploitation" of religion to achieve political influence. It is almost impossible for any devout Muslim in politics not to make reference to the religious beliefs that person shares with his or her supporters. Regardless of their perspectives, all politicians, as political leaders by definition, must necessarily refer to concepts and ideas they share with their constituents to motivate and mobilize people.[58]

Second, the phrase "for political influence" used in Article 24 indicates that this prohibition also applies to civil liberties, especially to freedom of speech and of association. This makes the prohibition applicable, for example, to those who organize religious endowments or charities, or found a newspaper. Even people undertaking nonreligious enterprises occasionally use religious ideas and concepts when those ideas and concepts are an integral part of that individual's worldview.[59] Third, Article 24 prohibits religious persons from making any explicit claims on "social order."

Articles 13 and 14, in conjunction with freedom of religion as set forth in Article 24, provide the opportunity to restrict freedom of religion if it is perceived to "endanger the existence of the…secular order of the Turkish Republic." The government may punish an individual on the basis of a person's intent alone, without taking into account the danger, if any, that may result from a particular action. The logical implication is that religiously motivated acts in civil and public life are considered illegal and punishable by law.[60]

According to Article 24, paragraph 2, education and instruction shall take place "under the supervision and control of the state." The constitution does not include any clause that recognizes religious education as an aspect of religious freedom. In practical terms, this means that there is no place for private educational institutions of religious persuasions in Turkey. In fact, the 1924 Law on Unification of Education, still in effect, had already nationalized and monopolized the Turkish educational system. This is quite different from the European and American systems. For instance, unlike in Turkey, restrictions on wearing the headscarf, if any, would only be applicable to public schools in the United States, where private schools are exempt from public control.

Ambiguous Practices

Despite the general affirmation of international human rights principles in the Turkish Constitution, the application of strict secularism makes it impossible to conclude that Turkey has upheld freedom of religion in a manner compatible with international human rights standards. The incompatibility arises because of the particular Turkish variant of secularism. Although there is no uniform and universal understanding of secularism, each country, on the basis of its social, political, and historical background, develops its own conception. Moreover, because of evolving social, cultural, and political attitudes, no fixed and irrevocable understanding of secularism exists even within the same society. In a liberal democracy, the wall between religion and politics constantly moves. In Turkey, however, the concept of secularism is complex and frozen; ambiguous institutional structures distinguish it from what may appear to be a similar version of secularism in other countries. Two examples of such differences follow.

Directorate of Religious Affairs

The first controversial issue is the existence of a government-controlled Directorate of Religious Affairs (DIB) that supervises and regulates Islam appoints and pays the country's imams and issues standardized sermons to be read aloud in thousands of mosques each Friday.[61] There are more that seventy thousand mosques in Turkey, and the DIB receives considerable funds from the state budget, but it offers almost no services to non-Sunni Muslim organizations.[62] According to Article 136 of the constitution, the DIB is instructed to exercise its duties "in accordance with the principles of secularism, removed from all political views and ideas." Even though the establishment and justification of this institution occurred in 1924, well before secularism had been inserted into the constitution, it was meant to regulate religion in the country and ensure that religious officials and imams did not promote fundamentalist ideas. This has caused the propagation of an official version of Islam that is shaped and determined by the state.

During the period between 1950 and 1960, the Turkish government moderated strict secularism by using this institution effectively to disseminate religion-friendly views, but this period ended with the military coup. Throughout the history of the Turkish Republic, the DIB has, on occasion crossed, the fine line between the regulation of religion and the political use of religion. Nevertheless, the military-backed constitution of 1982, despite its strong secularist slant, preferred to retain this institution rather than abolish it. The secularists' interest is more concerned with preserving and controlling the influence of religion on societal issues than with establishing a genuine separation between religion and politics. The idea behind the establishment of the DIB was to exert control over Sunni Islam-oriented religious practices and to exclude Sufi Islam from the benefits of state support.

Throughout the history of Turkey, Sufis (*tarikats*), identified as proponents of a civil-society version of Islam as opposed to the state-controlled ideology of Islam, had always occupied an important place in the social, economic, and political life of the country. Sufis were at the center of religious culture and education. During the Ataturk period, the state outlawed their activities and cut their funds because of their support of the Ottoman dynasty during the War of Independence. Sufis were also accused of being at the center of unrest. However, the Sufis continued to exist and influence social and political life in Turkey in subtle ways. Today, even though their existence is illegal, numerous Sufi activities persist in Turkey and in Europe, especially in Germany, where more than five million Turks reside.[63]

Another problematic feature of the DIB is that its jurisdiction extends only to Muslims, as the Treaty of Lausanne protects the rights of non-Muslims. At first glance, this seems to violate the equality principle of the constitution by delegating the administration of Muslim and non-Muslim affairs to two different government agencies. This seems to be a continuation of the Ottoman tradition, which had developed and used an early multicultural system for non-Muslims for many centuries that was different than for its Muslim majority.[64] Although each religious minority has the same rights as the country's Muslim citizens, their citizenship rights are somewhat limited when compared to the established religion of Islam.[65] One of the reasons for this limitation is the nature of the Turkish Republic, which was established with the overriding goal of achieving a unified nation-state. In recent years, the government has taken significant steps to improve the treatment of religious minorities. One of the reasons for these actions is pressure from the EU associated with the accession process. The recovery of property rights of religious minorities was a delicate issue in the negotiations between Turkey and the EU. The AKP, again, acted progressively on this issue, unlike several earlier secular Turkish governments, and the Turkish Parliament enacted a new law to correct unjust practices.[66]

Mandatory Religious Education

Turkey mentions no official state religion in its constitution. However, in a provision added by the military in 1982, the constitution obliges the state to provide Muslim religious education in elementary and secondary schools, a regulation that would appear to conflict with the principles of a modern, secular state.[67] According to some commentators, this significant policy shift discourages religious parents who want their children to obtain an education in Islam from sending them to private religious classes—some of which are suspected of having ties to Islamic fundamentalist organizations. The danger of fundamentalism, however, was not the main reason for the policy; rather, it seems to have been an expression of Cold War policies. The Turkish military, preoccupied with the threat of communist ideology, had displaced the democratically elected civilian government and wanted to cleanse society of communist ideology; at the time, the promotion of religion seemed to be the lesser evil.

After the military coup in the 1980s, not only was mandatory religious education initiated, but also many Imam Hatip schools were established all over the country, especially in Anatolia. These schools originally had produced professional imams in the 1920s and were the only alternative to secular public schools. In 1997, to discourage public expression of Islamist ideas due to the rise of Muslim political parties, the government extended the required period of secular mandatory education from five years to eight years for all children. The goal was to limit attendance at the public Imam Hatip schools that were popular among religious and conservative sectors of the population. Under the 1997 law, students could pursue their studies in these religious schools only after completing eight years of compulsory secular education. This law practically eliminated Imam Hatip middle schools and also, indirectly, had a negative impact on girls. Since girls are not allowed to wear a headscarf in secular public schools, many of them terminated their education. Because the Treaty of Lausanne protects minority religions in Turkey, mandatory religious education did not create any new problems for non-Muslims, who had their own schools and an independent religious education system. However, 15 million Turkish Alevis were affected negatively; a serious violation of their religious rights.[68] The European Court of Human Rights (ECHR) recently criticized Turkey for not providing religious education for the Alevi minorities.[69]

6. The Jurisprudence of the Constitutional Court on Islam

The Turkish Constitutional Court's view of religious liberties and how they affect Turkish secularism has thus far projected the underlying political philosophy of the constitution. One of the distinct features of the Constitutional Court is its power to interfere in Turkish political life by dismantling democratically constituted, and even elected, political parties.[70] If we look at the jurisprudence of the Constitutional Court since its establishment, it is rather remarkable that the Court has been so active in imposing control over the political structure of the Turkish system. It has also been a staunch and consistent protector of the interests of the state. In fact, the Court's rulings regarding human rights issues have not been compatible with liberal democratic goals, as the Court regards the exercise of fundamental liberties as potentially threatening to state authority.[71] In liberal democracies, the constitution is supposed to give priority to the rights and freedoms of its citizens, or at worst to strike a balance between societal and state interests. From this perspective it is impossible to view the jurisprudence of the Turkish Constitutional Court as compatible with the minimum standards of a liberal democracy.

The referral of the secular-religious clash to the Turkish judiciary became an attractive option for powerful secular interests seeking to combat the alleged threat of religious fundamentalism while maintaining a facade of legality and Western-style constitutional democracy. The result has been the emergence of the Constitutional Court as an important venue for constraining political Islam and removing its policy preferences from the purview of legitimate political discourse. The jurisprudence of the Constitutional Court in relation to freedom of religion and secularism can be assessed from two perspectives: closure of political parties because of activities against secularism, and annulment of laws authorizing headscarf use in universities.

The Closure of Political Parties

Since the birth of the multiparty political system in Turkey in 1946, a fundamental problem threatening the freedom of Turkish political life has been the existence of certain legal and constitutional restrictions on the formation and management of political parties. Political parties have been dissolved by military coups, as happened in 1960 and again in 1980; prevented from forming in the first place; or shut down by means of legislation. Under Articles 68 and 69 of the constitution and the Political Parties Act, the Constitutional Court dissolved several parties and banned their leaders from engaging in politics for some years.[72] The irony is that, almost overnight, the dissolved parties reemerge with the same ideology and even the same permanent staff and resources—but with a new name.[73] Some decisions of the Turkish Constitutional Court have been appealed before the ECHR, only to meet with disappointment when the ECHR upheld the Turkish court's rulings.[74]

In 1995, the Parliament amended the Constitution to limit the power of the Constitutional Court over political parties and to ensure that the Court could not dissolve a political party merely on the grounds that its statutes or programs contradicted the provisions of the constitution or on the basis of disapproval of one or two activities conducted by the party. Nevertheless, in

1998 the Constitutional Court declared the Welfare Party unconstitutional. In reaction, more rigid criteria were inserted into the text of Article 69 of the constitution through an amendment in 2001, but the Virtue Party was dismantled in the same year. The 2001 constitutional amendment, which made it more difficult to dissolve political parties, was a requirement for EU membership.[75]

The aim of the constitutional amendment was to establish a delicate balance between electoral democracy and judicial oversight. This legislative move was a reaction against the invalidation of electoral outcomes that increased the number of representatives from Islam-friendly or Kurdish-friendly political parties. So far, the most prevalent ground for closure has been the violation of the constitutional statement concerning the "indivisible integrity of the State's territory and nation." Several political parties, including those accused of having connections with the PKK (Kurdistan Workers' Party), have been shut down for supporting a separatist organization in Turkey or for taking positions on the Kurdish issue that appear to conflict with the official line. The Constitutional Court interprets the principles of the unity of the state and of secularism in a rigid and exclusive way. Its approach imposes compulsory common standards that must be accepted by all political parties if they seek to survive. This position is inconsistent with the freedom of political parties in a democratic country.

The reasoning of the many judicial decisions defining antisecular activities is simply as follows: "Political parties advocated the transformation of the principle of secularism defined in the constitution and the laws."[76] For instance, the Welfare Party (Refah, 1998) and the Virtue Party (Fazilet, 2001) were dismantled because both parties advocated lifting the headscarf ban, allegedly supported a plural legal system, and allowed the wearing of headscarves in a reception at the residence of the prime minister. Therefore, allegedly, they violated the laws of the revolution.

The most recent party closure case was the most controversial. As indicated earlier, in 2008 despite the stricter legal conditions, Turkey's chief prosecutor brought a case against two parties, the DTP (Kurdish Party) and the AKP, the sole governing party, each for different reasons.[77] The challenge to the validity of the AKP triggered great political turmoil, which threatened the stability of the country. The leader of the AKP, Prime Minister Recep Tayyip Erdogan, has a long history of being banned from politics. Indeed, when he was mayor of Istanbul in 1998, after reciting a provocative poem during a political rally, Erdogan was sentenced to a prison term and banned from holding political office. The Constitutional Court had interpreted the speech at the rally as "advocating Islamic revolution," given its political context.[78] Experience had taught the AKP leadership to be extremely careful not to be trapped again, yet the party did not altogether escape this destiny, because the Court nearly closed it down. Early in the party's course, the secular establishment followed the AKP's legislative activities very closely. It opposed AKP initiatives, such as a failed attempt to recriminalize adultery and a tax on the wine industry, which were considered by many to be punitive. When Erdogan spoke publicly against contraception and abortion, his stance was interpreted as Islamic, and, finally, any comment he might make in support of lifting the headscarf ban would cross a dangerous red line drawn by seculars.

The principal reason for initiating the AKP closure in 2008 was the passage of a constitutional amendment that lifted the headscarf ban. By its nonadherence to the rules set out in the constitution, the Court eroded the separation of powers and acted in a manner that seemed to defy the legal order. The Turkish Constitutional Court demonstrated once again that it does not respect fundamental human rights, particularly the right of equality before the law. The Court's expansionist interpretation of the rights of the state, and its corresponding restrictive position regarding the rights of the individual, has been one of the major impediments to the progress of Turkish democracy. Instead of upholding the basic rights of Turkey's citizens, the judiciary has opted instead to restrict these rights and liberties in order to protect the state and maintain the status quo.[79]

Headscarf Decisions

Turkish high courts such as the Constitutional Court and the Administrative Supreme Court (Danistay) have played an important role in the last few decades because of their highly political decisions in support of the headscarf ban. The competing arguments in the headscarf debate are always more political than legal. Yet, because of the sharp polarity of the two sides, there is no societal agreement on which interpretation of the law was correct. On the secular front, the legal basis for the ban rests on the decision of the Constitutional Court. According to the secularists, the headscarf issue is not a question of individual rights and freedoms, but a matter of disallowing a symbol of political Islam and protecting the sanctity of the secular state.

Critics of the headscarf ban argue that there is no adequate legal ground prohibiting headscarves, especially considering that wearing a headscarf is a religious requirement for many Muslim women. Additionally, these critics claim that the freedom to wear headscarves is an integral aspect of the freedom of religion and freedom of speech, and that, therefore, the decision of the Constitutional Court should not be treated as a sufficient basis for the implementation of the headscarf ban. They contend that the imposition of the headscarf ban was a de facto, oppressive initiative resulting from the post-modern military coup and not an instance of valid law. The legal and political arguments used by the Turkish high courts and the counterarguments of the defense are set forth below.

The Legal Arguments

A. Did Turkey's Constitutional Court ban the headscarf? According to head-scarf users, the answer to this question is no, and according to the seculars, yes. Headscarf proponents, first of all, argue that there is no rule about how to dress in the constitution. Moreover, Article 12 dictates that, "Everyone has individual, untouchable, non-derogable fundamental rights and freedom." Therefore, it is impossible to interpret any article of the constitution as autho-rizing the headscarf ban because freedom of dress is part of the equal rights and freedoms accorded to every individual. Article 42 gives the right to an education to all; Article 24 defines freedom of belief, religion, and religious practice. Finally, Article 70 gives everyone the right to become a civil ser-vant. Women who wear a headscarf are discriminated against and denied all of these rights guaranteed under the constitution.

B. Is there any law that denies the headscarf? In the entire Turkish legal sys-tem, there are only two laws that deal with attire, both concern men only. The first one, enacted in 1925, obliges members of Parliament and civil servants to wear a hat.[80] The second law, enacted in 1934, deals with religious dress and is applied to clergy, boy scouts, sportsmen, foreign diplomats, and military servicemen.[81] It is impossible to use either of these laws to ban the wearing of the headscarf by women in Turkey.

C. Does the Higher Education Law permit discriminatory implementa-tion with respect to headscarf wearing? Article 17 of the Higher Education Law provides for "freedom of dress in higher education institutions, and this can only be changed by law." Because no Turkish law bans the headscarf, this would seem to mean that headscarf use is legitimate. A Constitutional Court decision cannot change this reality by interpreting this rule without invalidating it.[82]

D. Are decisions of the Constitutional Court the highest legal authority? One of the major legal disagreements relating to the headscarf debate is whether the Parliament could issue a law, without changing the constitution, allow-ing headscarf use in universities. This legal argument created a huge political outcry in Turkey. According to secularists, neither changing the law, nor issuing a new law, nor changing the constitution can legitimize the wearing of a headscarf, because a decision of the Constitutional Court represents the highest legal authority. This absurd argument attracted many followers among the secular elites, especially in light of the 2005 *Sahin* headscarf decision of the European Court of Human Rights.

E. *Is it possible to reverse freedom of dress despite the existing law?* The Constitutional Court did not invalidate the addendum Article 17 of the Higher Education Law, which means that this law is still applicable. Eight years after the Constitutional Court decision, in 1998, university administrations cannot rely on an administrative order that is based on an interpretation of the Court's decision.[83] The separation of powers is a fundamental principle of a democratic system. The Constitutional Court can annul a law, but it cannot interfere with how laws are implemented.[84]

F. *What rules and principles limit human rights and individual freedom in a democratic society?* Article 13 of the constitution set forth the rules limiting fundamental human rights and freedoms. According to Article 13: (1) a law should establish limitations; (2) such limitations should not violate the spirit of the constitution, the rules and principles of a democratic society, the secularity principle, or the proportionality principle; (3) any limitation should not interfere with the fundamental spirit of rights and freedoms. Since there is no law against headscarf use in the Turkish legal system, any ban would violate Article 13 (2) consistent with the Court's own decisions. Thus, any limitation on headscarf use should be considered unlawful.[85]

The Political Arguments

A. *The headscarf is considered an ideological symbol.* Women who wear headscarves do not wear them just because they are sincerely religious. The real reason they wear them is to express an ideological and political commitment.

Counterargument: There is no homogenous group of women who wear the headscarf; wearing a headscarf has multiple meanings, which involve religious belief, culture, habit, ideological tool, freedom, democratic right, fear, security, family pressure, and identity. Therefore, to indiscriminately punish all women who wear headscarves because some women wear them for political and ideological reasons is grossly unfair. Moreover, traditional headscarf use remains highly acceptable in Turkish society, as long as the headscarf wearer does not attempt to participate in the "modern," which is defined by the Turkish state as the "public sphere." But in Turkey's legal system, public space is broadly defined to include any place where public services are offered, such as universities, courts, hospitals, libraries, and other public buildings. Headscarf wearers cannot receive many of the services normally provided by the Turkish state to its citizens and creates significant discrimination against these women.[86]

B. The wearing of a headscarf by civil servants is against the neutrality principle of the state.

Counterargument: In Turkey the principle of neutrality is misunderstood and is not implemented correctly. The state identifies itself with a certain ideology, but considers itself to be neutral and rejects alternative views. Considering that in Turkey, more that 60 percent of women wear a headscarf, it is unfair to disallow them from providing public services. When the state hires female civil servants other than for uniformed positions, such as security or military officers, it should consider only the skills necessary for a particular job and not dress, personal belief, or ideology, as long as the civil servant understands the duty to act in a neutral, objective manner.

C. Removing the headscarf should be considered as a way to gain freedom and independence. Seculars claim that the headscarf ban is actually beneficial for women. Wearing a headscarf automatically forces a woman into a secondary position in society, precludes her from participating in the public sphere, and situates her within a group that holds a worldview hostile to freedom.

Counterargument: This view confuses the concepts of freedom and emancipation. Individuals must be able to choose for themselves what is acceptable and desirable; otherwise, there is no freedom. The decision to wear a headscarf should belong to an individual, not to the state. Pushing women to conform against their free will is a characteristic of antidemocratic societies. Moreover, in some instances, the headscarf can be a tool for freedom—as a protector of women that enables them to enter the public sphere and attend universities. The denial of access to the public sphere and the right to receive public services takes freedom away from religious women.

D. In order to protect women from a future possible regime that would make headscarf use mandatory, it is legitimate for the state to ban headscarf use.

Counterargument: A legitimate fear of antidemocratic regimes and attempts to protect society from such an outcome are unobjectionable. However, to deny part of a society their legitimate human rights in order to protect the rest is not an acceptable policy. Moreover, there is no evidence that a headscarf ban would prevent a society from becoming antidemocratic. To favor the ban is to dissolve the differences between antidemocratic countries such as Saudi Arabia and Iran that require the headscarf and Turkey that prohibits it. These governments control the lifestyle, as well as the ethnic, cultural, and religious activities of women subject to their authority. All regulate women's dress according to ideological state policy and choice is greatly reduced for women in such countries. Restricted from making their own individual decisions, women are not free and need to be emancipated. From the perspective of the principles of universal human rights, Turkey's approach to the headscarf is identical to that of countries subject to strict Islamic governance.

7. Judicial Activism of the Constitutional Court

The Constitutional Court's self-empowering interpretation sets a dangerous precedent for any political-legal order and in particular for those of a democratic polity. The interference with constitutional democracy gives a green light to dangerous scenarios. If, in the future, a fascist, totalitarian, or fundamentalist cohort of judges were to dominate the Court and seek to impose their worldviews on society, they would appear entitled to do so, given this precedent. Such an imbalance of power delegitimizes the entire political system. Rather than keeping its distance from the fray, the Constitutional Court is increasingly viewed as a player in partisan politics. The precedent set by the court's actions could undermine the stability of the country by eroding the rule of law and undermining the judiciary's role as a neutral arbiter. It harms the judiciary's image, and, in turn, diminishes the sense of justice and respect for law and order among the Turkish citizenry.

Recent developments in the Turkish constitutional debate suggest that the real division derives not from the interpretation and implementation of secularism but, instead, from a struggle for influence and power among various state institutions. From the outset, strong supporters of strict secularism have been frightened by the rise of political Islam and fought hard to resist a transition from strict to liberal secularism. They claim that the current government would allow fundamentalist political Islam to emerge, slowly and gradually, in such a permissive environment. It is reasonable to take seriously the danger of a radical Islamic movement in Turkey. There are Turkish Islamist groups, as elsewhere, that are antimodern and antisecular, and ideologically adhere to fundamentalist Islamic views.[87] However, such groups are politically and culturally quite marginal in Turkey. Some groups are more rigid than others with regard to the promotion of women's rights and women's desire to participate in public life in Turkey. The real danger of radical Islamism in Turkey might very well be a reaction to the secular exclusionary system that denies female citizens access to education and employment opportunities, pushes them out of social and public spaces, keeps them at home, and gives women no alternative means for achieving normalcy. This is a dangerous road that could, over time, give rise to a radical Islamist movement. Such a development would be a greater danger to Turkish secularism than allowing women to participate in public life today.

A secular democratic state should be neutral in regard to religion. Neutrality means the government shall neither favor nor burden any particular religion. In Turkey, however, neutrality is supposed to apply among religions, sects, and denominations, but not between the state and religion. From a liberal perspective, it is, of course, valuable not to favor or burden any religious belief, but what about the Turkish government's own strict commitment to secular values? In the Turkish case, *laïcité*, or secularism, unlike the liberal concept of secularism, does not produce "neutrality." An underlying principle and a specific duty of the state is to modernize Turkish society in line with secularist ideals. In other words, secularism is not a negative norm, which implies simple abstention on the part of the government, but a positive one, which effectively demands support for nonreligious values and even action, on occasion, against religious beliefs and practices. When implementing strict secularism, the state exerts control over religious life while supposedly excluding personal beliefs from public life. This is the expected result of the secularization processes initiated in many parts of the world in the early twentieth century. One reason for the strict implementation of secularism in Turkey is the expectation that the process will lead to de-Islamization. However, a misguided secularism, based on the claim of a government to control religious life, tends to produce a tension between state and society, and this is dangerous for democracy. Policies based on controlling society often impose unfair, arbitrary, and discriminatory restrictions on civilian and political rights. This brings about a decline of the legitimacy of the state and its political system. In most cases, the state will disallow the normal political participation of religious actors and be inclined to oppress them. In Turkey, such authoritarian policies do not provoke violent responses from Islamic organizations, but in other countries they have led to violence and widespread unrest.[88]

At the beginning of the republic, Turkey deliberately chose an authoritarian path to modernization. Indeed, the main concern of the political elite was the modernization of Turkish society without any effort to establish a democratic form of government. Political activity was limited to political parties that fully accepted the republican ideology, which consists, essentially, of nationalism and secularism. In this context, references to religious values and symbols in public and political realms, as well as in civil-societal life, were forbidden and punished by the state. The Turkish model of secularism as one of the most important and unchangeable principles of the Turkish Constitution does not possess the flexibility needed for adjusting to the changing social and political needs of Turkish society. As a frozen concept, strict secularism completely rejects any role for religion in any public space and consequently excludes religiously devout citizens from public participation. In contrast, liberal secularism gives opportunities to its citizens without discriminating against people with ethnic and religious orientations. In strong democratic cultures, the social role of religion is not regarded as a threat to the secular order. Turkey's exclusionary secularism restricts the options of devout Turkish Muslim women and has been used to ban headscarf use by the Turkish judicial establishment. Moreover, the secularist legal and political arguments of the Turkish courts have reached the ECHR and significantly influenced European jurisprudence. The next chapter discusses ECHR decisions concerning the headscarf debate and evaluates whether the European court has effectively protected Muslim women's freedom of religion in its rulings on headscarf use in schools.

4

The Role of the European Court of Human Rights

> [It] appears difficult to reconcile the wearing of an Islamic scarf with the message of tolerance, respect for others, and, above all, equality and non–discrimination.
>
> JUDGMENT OF THE EUROPEAN COURT OF HUMAN RIGHTS, Dahlab v. Switzerland

In national and international courts, cases concerning freedom of religion and religious symbols raise critical questions about the limits of religious freedom in the increasingly diverse societies of the West, in the European Union, and beyond. On the one hand, these cases signify a growing tension between cultural extension and the legal enforcement of human rights, including freedom of religion and belief; on the other hand, the cases reflect an increased vigilance in relation to religious practices, especially those that reflect Huntington's "clash of civilizations" and consider restrictions on religious freedom in the name of public order.[1] The cases, especially in Europe, also disclose "the growth of pan-European legal discourse of religious symbols not only as text, but as a mechanism, however broad and ambiguous, of social control."[2] Decisions of the European Court of Human Rights (ECHR) in these cases illustrate the pertinence of such a statement.

Although the European Convention on Human Rights (the Convention), created by the Council of Europe as a regional agreement, was strongly influenced by the Universal Declaration of Human Rights, it contains a more precise expression of specific rights and has made a great contribution by raising awareness of human rights issues on the European continent.[3] The ECHR, established by the Convention, receives a complaint from an individual after the applicant has exhausted all domestic remedies and alleges to be a victim of a violation of the Convention by a contracting state.[4] International lawyers generally regard the European human rights system as the "most effective and advanced" supranational human rights regime in the world and "a striking example of what a well-conceived instrument can accomplish in a promising environment."[5] Compliance has been so consistent that the ECHR's decisions are considered "as effective as those any domestic court, and a rare success story in the international arena."[6] According to some political scientists, through its judicial decisions the court has helped to "consolidate democratic institutions and anchor liberal reforms."[7] Sometimes the ECHR is heralded, if not unanimously, as the "Constitutional Court of Europe."[8]

1. ECHR Decisions in Headscarf Cases

In keeping with the ECHR's important role for its member states, the court's decisions in headscarf cases have exerted a major influence in important legal arenas in Europe and beyond. Unfortunately, the ECHR's adopted approach to restrictions on the wearing of headscarves allows states to violate the rights of individuals, specifically those who belong to non-Christian religions and wish to wear certain articles of clothing in public for religious reasons. The ECHR has set an easy standard for states that seek to limit the rights of those within their jurisdiction who use these forms of religious expression. In many European states, the rights of minority religions have routinely been limited, and the ECHR has not repudiated such limitations. The judges of the ECHR find it difficult to move outside of the (broadly) Christian and secular religious and political paradigms that predominate in Europe, and thus they have been unable to address non-Christian religions in a respectful and culturally sensitive manner.[9] The headscarf cases discussed below provide some examples of how religious freedom has been limited by the ECHR's interpretation of Article 9, paragraphs 1 and 2 of the Convention:

> Convention Article 9 (1): Everyone has the right to freedom of thought, conscience and religion; this right includes freedom to change his religion or belief and freedom, either alone or in community with others and in public or private, to manifest his religion or belief and freedom, wither alone or in community with others and in public or private, to manifest his religion or belief, in worship, teaching, protect or observance.

> Convention Article 9 (2): Freedom to manifest one's religion or belief shall be subject only to such limitations as are prescribed by law and are necessary in a democratic society in the interest of public safety, for the protection of public order, health and morals, or for the protection of the rights and freedom of others.

The headscarf cases also demonstrate the extent to which the court has been prepared to rely on unexamined governmental claims about Islam and the wearing of headscarves, assertions unsubstantiated by either evidence or reasoning. These pivotal decisions suggest the complexity of cases that attempt to limit religious freedom in the name of state neutrality, secularism, and even, in a twisted way, gender equality—all principles that are strongly protected by the constitutions of liberal states. The international and national judicial decisions, together with the domestic legislation of individual states, illustrate, in this instance, the perverse application of judicial oversight.

In an increasingly globalized world with frequent interaction between international and national law, the influence of legal standards established by an important international court is of vital significance. Until 1992, despite numerous complaints based on Article 9, the court did not issue a single judgment in which the right to religious freedom was given full and proper consideration. For more than thirty years, these applications were deemed inadmissible as "manifestly ill-founded" under Article 27 (2) of the Convention.[10] Since then, a substantial evolution has occurred in the case law of the ECHR that indicates, as Julie Ringelheim put it, "an increasing attempt at going beyond casuistry and building a consistent vision of religious freedom and of its implications for the relations between states and religions in a democratic society, valid across Europe."[11] As of 2011, the ECHR had dealt with sixteen lawsuits, most of them after 2000, filed by individuals banned from wearing religious symbols in various circumstances.

Among the sixteen cases, twelve are related to the ban of Islamic headscarves in public education (six concerning students and six teachers),[12] and three consider the Sikh turban in the context of safety regulations.[13] More recently, a case related to safety regulations involved a Muslim woman in France.[14] Apart from one case relating to the United Kingdom and another to Switzerland, five cases concern France, and the remaining nine cases involve Turkey. It is remarkable that, apart from the famous *Leyla Sahin v. Turkey* decision by the ECHR Grand Chamber in November 2005, now a cornerstone of the court's jurisprudence, and two cases in December 2008, all of the rulings in these cases were "non-admissibility" decisions, meaning the court did not address the merits of the cases. Below we discuss and analyze two important ECHR decisions in religious clothing or headscarf cases: *Dahlab v. Switzerland* and *Leyla Sahin v. Turkey*.

Dahlab v. Switzerland

In 2001, Lucia Dahlab, a primary schoolteacher who had converted to Islam, filed the first case of this type against Switzerland. Until 2001, there had been no complaints about her modest clothing style and headscarf from her colleagues, her pupils, or their parents in the school where she taught, in the canton of Geneva. The ECHR dismissed the application as inadmissible, and Dahlab was subsequently prohibited from wearing traditional, modest clothing, including a headscarf.[15] Sensitive to the norm that she should not proselytize, when her students asked her why she covered her head, rather than identifying herself as a Muslim, she answered to keep her ears warm.[16] Post-9/11, however, a school inspector reported that Dahlab was wearing Islamic dress. The school administration issued a directive ordering her to stop wearing the garments at school. She refused and challenged this decision in the Swiss courts. After she lost, she brought the case to the ECHR.[17]

The ECHR upheld the government's right to require a Muslim teacher to remove her headscarf on the grounds that the law did not target the plaintiff's religious belief; rather, it aimed "to protect others' freedom and security of public order." It also protected the young, four- to eight-year-old children in Dahlab's classes, who were "more easily influenced by such a powerful external symbol" than the older children.[18] The ECHR concurred with the view of the Swiss Federal Court that the prohibition on wearing a headscarf in the context of the applicant's activities as a teacher was "justified by the potential interference with the religious beliefs of her pupils at the school and the pupils' parents, and by the breach of the principle of denominational neutrality in schools." The ECHR did not consider that among the pupils and families there might also be Muslims. Switzerland is a country with significant immigrant populations, a majority of them from Turkey. The ECHR's decision had a significant negative impact on Muslim minorities in the particular school district.

According to Carolyn Evans, the court's reasoning in *Dahlab* had three key elements: (1) the wearing of an Islamic headscarf could have a proselytizing effect;[19] (2) the headscarf is incompatible with gender equality; and (3) the headscarf is incompatible with tolerance and respect. None of these arguments were adequately supported by evidence or facts. With this judgment, a teacher with an otherwise spotless employment record, who had spent years wearing Islamic clothing to which no one objected, had been effectively fired because of her headscarf—more important, because of post-9/11 Islamophobia. In line with the general atmosphere in Europe post-9/11, the case was considered so clear that it did not merit a full and proper consideration by the ECHR.[20] Although the *Dahlab* decision was one of non-admissibility, the decision disclosed distrust on the part of the ECHR toward the Islamic headscarf itself.[21] The decision did not seem important at the time, but *Dahlab* provided the legal reasoning used over and over again in future cases of the ECHR, repeated in both *Leyla Sahin* (2005) and *Dogru* (2008).

Leyla Sahin v. Turkey

Leyla Sahin v. Turkey is one of the most important ECHR decisions on the headscarf, because it was the Grand Chamber of the court that heard the case.[22] Leyla Sahin, a twenty-four-year-old, fifth-year female medical student at the Faculty of Medicine of the University of Istanbul, had transferred to Istanbul after four years at the University of Bursa. During those four years, she wore a headscarf, and she continued to wear it at the University of Istanbul until February 1998. On February 23, 1998, the vice-chancellor of the University of Istanbul issued a "circular" (an official statement) declaring that students wearing headscarves may not be admitted to lectures, courses, and examinations.[23] Ms. Sahin was not allowed to take certain examinations and was excluded from classes because she refused to remove her headscarf. She had also participated in what the court described as an "unauthorized assembly" outside the university's Faculty of Medicine, protesting against the rules on dress, and she was consequently suspended for a semester. Sahin left the University of Istanbul and completed her studies in Austria.[24] After exhausting legal remedies in Turkey, she brought an ECHR suit against Turkey for upholding the decision of the University of Istanbul.[25]

A seven-judge chamber decision of the ECHR on June 29, 2004, held unanimously that there had been no violation of Sahin's freedom of religion under Article 9.[26] In reaching its decision, the ECHR chamber drew on the Turkish Constitution and on legal practice related to Turkey's development as a secular state, as well as on the case law of the Constitutional Court of Turkey. Importantly, the ECHR also based its decision on comparative law, including court decisions and legal debates concerning the wearing of the Islamic headscarf in state schools in Belgium, France, Germany, the Netherlands, Switzerland, and the United Kingdom. The court's analysis of comparative law, however, was sloppy and full of inaccurate information.[27]

The ECHR chamber also referred to the French National Assembly bill of February 2004, which became law in March 2004, that banned "ostentatious" religious symbols in state primary and secondary schools. The French bill was not relevant to the Turkish case, yet the court wanted to allude to European sentiment regarding banning the headscarf in middle and high schools, despite the fact that Sahin had been a university student.

On September 27, 2004, the applicant requested that the chamber case be referred to the Grand Chamber of the ECHR. The court agreed to hear the case in Grand Chamber, and, one year later, a seventeen-judge panel handed down a fifty-one-page decision that included a separate, concurring opinion by two judges and one dissenting opinion. The majority decision of the Grand Chamber confirmed the earlier chamber's decision on the grounds that Turkey's political concerns about maintaining secularism legitimated interfering with Leyla Sahin's freedom of religion. Instead of invoking the alleged proselytizing effect of a headscarf, as in *Dahlab,* the Grand Chamber emphasized "pressure on students, who do not wear a headscarf" and relied in part on *Dahlab* with respect to gender equality and tolerance, citing the relevant section of the *Dahlab* decision as its conclusion.[28]

The Grand Chamber's key concerns in *Sahin* included (1) the possibility that an Islamic political party might rise in popularity and move to create a fully Islamic state in Turkey;[29] (2) the headscarf as a sign of gender inequality; and (3) the headscarf as associated with intolerance and as a threat to Turkish secularism.

Although the Turkish state's concerns were highly questionable, they were similar to the concerns of the European public at the time. The ECHR took these concerns seriously.[30] The ECHR also made clear that the legitimacy of a headscarf ban, in terms of human rights, was highly context-specific. This left the door wide open for different judgments in different sociopolitical circumstances, and many commentators have interpreted this as an implied reference to the 2004 French law that banned religious symbols in public schools.[31]

The Standard Review Process of the ECHR and the Sahin *Judgment*

The ECHR has established a standard procedure in cases concerning freedom of religion, based on Article 9 of the Convention. First, the court determines whether a state interfered with an individual's rights to freedom of religion as set forth in the provision. Then, the court investigates whether a state could justify restrictions placed on the behavior (in these cases, the restriction of headscarf use) by reference to the criteria set out in Article 9 (2).

In following this standard review process in the two chambers, the ECHR first decided that Turkey had interfered with Sahin's right to manifest her religious belief.[32] Scholars have interpreted this important part of the decision as a significant departure from the ECHR's earlier decisions regarding headscarf use.[33] The second step for the court is to consider in a specific case whether the conditions of paragraph 2 constitute an acceptable basis on which to limit freedom of religion, as follows:

   i. *The restriction should be prescribed by law:* The court first had to address how to interpret a condition of "prescribed by law." As discussed earlier, there was no statute banning the headscarf in the Turkish legal system. Sahin was expelled from the university because of an administrative regulation. In order to justify the headscarf ban, the ECHR observed that it "has always understood that the term "law" is a "substantive" not a "formal" one; it includes both "written law…and regulatory measures taken by professional regulatory bodies under independent rule-making powers delegated to them by parliament…and unwritten law…In sum, the 'law' is the provision in force as the competent courts have interpreted it."[34] In using this language, the ECHR endorsed the decision-making powers of university authorities, a prerogative previously granted only to national governments. With this deferential interpretation by the court, a circular issued by the vice-chancellor of the University of Istanbul was elevated to the status of law.[35] Furthermore, the court based its decision that the circular was prescribed on a prior opinion of Turkey's Constitutional Court, which had held that wearing headscarves in public schools was inconsistent with its understanding of secularity and also with the Turkish Constitution.[36] Thus, through the actions of one vice-chancellor, the dicta espoused in the Constitutional Court of Turkey became law and were then relied on to justify an abrogation of Sahin's rights and treated as sufficient to satisfy the "prescribed by law" requirement.

   ii. *The restriction should be necessary in a democratic society:* The second condition for the limitation of religious freedom was the most problematic part of the decision.[37] The ECHR interpreted various liberal principles literally, point by point, closely following the Turkish government's rationale for upholding the headscarf ban rather than adhering to European human rights principles based on the European Convention and the court's own jurisprudence. What is most troublesome is the court's failure to evaluate these abstract liberal principles in the context of this specific case.[38]

   In so doing, the ECHR opened the door to a dangerous extension of the margin of appreciation principle in the context of freedom of religion.[39] The idea behind this principle is that national legal systems and democratically elected authorities are often better placed to address issues arising within their territories than supranational judicial authorities. This presented the court with an easy way to decide the case, with the help of the Turkish authorities, to reach the conclusion that there had been no violation of Article 9 of the Convention.[40] However, in its earlier decisions, the ECHR had pointed out that "the margin of appreciation goes hand in hand with a European supervision," encompassing both the law and the decision applying it. In *Sahin* the court did not even try to assess this aspect of "European supervision."

In delimiting the margin of appreciation in *Sahin,* the ECHR designated what was at stake; namely, "the need to protect the rights and freedom of others, to preserve public order, and to secure civil peace and true religious pluralism."[41] Referring to an earlier case, *Karaduman v. Turkey,* the ECHR contended that "measures taken in universities were to prevent certain fundamentalist religious movements from exerting pressure on students who did not practice their religion or who belong to another religion were found to be justified by the Convention."[42]

According to the ECHR "there had to be borne in mind the impact which wearing such a symbol, which was presented or perceived as a compulsory religious duty, may have on those who choose not to wear it"[43]—a rather unusual argument for a human rights court. In the words of Jeremy Gunn, "we would not normally expect a human rights tribunal to be more solicitous of the sensibilities of those who do not like religious expression (which is not guaranteed by the European Convention)."[44] Moreover, Turkey presented no evidence at all that wearing a headscarf in schools creates social pressure on students who choose not to wear it, and the ECHR did not bother to search for such examples. The ECHR, however, could have looked in numerous places for evidence of Islamist pressure on women to wear the headscarf in universities, as in Sahin's story, or by consulting social scientific research, opinion polls, or human rights organizations.[45]

iii. Proportionality: According to the ECHR's standard procedure, proportionality between means and ends should be determined in each specific case. The ECHR never analyzed this critical issue of proportionality in *Sahin.*[46] Instead, the ECHR set forth its own "relevant factors." First, the court stated, "Practicing Islam in Turkish universities are free, within the limits imposed by educational organizational constraints, to manifest their religion in accordance with habitual forms of Muslim observance."[47] This was simply not true, as students prohibited from wearing the headscarf certainly are not free to observe their religion. Moreover, the ECHR is not competent to make a decision based on its knowledge of Islam "whether the headscarf is a habitual form of Muslim observance or not." Because the ECHR did not use expert witnesses, as some courts in the United States do under comparable circumstances,[48] it should have accepted the individual's interpretation about the content under observation in a particular religion.[49] As Judge Tulkens wrote in her dissent, "it is not the Court's role to make an appraisal…of a religion or a religious practice."[50]

Second, the long and complex history that produced various regulations on headscarves in universities was taken by the court as an example of a "continued dialog" among various groups and students. The practice of establishing "convincing offices" or "persuasion offices" that negotiate with students to voluntarily take off their headscarves so the students can enter university buildings,[51] rather than engaging in dialogue, is widely criticized in Turkey, because it creates an extra burden on and stigmatizes students. Headscarf regulations constantly changed in Turkey because of the changing political purposes of successive governments and not because of "continuing dialog" as the court wrongly insisted.

Third, the ECHR accepted fully the conclusions reached by Turkey's legislature and court system, despite the fact that both are heavily influenced by an unelected, strictly secularist military, and by high-level civil servants and high court judges. The headscarf had become a major controversial issue in Turkey, raised by political parties in the electoral process. Constant interference with democratically elected governments, in the name of the protection of Turkish secularism, led to ongoing negotiations about headscarf regulation. Rather than acknowledging this uncertainty in Turkey, the ECHR selectively recited the history of headscarf regulation.

The omission of relevant history is rendered more serious when it is coupled with the very wide margin of appreciation that the court determined was appropriate to examine Turkey's institutional determination.[52] With respect to the proportionality principle, the ECHR should have explained the reasons behind its reliance on a Turkish ruling that effectively precludes a very large number of women from pursuing higher education in Turkey. The court never balanced the right of women to manifest their religion by wearing headscarves against the right of other students to avoid proselytism.[53] The ECHR's interpretation of Article 9 in *Sahin* could perhaps be better understood as an acknowledgment that "the right to manifest one's religious belief can be abrogated as long as your government has outlawed that right, and has done so for appropriate purposes, as determined by the government itself."[54] The ECHR has apparently repeated similar arguments in all headscarf cases brought before it, including in its most recent case *Dogru v. France*, discussed below.

Significant Considerations Overlooked in Dahlab *and* Sahin

i. The meaning of headscarf use: In *Dahlab* and *Sahin*, the ECHR oversimplified the use of a headscarf in Turkey as an indicator of a polarizing opposition between the threat of fundamentalist Islam and the secularists seeking to retain a democracy and a secular legal system. As suggested earlier, wearing a headscarf has multiple meanings in modern Turkey and clarification of the various distinctions is easily accessible.[55] Statistics support this view, and respectable international human rights NGOs have reported on it.[56] There was no claim or conclusion in either of the two ECHR decisions that women wearing the headscarf, in Switzerland or in Turkey, were forced to do so. The wearing of a headscarf by educated, intelligent women might be better described as voluntary compliance with what they perceive to be a religious obligation.

ii. Stereotyping Islam: Moreover, the ECHR used highly questionable language in its *Dahlab* and *Sahin* judgments in referring to the Quranic view of the headscarf without detailed discussion of varying Islamic teachings by different Muslim scholars or of clothing in different Muslim societies.[57] The ECHR's broad, vague approach seems to reflect the popular Western view that the Quran and Islam are oppressive to women, and there is no need to be more specific because it is a self-evident, shared understanding of Islam.[58]

iii. One size fits all: Furthermore when the ECHR referred in *Sahin* to its earlier *Dahlab* case, it did not take into account the significant differences between *Dahlab* and *Sahin*, and the differences are crucial. Dahlab lived in Switzerland, a predominantly Christian country, as opposed to Sahin in Turkey, a predominantly Muslim country; Dahlab was a teacher, Sahin was a university student. Such differences were treated as irrelevant, and did not move the court to demonstrate that the value judgments being made were not merely reflections of stereotypes. Commenting on the *Dahlab* and *Sahin* cases, Carolyn Evans has convincingly argued that the court "uses both stereotypes of Muslim women without any recognition of the inherent contradiction between the two cases and with minimal evidence to demonstrate that either stereotype is accurate with respect either to the applicants or to Muslim women more generally."[59] On the one hand, the Muslim woman appears as "the victim of a gender oppressive religion, needing protection from abusive, violent male relatives, and passive, unable to help herself in the face of a culture of male dominance. On the other hand, the Muslim woman is also linked to the figure of the aggressor as she is "inherently and unavoidably engaged in ruthlessly propagating her views."[60] However, neither Dahlab nor Sahin belonged to a religious organization or a political movement that promoted Islamic fundamentalism, nor did they participate in civil disobedience at their school or workplace, and the court presented no evidence of the applicants' prejudices. The court seems to be saying that anyone who is sufficiently serious about advertising the fact that they are Muslim must by definition be intolerant. This argument demonstrates the importance of separating the decisions of a human rights court from the dominant populist stereotypes disseminated in European media.

iv. Interpreting secularism and Islam: The ECHR interpreted the concept of secularism as the opposite of Islam's intolerance, casting political Islam as inconsistent with the classic liberal state's role in addressing religious disputes and accepting that the liberal state, by definition, ensures that all religions and beliefs are treated fairly and equally.[61] However, there is in practice no assurance that secularism consistently upholds democracy with respect to religious freedom. On the contrary, the history of secularism is full of examples of the opposite, which were available to the court had it wished to expose itself to the full complexity of the opposing argument.[62]

v. Celebrating Turkish secularism: While adopting a highly problematic concept of secularism in general, the court took a further step by endorsing the more problematic aspects of Turkish secularism. The ECHR, in an almost self-congratulatory tone, found that Turkish secularism was consistent with the values underpinning the Convention, a rather unexpected historical validation.[63] For some commentators, the ECHR's deference to Turkey's principle of secularism was decisive in shaping the outcome in *Sahin*, and they harshly criticized the court's judgment.[64] The ECHR never mentioned Turkey's domestic political turmoil during the period when several contradictory regulations on the headscarf were issued. It never considered the military interventions in Turkish politics and their impact on secularist principles, let alone the thoroughly antidemocratic imposition of the entire Turkish Constitution by the military.

Turkish secularism was represented by the court as promoting gender equality and as the guarantor of democratic values, as the ECHR put it, seeking the "meeting point of liberty and equality." The ECHR also claimed that when Turkey became a secular state, there appeared to be an historic opportunity for women to be freed from traditional religious restraints and societal pressures. This argument requires elaborate research before reaching such an authoritative result about gender development in Turkey. Assuredly, the establishment of the republic brought about significant developments in the legal status of women during a period when Turkey was not completely secular. Nevertheless, a huge, well-documented gap exists between women's legal rights in the law books and their realization in the Turkish social structure, which merited no reference in the court's judgment. In practice, banning the headscarf in Turkey has had a negative impact on women, the majority of the population, but the ECHR never addressed the argument that characterizes the ban as "a backdoor means to deprive girls of education."[65]

In the headscarf cases, the ECHR knowingly chose not to look critically at Turkish politics. It seems probable that the judges, aware that Islam was becoming a European problem, deemed it better policy to take a critical view of Islam in arguments that had originated in a Muslim country rather than in Christian Europe.

Dogru v. France and *Kervanci v. France*

In November and December 2008, the ECHR was presented with two cases concerning restrictions of religious freedom for non-Christians. Two Muslim girls of Turkish origin, aged eleven at the time, were enrolled in the first year of a state secondary school in Flers for the academic year 1998–1999. From January 1999 onward, they wore headscarves to school and attended physical education classes wearing them. The girls refused to remove their headscarves despite repeated requests to do so by their teacher, who explained to them that wearing a headscarf was incompatible with physical education classes. They were expelled from the school in February 1999 due to their refusal to remove their headscarves.[66] The girls' parents proposed that they could wear hats instead of headscarves, but the school rejected this accommodation. When the two cases ended up in the ECHR, the court, in line with its recent jurisprudence, found no violation of the freedom of religion, stating that the girls, by insisting on their headscarves, had made an "ostentatious" display that was not consistent with French secularism.[67] This judicial response seemed odd, considering that the only issue raised was whether a headscarf or hat is incompatible with participation in a physical education class. The ECHR found the expulsions not to be disproportionate, because the girls could continue their education by taking a correspondence course and did not consider arguments that their right to an education was being violated.

These cases were important because they were the first cases against France after the French law of 2004 banning religious symbols in public schools came into force, although the cases had been initiated earlier. The court refused to apply the French headscarf law retroactively and instead noted that the domestic authorities had justified the measures based on statutory and regulatory provisions, internal documents, and a decision of the Conseil d'Etat (the Supreme Administrative Court in France).[68] These factors made the school action reasonable, based on (1) the duty to attend classes regularly; (2) the requirements of safety; and (3) the necessity of appropriate dress for sports activities.[69]

The ECHR's judgment contained, as in *Sahin,* a long paragraph describing French *laïcité* dating back to 1789. It noted that, from the 1980s, the French secular model was challenged by the presence of Muslims in society, particularly in schools. Quoting a paragraph from the Stasi Commission that gave birth to the 2004 law, the court stated, "In France, the troubles have given rise to various forms of collective mobilization regarding the question of the place of Islam in Republican society."[70]

The ECHR pursued its regular procedure in dealing with several headscarf decisions of the Conseil d'Etat and declarations and circulars of the French Ministry of Education, in order to reach the conclusion that any "restriction should be prescribed by law."[71] The ECHR also referred to a French government report on the application of the 2004 law and accepted the French government's argument that the law was effective and successful in eliminating headscarves from schools without causing significant negative effects. No evidence was produced by the court to back up this claim.

In order to show that the interference had been "necessary in a democratic society," the ECHR referred to its judgment in *Sahin* and recommended that the "same solution be adopted in the recent case, having regard to the fact that the measure in question had mainly been based on the constitutional principles of secularism and gender equality."[72] The ECHR repeatedly associated the secularism argument with the neutrality required of the state. Moreover, the court added that respect for religious freedom does not mean that manifestations of religious beliefs cannot be subject to restriction.[73] The Convention, however, makes it clear that religious freedom is not limited to beliefs but extends to manifestations.[74]

The ECHR also cited *Dahlab,* using the "powerful external symbol" argument, because of the supposed effects of this behavior on the other pupils in the eleven-year-old applicant's class. The court did not make a distinction between *Dahlab,* which concerned a teacher, and *Dogru* and/or *Kervanci,* which involved children and asserted that the eleven-year-old girls' headscarves were likely to have an impact on other children.

The ECHR did rely literally and consistently on its earlier decisions, especially the *Sahin* decision, in the *Dogru* and *Kervanci* cases. Other than a few paragraphs that were specific to *Dogru* and *Kervanci,* the court proposed no new argument and saw no need to make an adjustment in view of the much different set of facts in the case of children's headscarves in a physical education class. To validate its conclusion, the ECHR formulated a more general argument: "In France, as in Turkey or Switzerland, secularism is a constitutional principle, and a founding principle of the Republic to which the entire population adheres, and the protection of which appears to be of prime importance, in particular in schools. The Court reiterates that an attitude which fails to respect that principle will not necessarily be accepted as being covered by the freedom to manifest one's religion and will not enjoy the protection of Article 9 of the Convention (see: *Refah Partisi and others v. Turkey*)."[75]

This is a monumental paragraph. The ECHR explained its recent decisions in *Dogru* and *Kervanci* as confirming that decisions by Turkish courts, whether on the headscarf or on political party closures (Refah), played a pivotal role in formulating the court's approach in other cases related to Islam. There is little doubt that any case pertaining to Islam that comes before the ECHR, no matter which country is involved, will have a predictable outcome.

El Morsli v. France

In a case decided in March of 2008, Ms. El Morsli was denied access to the French general consulate in Marrakesh because she refused to take off her headscarf while going through the identity check.[76] Although she was ready to remove her headscarf in the presence of a woman, this option was refused. In light of this experience, she unsuccessfully requested a visa for entry into France by registered mail. The reason for its refusal was that she needed to follow normal procedures to obtain a visa by going in person to the consulate. She complained to the ECHR that she was being denied her rights, based on Article 9 (freedom of religion), Article 14 (discrimination based on religion), and Article 8 (right to family). According to the ECHR, the French authorities did not infringe upon her freedom of religion. In the court's opinion, these security checks are necessary in the interests of public safety and the arrangements for implementing them fall within the state's margin of appreciation.[77] It is striking that, in this case, the court failed to take into account the fact that El Morsli was ready to accommodate the security rules by offering to be inspected by a woman, despite the result that El Morsli was denied a French visa. Moreover, this case was not about a continuing relationship that might erode secularism, nor an illustration of the neutrality argument relied on in earlier judgments of the court to protect students and teachers from adverse impacts. This case has more severe consequences for wider concerns about the headscarf ban, especially bearing on whether Muslim women wearing headscarves can enter public places.

The Sikh Turban Cases

Mann Singh

In 2007, the EHCR dealt with another Article 9 case, this time in relation to the Sikh turban. Mann Singh had for twenty years held a driver's license that had a photo of him wearing a turban. In 2004, he was unable to renew his license with a similar photo, and he viewed the refusal as a fundamental violation of his religion.[78] The ECHR rejected the case outright on admissibility without a hearing. Essentially, the ECHR took on board the government's argument that bareheaded photos were necessary for identification purposes without considering that the authorities had accepted photos of persons wearing turbans until 2004. Subsequently, the French government issued a directive stating that in all official identity photos the subject had to be bareheaded. The *Dahlab* and *Mann Singh v. France* decisions are significant in that they demonstrate that the 9/11 terrorist attacks on the United States in 2001 appear to have had an impact on the ECHR's decisions regarding the delimiting of the freedom of religion. Both cases reflected a restrictive change in government policy concerning the wearing of religious headgear following 9/11, and the court accepted without inquiry the newly imposed limits on freedom of religion.

Jaswir Singh v. France and Ranjit Singh v. France

In the first cases brought against France since it passed its controversial legislation in March 2004, two Sikh students, fourteen and seventeen years old at the time, filed complaints with the ECHR on May 30, 2008, following their expulsion from a high school in Paris for wearing *keskis* (small turbans). After being out of school for one year, they were admitted to the Fenelon Catholic High School, where many Muslim girls who wore headscarves were enrolled. Islam and Sikhism, two different religions, are not treated as equivalent in France. There is, however, an acceptable argument in these cases relating to safety and security. If the court were to go against its jurisprudence on religious symbols in this case, it might invite criticism that the ECHR uses a different and harsher standard for Islam. Therefore, the outcomes of these cases will be of enormous importance to the member states of the ECHR and for the Muslim citizens of Europe. The president of the ECHR, French judge Jean Paul Costa, had stated in October 2003, during a discussion of France's 2004 law before the French Stasi Commission on *laïcité*, that "in the event that such a statute was reviewed by our Court, it would be considered as complying with the French model of secularism, and consequently not in breach of the European Convention of Human Rights."[79] Judge Costa thereby revealed his view, relevant to the upcoming case and other future cases. The question remains open as to whether Judge Costa will be entitled to hear the Singh cases, given the requirements for a fair hearing and impartiality.[80]

2. The Legal and Political Influence of the ECHR on the Headscarf Controversy

A consideration of ECHR jurisprudence in all of the above cases yields the discouraging conclusion that Article 9, addressing freedom of religion, has received only limited protection. Unless the court rules that a religious practice does not interfere with secularism, the ways to apply Article 9 become highly questionable, given the different constitutional rules of EU member countries. If the case is related to Muslim women, gender equality has a negative relevance rather than a positive one; more important, although it sits in Europe and acts as the constitutional court of the EU, the court does not seem to appreciate European pluralism and antidiscrimination principles.

The ECHR headscarf decisions, broadly, raise crucial questions in regard to Islam. Does wearing an Islamic headscarf in public schools have an important political significance that threatens public order and individual freedom in a democracy? If so, what is that significance? And does it provide a sufficient basis for government restrictions on religious expression? What role does the concept of secularism/*laïcité* play in relation to the headscarf problem? Does the identity of the majority religion in a country make a difference in how such questions are approached? Does the degree of religiosity make a difference? Should there be a difference in treatment between universities and primary and secondary schools? In applying these restrictions, can we make a distinction between students and teachers or other civil servants? What is the appropriate allocation among governmental institutions of decision-making authority concerning these divisive issues? Are local government authorities, school administrators, central governments, or national and international courts in a better position to shape policies regarding these issues? The countries discussed have committed themselves to accept the authority of an international arbiter of human rights, the ECHR. Therefore, it is appropriate to ask how best to evaluate the role of a supranational human rights court in relation to domestic laws and national court decisions, given the human rights obligations of member countries and the pivotal role of the ECHR in relation to domestic legal developments.

The conclusion here is that the ECHR, arguably the most respected and effective regional human rights institution in the world, has played a harmful, not a protective, role in these cases, resulting in significant discrimination against devout religious women while leaving equally religious men untouched. This discrimination has been most visible in Turkey, where it affects the overwhelming majority of Turkish women. Unfortunately, the ECHR, instead of playing a constructive role, placed excessive reliance on Turkey's arguments and accorded Turkey an overly generous margin of appreciation.

In 2005, when the ECHR delivered its judgment against Sahin, it elevated the headscarf battle from the national to the international level, an outcome much celebrated in the Turkish secular media. Arguments between pro-headscarf and anti-headscarf groups became intense. Several incidents were reported by human rights organizations regarding the violation of the rights to public and political life, education, and health in Turkey.[81] In 2006 a doctor refused to treat a five-year-old boy because his mother wore the niqab.[82] In December 2007 a similar incident took place in a university hospital.[83] These cases indicate that the *Sahin* decision has had a larger, deeper, and lasting impact on Turkey than might be suggested by the particular facts of Sahin's complaint.

The headscarf decision has been interpreted in Turkey rather differently from what the ECHR seemed to have had in mind. According to the Turkish Constitutional Court and other secular forces, the ECHR's decision brought an effective end to the national headscarf debate, as the *Sahin* judgment was considered to be the final word because the ECHR should be viewed as the final decision-making venue. The Turkish judicial authorities' interpretation lent the ECHR a very strong authority that exceeded the limits generally imposed on democratically elected, national legislative institutions.

The ECHR had in fact evaded a proper evaluation of the issue by leaving the decision on the headscarf ban up to Turkey. Its partisan and evasive language, however, made it difficult to realize that the court had avoided making a final decision and left it to national authorities. Turkish authorities are not always respectful of ECHR decisions, and Turkey has a poor track record of compliance with ECHR decisions on human rights that challenge its national policy. Only a decision that restricts Islam is likely to achieve this sui generis solidarity between the Turkish secular judicial establishment and the ECHR.

The ECHR seemed not to appreciate the political and social changes taking place in Turkey between the 1980s and the first decade of the twenty-first century. In 2004 when the ECHR was hearing *Sahin*, Turkey was at the negotiating table with EU officials in the course of a complex accession process. The strictly secular Turkish government had lost power, and a new, conservative political party, the AKP, had prevailed with a significant majority. The supporters of strict secular order in Turkey were creating a furor over the country's alleged move away from Europe. The ECHR was a perfect venue for sending a warning to the new Turkish government about Europe's deep attachment to secularism. While this interpretation is speculative, it seems a real possibility that the supranational human rights court considered itself, consciously or not, as a messenger for the European Union. But if the court wants to prohibit headscarf use in Europe, then it should do so on the basis of its own reasoning. Because the Turkish court system is highly politicized, and because the relationship between Islam and politics has a complex history, Turkey cannot provide a positive example of how to deal with European Muslims.

On the contrary, many of the Turkish courts' arguments have been completely accepted and dutifully repeated in the judgments of the ECHR in headscarf controversies. Elevated by the ECHR, some of these arguments have become a major source of international human rights jurisprudence. It is very likely that many countries in Europe, if they have not done so already, will include such arguments as authoritative in their own future domestic legislation and judicial decisions.

An Unintended Consequence: The Influence of Turkish Court Decisions on European Jurisprudence over Headscarf Use

After nearly a century of receiving European jurisprudence in the name of European modernity and Western Enlightenment ideas, Turkish jurisprudence has exerted a strong influence on European courts and lawmakers in resolving the headscarf debate through the ECHR judgments. It is astonishing that Turkey, which has earned a bad reputation for bringing an excessive caseload to the ECHR, nevertheless received such respect and deference from the court.[84] For more than a decade, the ECHR had been delivering a stream of adverse rulings against Turkey, most involving Kurdish issues. The government of Turkey has won only 10 percent of these cases,[85] and, revealingly, the only cases won by Turkey concerned the expulsion of students and teachers because of their headscarves, employment discrimination or expulsion from the military because of religion,[86] and the dismantling of religious parties. The court's track record is hardly encouraging to future Turkish applicants for relief. In apparent recognition of this, there seems to be a strong recent tendency among Turkish Muslim citizens not to bring their freedom of religion cases to the ECHR.

The specific arguments of the Turkish courts that were subsequently relied on in the ECHR's judgments include the following:[87]

1. *Peer Pressure:* In *Sahin* one of the major reasons given by the court against the applicant was that wearing a headscarf would create pressure on those students who choose not to wear one, an argument routinely stressed by the Turkish court since 1983 and referred to in several ECHR judgments.[88] One major criticism directed at the ECHR judgment was that this important argument was used without any supporting evidence and only on the authority of its earlier judgments. The court first used this argument in 1993, and twelve years later used the same argument in *Sahin*, without investigating whether, during the interval, students who do not wear the headscarf experienced pressure in Turkish universities.

2. *Fear of Islam:* The ECHR's second major argument in *Sahin* raised "the possibility of transformation of the State to an Islamic order in Turkey." The court tried to develop this argument more elaborately by relying heavily on its *Refah* judgment on the closing of an Islamic-oriented party by the Turkish Constitutional Court for alleged antisecular activities. In its conclusion, the court merely repeated the Turkish government's argument with its reasoning, highly questionable given that much of its defense in *Refah* rested on unsubstantiated accusations.[89] In according excessive deference to the Turkish judicial establishment and to the viewpoint of Turkey's secular elite, the ECHR compromises its own stature as a widely respected, supranational human rights court.[90] In a striking similarity of legal reasoning, both the Turkish Constitutional Court and the ECHR claimed that the headscarf-friendly policies of Islamic political parties qualified as evidence of antisecular activities—a political ploy of Turkey's secular establishment.

Again borrowing from Turkish court decisions, the ECHR also discussed the historical conditions in Turkey that justified a fear of political Islam. The evaluation of the *Refah* judgment is beyond the subject of this book, but what is relevant here is the doubtful validity of the ECHR's views in light of its unexamined stereotyping of Islam.

The correlation between the two sets of judgments regarding political party closures and headscarf ban leads to three conclusions:

i) The Turkish Constitutional Court and the ECHR considered that Turkish women who wear the headscarf "automatically and coercively" are connected with an Islamic political party that has been properly abolished because of its illegal, antisecular, and antidemocratic activities.

ii) Given the fundamental differences between the two kinds of cases with regard to the applicants (party members versus an individual), subject matter (political party versus headscarf use) and their contents, it is highly questionable to rely on the same arguments in the two different judgments. Neither the Turkish court nor the ECHR hesitated to merge them, although their only similarities were that both dealt with Islam, secularism, and Turkey.

iii) If these two cases (party closure and headscarf use) were treated as related, why did the ECHR fail to consider evaluating the headscarf issue under Article 10 of the Convention?[91] The ECHR is normally a strong supporter of freedom of thought and speech as the foundation of a democratic society. The headscarf clearly should have been protected by the ECHR within the limits of freedom of thought and speech, as articulated in Article 10. Or, we can ask a rhetorical question: Turkey is notorious for its restrictions on freedom of speech, especially on its application of Turkish Penal Code Article 301 that criminalizes "insulting Turkishness," and it received significant criticism on these counts from EU officials in the context of the accession process. On this basis, it is difficult to justify why the ECHR followed a Turkish approach by not giving Article 10 protection to Leyla Sahin in its decision.

3. *The Headscarf as a Powerful Symbol:* The Turkish Constitutional Court in its 1989 judgment referred to the "turban" (not the headscarf) as a "powerful political symbol." In its *Dahlab, Sahin,* and *Dogru* judgments, the ECHR extended the same concept to the headscarf, as a "powerful external symbol."[92] If wearing a headscarf is considered to be a religious duty—Leyla Sahin's contention, agreed to by the court—then it should have been viewed as an aspect of religious freedom. Yet, the ECHR follows the Turkish court's argument that the headscarf is a powerful religious symbol rather than the expression of a religious duty. As a result, beginning in the mid-1990s, France, Germany, and some other member countries of the Council of Europe accepted this view, which underpins the international (European) discourse to the effect that a certain form of female dress is not acceptable in a democratic society. Dissenting Judge Tulken, in *Sahin,* criticized the court and raised an issue that is increasingly contested across Europe: "Merely wearing the headscarf

cannot be associated with fundamentalism, and it is vital to distinguish between those who wear the headscarf and 'extremists' who seek to impose the headscarf as they do other religious symbols." Furthermore, she asked, "What in fact, is the connection between the ban and sexual equality?"[93]

The fundamental question is to what extent is the wearing of the Islamic headscarf a freely chosen individual act of religious freedom that is to be guaranteed and protected? And to what extent might the headscarf reflect the religious coercion of women, thereby threatening the protection of equality between men and women and resulting in discrimination?[94] Nowhere in Sahin did the ECHR address the latter question.

4. *Gender Equality:* The ECHR analysis involving its treatment of gender equality in the context of the headscarf controversy is ambiguous. The Turkish Constitutional Court in its 1989 decision posed this issue by noting, "to allow the Islamic headscarf in universities is against the equality principle." The Constitutional Court did not mean that the use of a headscarf is by itself against the equality principle, but that the Turkish headscarf law under review was formulated in a way that was not compatible with the equality principle because it targeted only female Muslim students.[95] Therefore, the Constitutional Court correctly annulled this law based on the equality principle. However, in the *Sahin* judgment of the ECHR, the Turkish headscarf law differed from the 1989 law in that it was an administrative directive of a university. The ECHR did not appreciate the difference between the two kinds of regulatory decrees and simply repeated the Turkish judgment of 1989, holding, without any evident inquiry, that the "headscarf is against the equality principle." Underlying this reasoning by the ECHR was the assumption that "Islam is against women's rights, and therefore it is also against gender equality," a rather absurd argument. Instead of making its own independent assessment, the ECHR referred to abstract principles contained in the Turkish Constitution calling for the promotion of women's rights in Turkey. It also cited a Constitutional Court decision on "sexual" equality.[96] This suggests that the ECHR paid very little attention to the complex actualities of headscarf politics in Turkey and elsewhere or to legal and technical developments of different times. These issues, in their details, illuminate the real power politics at work beneath the surface of the legal argument. In the end, the ECHR's heavy reliance on the margin of appreciation principle in this kind of case is questionable, especially when taking into account Turkey's poor human rights record.

5. *Laïcité:* As discussed earlier, the Turkish Constitutional Court makes a clear distinction between Turkish *laïcité* and other forms of secularism

in Western countries, including France. Although the concept was initially imported from France, Turkey implements the principle in its own particular way. The ECHR's *Sahin* judgment acknowledged the special position of Turkey as being threatened by an Islamic fundamentalist movement. This approving recognition of its strictly defined principle of *laïcité* by the ECHR represented a remarkable success for the Turkish Constitutional Court. The ECHR repeated this approval in *Dogru*, its most recent decision, and while affirming French *laïcité*, also endorsed Turkish *laïcité*, treating the two as equivalent.

6. *The Public and Private Spheres:* In the *Sahin* judgment the Turkish government stated in its defense, "There is no headscarf ban in private spheres, or communal areas [in Turkey]."[97] With this defense, the distinction between the private and the public spheres entered into international law via the ECHR's judgment. This distinction between the public and private spheres is a muddy business. It is not clear yet whether the ECHR will use this distinction in its future judgments. If it does, this will restrict headscarf use in public places not only in Turkey, but also in Europe.

The Turkish Constitutional Court, in its decisions, had difficulty differentiating the vast majority of Turkish women who wear headscarves routinely in everyday life when it tried to ban headscarves in public places. The court noted that women are free to wear a headscarf in the private sphere and communal areas including streets, gardens, homes, private businesses, and other places. But if the headscarf is a religious symbol, then women cannot wear such headgear in common areas, according to Turkish law, which bans religious dress in common areas under a law passed during the early period of the Turkish Republic.[98] The Court unintentionally went beyond what it had been asked to do and positioned itself as a lawmaker, suggesting that certain dress is acceptable in some places and unacceptable in others.

The history of the public-private distinction in Turkish court decisions shows that the Constitutional Court for a long time had defined universities as headscarf-free "public spaces." However, the Turkish courts were well aware that the majority of Turkish women in Turkey wear the headscarf; the Turkish Court categorized some women as "traditional headscarf users" so as not to exclude them from the public sphere. This categorization was done without any scientific research and with no basis in any national criteria, and in so doing, the Court overstepped its legal limitations. The case in front of the Constitutional Court concerned university students, not all women. The categorization is also problematic in that every form of dress has its own historical and ideological meaning, whether modern, traditional, or religious. In Turkey, it is well known that clothing, especially women's clothing, was used to introduce Ataturk's ideological project of modernization. Therefore, the choice not to wear a headscarf must be also considered as an ideological stand.[99]

To understand the ECHR's deference to Turkish jurisprudence we need to take account of temporal, contextual, and geographical factors. The *Sahin* judgment was delivered in 2005, a time when Europe was facing Islamic terrorism, and European political winds were blowing very much against Islam. Further, the court is located in the city of Strasbourg, France, the nation where the 2004 law was enacted that banned religious symbols in public schools. Emerging Islamophobia and a growing right-wing political sentiment that targeted immigration from Muslim countries were influential in European public opinion.

Moreover, Turkey's negotiations for accession to EU membership officially began in 2005. With significant numbers of Muslim immigrants already present in most European states, the possibility of absorbing Turkey's population of 75 million Muslims was seen as a major threat to the cultural existence of the European Union. The presence of the Muslim "other" inside the boundaries of Europe has unleashed a massive controversy about the parameters of citizenship. These debates often focus on the bodies of women, and the headscarf is a flashpoint for politicians and the popular press, where it is often construed as a symbol of the oppression of women inconsistent with "European values."[100]

These circumstances made the ECHR's headscarf judgment not only a legal but also a political symbol of opposition to Islam in Europe. The EU, however, has committed itself with increasing specificity to mandating gender equality, human rights, and democracy as core European values. Therefore, the European Court may think it is a good idea to endorse the anti-headscarf view of the Turkish courts and deny the rights of headscarf users because it is a less burdensome choice than to properly evaluate the cases according to international human rights principles.

The ECHR's Capability to Deliver Justice

The headscarf debate is not a local Turkish issue, and the ECHR's judgment in *Sahin* has had an important influence on the legal order of other European countries. International tribunals need to be careful about how their decisions will be understood and implemented elsewhere. The strong influence of Turkish courts on the ECHR raises some questions about its capability to deliver justice in future cases, given its arguments in several areas.

1. *Wide Margin of Appreciation and European Supervision:* Considering the partisan language of the *Sahin* judgment, the author of the dissenting opinion, Judge Tulken, rightly questioned the nature of the court's legitimate authority to decide on headscarf policy, especially given its obligation to provide "European supervision." Tulken asked: "Who is best placed to decide how member states should discharge their Convention obligations in a sensitive area?"[101] The majority argument was that "a wide margin of appreciation was required because of the diversity of practice between the States on the issue of regulating the wearing of religious symbols in an educational institution." The Grand Chamber's judgment also implied that "a European consensus was lacking in this sphere."[102] Judge Tulken noted that none of the other member states had bans in place on religious attire at the university level, so this diversity of practice did not exist regarding the specific issue before the court. Furthermore, even as the majority chose to base its judgment on a margin of appreciation, the court was ignoring its obligation to provide the necessary European supervision: "The issue raised in the application…is not merely a 'local' issue, but one of importance to all the member states. European supervision cannot, therefore, be escaped simply by invoking the margin of appreciation."[103]

2. *Treatment of Islam:* A controversial question about the Grand Chamber's judgment in *Sahin* is whether the ECHR departed from its established jurisprudence on freedom of religion when dealing with cases about Islam. Strong criticism by a few human rights scholars has alleged that the ECHR adopted a double standard on freedom of religion cases that deal with Islam, despite the court's protective stance toward Islam when its status as a minority religion is at issue.[104] Careful and extensive research on ECHR decisions, including the commission's decisions in relation to Article 9 (and possibly also Article 10), is needed to evaluate these accusations in a responsible manner; an inquiry beyond the scope of this book. Yet the ECHR's jurisprudence concerning non-Christian religious clothing, predominantly the headscarf, is deeply problematic. The lack of sympathy and understanding from the European Court toward those affected by the headscarf bans is in marked contrast to its approach in cases that concern a need to protect devotees of the Christian religion.[105] An example is the famous *Otto Preminger Institut v. Austria* decision, in which the ECHR upheld the seizure by Austrian authorities of a film

because its content could have upset devout Christians. The court read into Article 9 the need to protect the "respect for the religious feelings of believers." However, when it comes to Muslim or Sikh manifestations of belief through particular clothing, or the dismantling of religious political parties, the court has been prepared to accept the denial of education and employment opportunities to girls and women, and the denial of essential documents such as driver's licenses, and the expulsion of military officers because of their religiosity. Most recently, the ECHR's Grand Chamber decision in *Lautsi v. Italy* (2010) allowing the Italian government to place the Christian cross in public schools gives the impression that the European Court, at least, is not well equipped to make reasonable decisions on issues related to Islam, or, at most, it has a prejudice against the new minority religion of Europe.[106]

3. *Consistency:* A third fundamental question raised by the *Sahin* judgment is whether the ECHR ignored its established jurisprudence on headscarf cases. The answer: it did not. A look at earlier ECHR judgments in relevant cases, including the commission's treatment of Article 9 and of Islam, reveals a consistent pattern, not only in the outcomes, but also in the court's investigative methods, procedural rules, and its disregard of applicants' legal status, specific conditions, and varied defendant countries.[107] The *Sahin* judgment did not come as a surprise, at least to Turkey.

4. *Lasting Impact:* A final question is whether the ECHR's *Sahin* judgment will have long-lasting effects in countries within the jurisdiction of the Convention. Although the general rules of applicability for ECHR decisions are limited to specific cases, the ECHR is known to refer to its earlier judgments in all cases and tends to exhibit continuity in its jurisprudence. The *Sahin* judgment, at first glance, appears to be applicable only to Turkey. The ECHR heavily relied on the special danger to secularism in a Muslim country and connected the wearing of a headscarf with possible interference with Turkish democracy by fundamentalist political parties, as seen in the party closure (Refah) case. It does not seem appropriate to rely, without explanation, on similar arguments in other European countries. Because Turkey is the only predominantly Muslim country that is a member of the Council of Europe, the argument in *Sahin* citing the danger of a fundamentalist Islamic government cannot be extended, on its face, to other countries. But the general reasoning of the court, which includes the emerging fear of Islamic fundamentalism and the headscarf as a powerful symbol or tool against gender equality, could be used in

future cases. The court's statement that the "headscarf is not compatible with pluralistic society and individual freedom" suggests a general applicability of ECHR's judgments whether a country is Muslim or not.[108] This is no longer an apprehension. In *Dogru v. France* and *Kervanci v. France* its most recent headscarf cases, the ECHR repeated all these arguments, despite the fact that the applicant country was France. The *Sahin* judgment, therefore, is likely to be treated as a persuasive precedent in future headscarf cases.

PART TWO

Europe and the United States

Show me just what Muhammad brought that was new,
and there you will find things only evil and inhuman,
such as his command to spread by the sword the faith
he preached.

POPE BENEDICT XVI, QUOTING A
FOURTEENTH-CENTURY BYZANTINE EMPEROR
September 12, 2006

5

Anti-Islamic Discourses in Europe

As the headscarf controversy continued to unfold in domestic politics in Turkey, fundamentalist Islamic movements were becoming a serious international security concern for non-Muslim countries. The preoccupation with Islam reached its height as a result of the 9/11 attacks on the United States, and the atmosphere of fear in the West led to the open expression of anti-Islamic sentiments, which had lain dormant for a long time. Geographically, the terrorist attacks on New York City and Washington, D.C. were remote from Europe, yet the impact on the continent was significant. Following additional terrorist attacks, in March 2004 and in London in July 2005, and the November 2004 assassination of Theo van Gogh in Amsterdam, fear of Islam rose to the level of hysteria all over Europe. Parallel to these developments, the headscarf became a symbol of the presence of Islam in the West. Because of its colonial past, Europe has strong historic connections with the Muslim world. In recent years, economic globalization engendered significant immigration from predominantly Muslim countries in Asia and Africa to the continent. As a result, in many European countries, soul-searching began concerning Islam; a new and threatening religious presence in a continent of Christianity.

Significant differences exist among Muslims in Europe due to the various reasons that brought them to Europe in the first place. Some Muslims came to European countries from former colonies; others had been invited to Europe in the 1960s as "guest workers"; and some Muslims are native to Europe, such as a number of citizens of Albania and the former Yugoslavia. Despite the enormous cultural and theological differences among Muslims and their Islamic practices, Islam is presented to the European public as a monolithic block. In this discourse, Islam is viewed as incompatible with Europe's fundamental values, such as democracy and individual freedom. As Islam was increasingly regarded as a threat to the achievements of the European age of

Enlightenment, approximately fifteen million Muslims in Europe gradually became unwanted "others." Anti-immigration sentiment related to anti-Middle Eastern and anti-North African feelings, the association of Islam with the Arab world, the political conflict between Palestinians and Israelis, and the growth of extreme right-wing movements may be considered significant reasons for such negative feelings.

Diverse political, theological, ideological, and historical reasons combined to cultivate opposition to Islam in Europe. Muslims are not only considered different from Europeans and their religion incompatible with European culture, but their presence is also regarded as a threat to the health of Europe. Historically, Europe was continually preoccupied with Islam as an external presence—Europe's "other"—and, predominantly, Muslims were considered part of the Ottoman Empire. The current phenomenon, however, is different, because the anti-Islamic viewpoint culminates in the claim that Europe is running a great risk of being conquered by Islam through immigration, naturalization, and high birthrates. Defenders of this argument are convinced that because of its growing Muslim communities, Europe is in danger of losing its Christian-based cultural identity. The believers in these fears spoke of "Eurabia" and made racist arguments against Muslims as represented by Arab immigrants and naturalized citizens. Topping off such anxieties, the prospect of Turkey becoming a member of the EU via the accession process aroused anti-Turkish sentiment, another facet of the anti-Islamic mood in Europe.

In the European context, the term "Islamophobia" itself is a focus of the critique. For many European commentators, Islamists used the term specifically as a means of hindering legitimate criticism of Islam and Muslims. According to this position, Muslims demonstrate their refusal to hear criticism of their religion by designating every critique of Islam and Muslims as Islamophobia. By doing so, this group affirms, the Muslim aggressors present themselves as victims when, in fact, they are the perpetrators.[1]

Islam is not the only minority religion in Europe, but a strong political dimension to the discussion of Islam runs deeper than in contemporary European treatment of other minority religions. Historical animosity toward Islam in Europe, reinforced by contemporary Islamophobia, fosters a profound hostility to Islam, especially with respect to matters of ethnic and cultural identity. The question of Islam in Europe, according to Olivier Roy, is more comprehensive than the critique of certain Muslim practices or theological differences. Rather, it is intimately related to the sovereignty of Europe and current debates about the nation-state, globalization, the deterritorialization of conflicts, and crises of identity.[2] Roy points out that Europeans reject Islam for different reasons, but each country constructs its own particular kind of negative identity. While France uses *laïcité* against Islam, other Western countries take different approaches.

Anti-Islamic sentiments often express a strong, underlying racism. According to Roy this sentiment is more prevalent in France than in other European countries because of its colonial relationship with North Africa. Racism and colonialism are part of the mix. The Western obsession with the headscarf is also linked to sexual fantasies harbored by colonialists who encountered veiled women abroad: "The veil was a sexual provocation and a denial of sex, a come-on and refusal."[3] A veiled woman was often portrayed as an unruly prostitute or a slave to her husband. For the confused colonial, "Islam was a cruel and irrational system of religious and social organization."[4] The reality of universal patriarchal domination means that some women's issues should be subject to scrutiny in any religion, yet, in terms of women's rights, Islam receives more crude criticism than any other religion. For a long time, a commonly raised justification for the rejection of Islam has been women's rights.

The Role of the Media

Despite the idea that the media should be objective and represent both sides of an argument, when it comes to Islam, and particularly Muslim women's sexuality, European media seems willing to adopt negative public attitudes rather than remain informative and balanced. Throughout Europe, it can be quite difficult to publish articles that try to offer a more balanced view of Islam and Muslims, while anti-Islamic actors are able to present their views easily, without hesitation or limitation. The European public certainly supported the penchant to search for anti-Islamic news. The politicians and intellectuals who hold anti-Islamic views and the so-called experts on Islam who openly express their anti-Islamic opinions seem to gain more publicity. They successfully present themselves as courageous tellers of the truth in the face of moral relativists or "naive multiculturalists" and dangerous Muslims.[5] Even prominent political leaders, such as French president Nicolas Sarkozy and former UK Prime Minister Gordon Brown did not hesitate to publicly condemn Islamic veiling practices. The more outspoken Italian Prime Minister Silvio Berlusconi adopted a racist tone when he publicly referred to "the superiority of the West."[6]

Although the post-9/11 discourse on Islam in Europe became more polemical than in the United States, some countries, such as Spain, seemed to be an exception. The Spanish media agreed not to use the term "Islamic terrorism" as a collective term but instead use the names of the assaulting terrorist groups.[7] The Spanish public and the government's behavior following the 2004 Madrid train bombings were remarkably different from the reactions of the other European governments and public. The Spanish did not organize anti-Islamic demonstrations and carefully differentiated between the Muslim terrorists and the religion of Islam. Their motto was "no to terror, no to war." This more attuned response might be due in part to Spain's long-term experience with Basque separatist terrorism, to the country's historical closeness with Islamic culture, and to its civilization that was formed by interactions with different religions and cultures. It was Spain that, along with Turkey, initiated the "Alliance of Civilizations" project under U.N. auspices—a negation of Huntington's notorious "clash of civilizations" argument.

Muslim Women Speak Out Against Islam?

The European media seem to show a particular interest in questions of gender, power, and politics. Western sexual equality is seen as the crucial point of difference between European and Islamic cultures. In this respect, using so-called authentic Muslim women as anti-Islamic actors became an important tool in addressing certain problematic issues in the European setting. The high profile of Muslim-born intellectuals in anti-Islam discourse was highly appreciated by the European general public, and therefore the media used more and more Muslim spokespersons to legitimize a harsh critique of Islam and Muslims. Their commentary is regarded as authentic and plausible because these individuals, like Ayaan Hirsi Ali in the Netherlands, and Necla Kelek and Seyran Ates in Germany, have Muslim family backgrounds and hold academic or political titles that seem to give them legitimate mandates and the authority to analyze phenomena such as forced marriages, honor killings, female circumcision, and domestic violence.[8]

Without hesitation, these European Muslims are willing to take part in a harsh critique of Islam as representatives of Islam in a non-Islamic-majority society. While at the beginning of their media careers Hirsi Ali and Kelek self-identified as experts on Islam, they later stated they no longer regarded themselves as Muslims, although the media and those in political circles continued to describe them as examples of "independent, secular Muslims."[9] When addressed as modern Muslim women, none of them reject their classification as Muslim feminists, because the combination positions them as authoritative and powerful voices in the discourse of Islam's oppression of women. Their best-selling books oscillate between political pamphleteering and the currently fashionable "veil literature." Their rhetoric is sharp. They provide no special interpretation of Islam beyond stating Islam is incompatible with democracy and sexual equality. To make their arguments more convincing to the masses, they mix empirical data and novel elements with narratives of their family histories.[10]

All three of these prominent women regard themselves as the voice of oppressed women, who cannot speak or are afraid to do so. Their common assumption is that all these practices are based on Islam and covered by Islamic law, disregarding that in the several cases of forced marriage, honor killing, and female circumcision that became public, the individuals involved were not Muslims but members of African or Oriental religious minorities. They also failed to consider the fatwas of leading European ulemas who pointed out that these practices are not covered by Islamic law.[11]

Ayaan Hirsi Ali, and Seyran Ates faced serious death threats because of their publicly expressed opinions on Islam and Muslim men. This has led, on the one hand, to further discussion of the value of freedom of speech in Europe but has also strengthened the symbolic role of the "threatened critics of Islam" in the discourse.[12] Ironically, it also strengthened the women's roles as authentic informants concerning the "real face of Islam," because it was regarded as evidence that Islam, as represented by the offenders, is in truth a religion of violence. Some of these personalities received several awards for their efforts on behalf of "freedom of speech, intercultural understanding and freedom in the world."[13] Thus, they gained a kind of official status as the "Oriental confirmer in duty" for the superiority of Western culture to Islam. This is a well-known figure in the modern literature of the East, where the "Western confirmer in duty" confirms that one who is part of the Western culture and knows Oriental culture very well can confirm that Western culture is superior.[14]

Among these, Somali-born Ayaan Hirsi Ali has gained international recognition. A former member of the Dutch Parliament, she was deported from the Netherlands when authorities discovered that she had lied about her background in her application for Dutch citizenship. She found a new home in the United States and a new conservative patron, the Heritage Foundation, to further her anti-Islam career. Her books became best sellers in the post-9/11 atmosphere in the United States, as the American public became interested in Islamic societies. Hirsi Ali's articles appear in prominent, mainstream news media, such as the *Wall Street Journal*, and are not supplemented with alternative, balancing perspectives. Her views are considered to be those of an expert, not only on cultural issues relating to Islam but also on politics and a wide range of current topics in the Islamic world generally.[15]

In reaction to such misrepresentation, some Muslim-born scholars launched their own forum to garner public attention, which focused on the integration of Muslim migrants rather than on stereotypes of Muslims and Islam. The responses from anti-Islam Muslim activists and well-known feminists were very sharp; many blamed the Muslim scholars as "a defender of the headscarf and a collaborator of Islamists." Unlike the former group, its efforts received no prominent interest in the media.[16]

"Problematic" Islamic Practices

The regulation of Islamic practices in Europe, which has been subject to much public debate and policy-making in recent years, requires us to look at several emblematic issues. Apart from the headscarf debate, for example, Islamic schools, mosques (their size, architectural style, location in the city), imams, and dietary restrictions are framed as "problematic." Specific aspects of Islam, its symbols, and practices became "emblematic" and fueled efforts to instigate the regulation of Muslim behavior, practices, and symbols.[17] In Great Britain, a multiculturalist country, the prohibition of Islamic rituals, such as the slaughtering of animals, is an indicator of such sentiment. In 2009 a campaign against the building of a minaret of a mosque in Switzerland included a poster depicting a woman with a headscarf carrying a gun shaped like a minaret—a telling example of the way Muslims are imagined by Europeans.

In the course of these developments, European countries encountered Islam and Islamic practices in a wider political and legal context. Each country regulates Islam and Islamic practices differently depending on particularities in state-church relations; views on freedom of religion, neutrality, and the concept of equal treatment; and specific legal traditions informed by the country's history. Yet Islam has become "a common problem" for many European countries where legal and political practices yield similar outcomes. Islam as a whole has been viewed as a societal problem in Europe. Immigration policies in relation to Muslims were the first area to become more regionally uniform in Europe.

In this atmosphere, the headscarf has become the primary symbol of all Muslims. As a disturbing tool of the supposed subordination of women in Muslim culture, it functions as a sign of incompatibility with European culture. French public discourse is most indicative in this regard. In France, the anti-Islam discourse extended from academic writings to popular magazines, from denunciations of fundamentalism to generalized attacks on Muslims and Islam. France was the first country to act on the headscarf controversy through legal means; the law of 2004 became a high point of the debate. The headscarf controversy arose in other European countries and beyond, where it took a different shape, significance, and symbolism in each national setting. Legal and political debates about the place of religion in schools in general, and wearing a headscarf in particular, spread across a number of European states. In the meantime, European courts, both national and international, were receiving legal complaints from Muslim women who had lost their jobs or been expelled from schools because of wearing headscarves at work and in public institutions.

From Headscarf to Burqa

Recently, headscarf debates have expanded to the burqa or other Islamic dress styles that include face coverings. The burqa has received wide media attention in Europe, particularly in France, the Netherlands, and, most recently, in Belgium and even Spain.[18] Yet the underlying issue remains the resentment of the commonly worn headscarf rather than the few examples of burqa wearing in Europe. A reasonable argument exists against covering one's face; thus, the politically correct solution may be to shift the restrictions on headscarf use to restrictions on burqa use. Public opinion on banning the burqa in the United States is quite different from European sentiment. A recent opinion poll in the Pew Global Attitudes Project Survey found the French public overwhelmingly endorsing such a measure: 82 percent approve of a ban on Muslim women wearing full veils in public, including schools, hospitals, and government offices, while seven percent disapprove. Majorities in Germany (71 percent), Britain (62 percent), and Spain (59 percent) would also support a similar ban in their countries. In contrast, most Americans would oppose such a measure: 65 percent say they would disapprove of a ban on Muslim women wearing full veils in public places, compared with 28 percent who say they would approve of the ban in hospitals and government offices.[19] To prohibit a citizen from wearing religious garb, be it a yarmulke, a clerical collar, or a Hare Krishna robe, would seem to be a violation of religious freedom. And that is how Americans see it.

In Europe, the plan is to outlaw face covering in all public places across Western Europe. Generally in European settings, the primary reason given for a ban on the burqa is that it constitutes a safety issue. Second, the burqa, as it blocks contact and conversation, is a tool for obstructing integration into and interaction with a given society. As a result, the face covering dramatically reduces the possibilities for women to find jobs in Europe and to participate in a great number of activities. A third reason is the popular belief that this particular form of dress violates the basic norms of a democratic society and goes beyond what may be accepted as reasonable ways of expressing difference through dress.[20]

Europe has also seen a great deal of opposition to the proposal for a general "burqa ban." The number of Muslim women who actually wear a burqa in France, for instance, is very small: approximately 2,000 women out of France's total population of approximately1.5 million adult Muslim women. The nuisance or true risk they might pose to societies is unclear, and a special law or ban seems primarily to serve political interests and further stigmatize Islam. In France and the Netherlands, both countries' legal experts and committees that are in charge of immigration called a burqa ban disproportional, and a violation of freedom of religion and the principle of nondiscrimination on religious grounds.[21] Moreover, such a law would very likely have perverse effects, possibly leading to more harassment or religiously motivated attacks against Muslim women, or to a greater number of women who will start wearing the veil as a sign of protest.[22] After Sarkozy publicly condemned the burqa, it seems, the chances of a ban being imposed have risen sharply. Although few women wear the full garment in France, mayors of cities with large Muslim populations report a steady increase in their numbers, not due to immigration but due to French-born women who converted to Islam adopting the burqa, as well as women from North African countries where the burqa is not traditionally worn.[23] Banning the burqa will only increase the oppression of Muslim women, since they will not be allowed to leave home and will thus be even more isolated from society, and, in many cases, be exposed to harsh treatment within forced marriages. Furthermore, the fine will exacerbate the problems of poverty and unemployment. It will punish the very women who are least likely to have control over their own economic conditions.

Multiculturalism or Assimilation?

In general, the West has two models for dealing with a minority population: (1) the multiculturalist model, usually associated with Anglo-Saxon systems (the United States, the UK, Canada, and Northern Europe); and (2) the assimilationist model, specific to France but also part of the American experience, as expressed by the metaphor of the "melting pot." The French consider Anglo-Saxon multiculturalism either as entailing the destruction of national unity or as an instrument of ghettoization, while assimilation is perceived by multiculturalists as the expression of an authoritarian, centralized state that refuses to recognize minority rights.[24] Recent tensions in Europe show that both of these models pose problems. In France, while some Muslim youth are integrated through language and education, many young Muslims complain of being second-class citizens and victims of racism. Moreover, by wearing the headscarf, Muslim girls demand to be recognized in the public space as religious believers. At the same time, the increased radicalization of a fraction of Muslim youth in the UK and in the Netherlands led to a shift in public opinion in these countries, resulting in the multicultural model to be called into question and accused of encouraging "separatism."[25]

The initial hostility of multiculturalist European countries toward the French model has turned into a renewed interest. One sign of this tendency is that a number of countries that embraced multiculturalism seem ready to restrict the wearing of the Islamic headscarf, including the Netherlands, the United Kingdom, Belgium, and Germany. The extent to which multiculturalism is seen to have failed invites attention to the alternative represented by the French model. France however, as the champion of secularism, or *laïcité*, is struggling with the application of this concept in dealing with Islam as a minority religion in Europe. In this sense, "integration" or "assimilation" in the French manner should not be an option. In French society, the perception that Islam and Islamic culture are dramatically different from French culture has gained so much ground that it can block any kind of assimilation and integration.

In the Netherlands, for example, positive multiculturalism was shattered and turned abruptly in a negative direction after the November 2004 assassination of the filmmaker Theo van Gogh by a young Muslim of Moroccan origin.[26] More often, Europe's hostility toward Islam is covered up by politically correct policies such as multiculturalism, interfaith dialogue, or minority rights. In conflict with Dutch multiculturalism, new policies for immigrant integration were implemented that included requirements for newcomers to learn about Dutch society, to learn the Dutch language, and to make an effort to adapt to prevailing societal norms and values. Some Dutch citizens even claimed that Islam and the Islamic culture are difficult to integrate into local Dutch culture. During the same time, various European countries converged in implementing tougher and more demanding assimilationist immigrant integration policies.[27]

Europe offers many examples of failed multiculturalist policies. One tale of a prestigious public high school in the Belgian port city of Antwerp is a good example. According to a report in the *Economist*, a school headmistress tried a new approach to counter the ban on headscarves in middle and high schools.[28] However, her "efforts to construct a haven of multicultural dialogue [were] wrecked by the intolerance of others."[29] As her school became a rare place where veils were permitted, instead of being a beacon of tolerance, her school was transformed into a "ghetto." "The proportion of headscarf-wearing girls went from 50% to 80% in three years, and girls who did not wear scarves found themselves under stronger and stronger pressure to cover up.

The school found itself 'targeted' by Islamist hardliners who began questioning certain lessons, school excursions, and trying to block the organization of mixed gender parents' meetings."[30] Finally, when a new term began, the headmistress banned the headscarf.

This case represented a poor model of a piecemeal approach, rather than the French model that generally prevails, or, more important, a more tolerant multiculturalist approach. The anonymous writer of the *Economist* piece provides a secular liberal sentiment of the multicultural Europe: "The arrival of traditional, pious immigrants in Europe does clearly test the liberal values that I hold dear. In short, how should a liberal, tolerant society protect the rights of a less liberal minority in its midst? Anyone with a quick answer to that one, I would suggest, is a fraud or a demagogue." This is a remarkable example of how European liberals turn from a multiculturalist approach to a strict, intolerant version of the French *laïcité* model. Even more dangerously, instead of celebrating differences, liberals hesitated to accept and tolerate it because of the few radical fundamentalists' actions. Minority but well-organized radical Islamists won one more battle in Europe.

"Inclusive" Europe

Finally, to understand the place of Islam in Europe, it is necessary to go beyond a narrow consideration of the French version of *laïcité*—itself an exception in Europe—and confront the more general question of the compatibility of Islam with Western secularism. In our time, in a multicultural and hybrid global world, it is difficult to retain the idea of nation-states as they existed in the nineteenth century. Nationalities, and nation-states, especially strong unitary republican models such as France and Turkey, induce politicians to treat their country as an essence rather than as a dynamic, fluid construct.[31] Nations are no longer, and never really were, homogeneous, and therefore "nation-sharing" is an obligation of contemporary multicultural societies.[32] Moreover, Europe is the first successful model of supranational regionalization in which national boundaries have supposedly disappeared and a culture of peace has emerged. Unfortunately, it turns out that in Europe, the Christian legacy was stronger than the culture of peace. From the perspective of real politics and economic interests, the conditions and principles for inclusion into Europe vary in each country's case, especially if the country has a significantly different culture and religion. Turkey's never ending accession process, in contrast with the easy entry of Eastern European countries, is a vital example of this European double standard.[33]

6

France

We cannot accept to have in our country women who
are prisoners behind netting, cut off from all social life,
deprived of identity.

FRENCH PRESIDENT NICOLAS SARKOZY, June 22, 2009

1. The Socioeconomic Conditions of French Muslims

France is the first European country where the headscarf controversy became
an important political problem and a legal issue that eventually led, in 2004,
to the adoption of a law that banned ostentatious religious symbols from public middle and high schools.[1] In France, Islam first became visible in public
spaces in the 1970s. Among immigrants and their descendants, religion frequently gives structure to their lives. Several surveys published on the Muslim
population in France confirm this strong relationship between Muslim immigrants and the practice of Islam. Historically, the question of Islam in France
was discussed only in relation to the political context of the Maghreb (western
North Africa) and its colonial past. As early as the 1870s, French authorities
set up a two-tier system in Algeria, giving Muslim citizens in North Africa a
particular personal status: local Catholics and Jews could become French citizens but Muslims could not. Officially, this policy was to protect the religious
identity of Muslims, but the real reason behind it was to provide a public
justification for discrimination against Muslims. Islam was seen as a barrier to
Frenchness, and, in one way or another, this is still is the case today. As heirs of
this colonial history, Muslim immigrants from North Africa have long considered themselves among the excluded in France and have lived their faith as
discreetly as possible.[2]

The French legal system forbids distinguishing or counting citizens or residents based on religious belief. Therefore, there is no official count of the number of Muslims living in France. However, estimates place the French Muslim population between 3.5 and 5 million, representing 6 to 8.5 percent of the total population (58.5 million). This total includes at least 2 million Muslims with French citizenship. The majority of Muslims in France trace their origins to North Africa—Algeria, Morocco, and Tunisia. There are also large Muslim groups who came from Turkey, the Middle East, and sub-Saharan Africa as workers. Muslim immigration to France significantly expanded after World War II, when French companies, in need of immigrants to fill gaps in the labor market, recruited workers from the Maghreb and the countries in the Sahel area (Senegal, Mali, and Mauritania), and later from Turkey.[3]

This first wave of economic immigration ended after the 1974 oil crisis, when France suspended the recruitment of workers and offered foreigners an option to stay and be joined by their families. Although tight restrictions were in place, many women and children joined the male immigrants and settled in France. In the second half of the 1980s, the next wave of immigration involved the arrival of Kurdish political refugees from Turkey, who were accommodated as asylum-seekers after the military coup d'état in 1980. The second generation of Muslim immigrants brought a new stage in the experience of Islam in France. In contrast to their parents, the children of Muslim immigrants embrace new religious attitudes and make a greater effort to adapt their beliefs and practices to the host society. These young people do not have the same history as their parents and do not have the same relationship to their religion. Most of them do not hesitate to define themselves as Muslims, although not all are believers. In 1975, the first demands for prayer rooms were taken into account; in 1976, during the month of Ramadan, a petition circulated that sought the establishment of a mosque. Islam often became a point of negotiation between employers and employees, perceived as a foundation for peaceful social relations. The management of public housing projects approved prayer rooms, yet mosques were generally located in basements. The 1979 Iranian Revolution, as well as the postcrisis influx of oil dollars, influenced French Muslims in terms of identity, and at the same time French society became more sensitive to the presence of Islam.

France's deteriorating economic and social conditions reinforced an anti-immigrant atmosphere in the late 1980s. The National Front, an extreme right-wing movement led by Jean-Marie Le Pen, expressed anti-immigrant sentiments, directed especially toward Arabs and Muslims. It rested its appeal to the French public on colonial stereotypes that portrayed Arabs as lazy, shifty, and disobedient. Public debate started to question the rights of Muslims and their children to stay in France, and young North Africans became the scapegoats of society's frustrations and fears and the targets of emerging, intense xenophobic attitudes. In contrast, the secular Socialist Party supported and to some degree facilitated the progressive integration of Islam in France.[4]

In 1989, the first controversy regarding whether to allow Muslim girls to wear headscarves arose, adding more of a religious element to the integration and immigration debate than previously had been the case. In the summer of 1995, the Algerian Armed Islamic Group planted bombs in a Paris subway to protest French support for the military regime in Algeria. A few years later, the attacks of 9/11 exerted a strong influence on French public opinion, consistently linking Islam with an array of negative images.

French Muslims suffer disproportionately from unemployment and encounter greater difficulties finding full-time, long-term employment. They occupy the lesser professional positions and are underrepresented in executive positions. The restructuring and layoffs in the industrial sector during the 1970s and 1980s had a disproportionate impact on French Muslims. Many currently find themselves unemployed or in early retirement. The concentration of Muslim immigrants in the industrial sectors also diminishes their ability to build strong professional and social networks that would enable them to help their children find employment. During the last decade, the proportion of female immigrants in the workplace increased. However, Muslim women are concentrated in precarious and part-time positions. In addition, Muslim women who wear the Islamic headscarf encounter resistance from employers.

Riots in the *Banlieues*

Muslim immigrants settled mainly in the poorest suburban neighborhoods of metropolitan cities—the *banlieues*, where industrial activities and cheap housing were concentrated, a pattern that continues to this day.[5] A strong geographical concentration of Muslims exists in socially disadvantaged city neighborhoods due to the government's effort to confine immigrants to housing projects. For a long time the French government referred to the housing problems of immigrants in terms of "social exclusion" but refused to admit the existence of racial discrimination.[6]

In October and November of 2005, a series of riots took place, chiefly involving young people of Algerian descent, who burned cars and public buildings to express their resentment of French government policy. The outbursts were triggered by the deaths of two Muslim teenagers during a chase with police who were carrying out an identity check.[7] Initially confined to the Paris area, the political vandalism spread to other areas and cities. The French Parliament declared a state of emergency. The riots served as a wake-up call, prompting the French government to reconsider its policy toward immigrants. A year later, civil unrest again flared up in the same suburbs. A wide range of commentary that attempted to link the turmoil to illegal immigration, Muslim separatism, and polygamous practices amplified the government's response to the riots. In fact, most of the rioters were second-generation immigrant youths, and the underlying issues were far more complex, involving social and economic exclusion and racial discrimination. At stake was the capability of the French Republic to respond to these challenges while maintaining its formal commitment to its distinctive model of the social integration of individuals no matter what their color or creed.[8]

Shortly after the rioting died down and after the state of emergency was lifted in January 2006, another set of protests broke out in central Paris and other French cities, this time largely by angry, white youths. The unrest was in response to a law, the First Employment Contract, that was perceived to compromise job security, impose lower wages, and infringe upon the rights of French workers. As a result of public pressure, the government revoked the youth employment law. Unlike its prompt response to the protests of 2006, the French government has failed to take any significant action to address the ever-growing crisis of social exclusion and racism affecting the French *banlieues*.[9] The drastically different responses by the French government to these two rather similar expressions of discontent reveal much about the social structure and current dominant mentality of the French.[10]

Discrimination against Muslims

For French Muslims, lack of citizenship is less of a barrier to employment than it is in other European countries, because many of them are French citizens. Rather, the problem lies in the fact that even second-generation French Muslims, who have lived in France all their lives, continue to be considered migrant workers. In interviews and surveys, many young people of North African origin say they have been victims of racial discrimination. In fact, religion may be as enduring a fault line in France as race is in the United States.[11] Farhad Khosrokhavar, a French sociologist, has found that Muslims, who constitute approximately "7 to 8 percent of the total French population, may account for more than 50 percent of the French prisoner population."

[12] He adds that this is the result of socioeconomic factors rather than religion. Nevertheless, the two—religion and socioeconomic factors—go hand in hand, because Muslims have difficulty finding jobs and integrating into the social fabric of France. In the early 1990s, 50 percent of the youth of Algerian nationality and 30 percent of Algerians with French nationality were unemployed, including many who had achieved some level of higher education.

With regard to the educational system, immigrant children in France also suffer from indirect discrimination. The ability of children with foreign origins to successfully integrate into the French school system is strongly linked to their migration experience.[13] The French educational system distributes pupils according to their place of residence. In 2004, another form of discrimination was created when France introduced a new law that prohibits the wearing of religious symbols in public schools. According to the Open Society Institute's 2007 *Muslims in the EU: Cities Report*, the majority of Muslim girls in France have either stopped wearing a headscarf while in school or given up their education due to the 2004 law. Some, with the financial means, have chosen to study at private schools or to be schooled at home so that they can continue to wear the headscarf.[14] One ironic and unintended consequence of the 2004 law was that private Catholic schools accept Muslims girls and permit them to wear headscarves freely while they receive a good education.[15]

2. The French "Foulard Affair"

In 1989, at the beginning of the school year, a number of incidents occurred in secondary schools, in particular at the lower secondary school in Creil near Paris. Three young women were suspended for refusing to remove their headscarves (*foulards*) despite being requested to do so by the teaching staff and the principal of the school. The case was widely discussed in public. It was the beginning of the *"Foulard* Affair," which raised important issues within French society regarding the republican model of social integration, the status of women in society, and possible changes in the school system. As there was no clear legal answer, the minister of education requested an advisory opinion of the Conseil d'Etat, the French Supreme Administrative Court, which stated that the headscarf and other religious signifiers were allowed in schools as long as they were not used to proselytize, to endanger students, or to interfere with instruction.[16] In the meantime, the French government tried to accommodate Islam in other ways as well, notably by considering the creation of an administrative unit that could manage the construction of mosques, as well as the training of imams and *halal* butchers.

The second significant headscarf controversy occurred in 1994, and this time the challenge was more severe. A new memorandum was issued delineating the difference between "discreet" religious symbols able to be brought into the classroom and "ostentatious" religious symbols (including the foulard), which were forbidden. For a long time, the French government had relied on mediation to solve headscarf conflicts between Muslim citizens and governmental institutions rather than issuing a single law applicable to all situations. Three hundred cases had been identified for mediation, and mediators at the Ministry of Education had received a number of complaints concerning the functioning of the Department of Education, a public utility. But the government's advisory opinion did not provide a lasting solution to the difficulties. More and more headscarf-related issues arose, and in 2002, 150 separate conflicts required the intervention of a mediator. According to the *Muslims in the EU: Cities Report*: "Very often, the situation was solved by mutual agreement. The girls agreed to take off their *hijab* in the classroom, rather than being in conflict with the school institution for several months."[17] Although no quantitative data is available on Muslim students who wear the headscarf, observers agree that the number of young women wearing headscarves in public schools had increased. More visibly, outside of schools, in the French *banlieues*, there was an increase in the wearing of headscarves.[18]

The post-9/11 atmosphere and the 2002 French presidential election, which focused on multiculturalism and the security agenda, encouraged anxieties among the citizenry about the headscarf. In a wider context, the discourse on the enlargement of Europe, the integration process accompanying Turkey's possible EU membership, and the international rhetoric of a "war on terror" contributed to the growing alarm over the headscarf. All these influences crystallized suspicions, and even fears, about the migrant population and the grim French inner-city immigrant neighborhoods.

In September 2003, after an article justifying a hard-line approach to the headscarf was published in the newspaper *Libération*, the media reported extensively on the exclusion of two young headscarved girls Alma and Lila Levy.[19] They were perceived to be exotic because their father was a militant atheist, raised Jewish, and a communist, and their mother was an Algerian teacher. It seemed that the use of the headscarf was intended to influence a family dispute. Within a few weeks, the Levy sisters became the main topic of public discourse, and discussions ranged far beyond the case of Alma and Lila. By the end of 2003, the leading editorials and opinion makers of the press had, with very few exceptions, accepted a monolithic interpretation of the headscarf as the signifier of an aggressive Islamism that challenges the most basic rules of republican coexistence. Media coverage strongly contributed to this negative view of veiling, and, more generally, of Islam. Encouraged by the media, several feminist associations and journals adopted similar Islamophobic rhetoric. The term "Muslim headscarf," or veil, is often linked to extremism, militancy, and jihadism, as if they belonged together naturally. Various exchanges among intellectuals, activists, politicians, and journalists have fueled alliances and disagreements over the headscarf.[20]

Stasi Commission

It was in this context, on July 1, 2003, that French President Jacques Chirac commissioned the Stasi Group, whose role was to study "the application of the principle of secularism in the Republic." The group began to work on multiple issues and recommendations, such as fighting labor discrimination or recognizing state holidays for Jews and Muslims. At the end, only the headscarf issue led to new legislation. According to a public survey, 69 percent of the French supported the law banning the headscarf in public schools. This support came from a wide political spectrum, including many Muslims in France.[21] 42 percent of Muslims favored the ban, and immigrant Muslim women in France revealed that despite having been raised in a society where many women veiled and/or had often veiled themselves while living in the Maghreb, none of them believed they must veil in order to be a "good" Muslim.[22] It should be acknowledged that Muslims in France do not represent a homogeneous group either ethnically or in their levels of religiosity.

The French government decided to follow the recommendation of the Stasi Commission and passed the law concerning *laïcité* and conspicuous religious symbols in schools on March 15, 2004, by a landslide majority of 494 to 36, driving the *Foulard* Affair to new heights.[23] Surprisingly, the law was issued despite the fact that the number of girls wearing headscarves in French schools had been declining for nearly a decade. The legislation prohibited the headscarf despite its infrequent use, which suggests that the veil had taken on a larger symbolic meaning in French society.[24]

The commission described the wearing of religious signs in middle and high schools as "a communitarian danger for the French national identity and social cohesion."[25] France now has one of the most restrictive legislative approaches to the headscarf in Europe. The backers of the law have particularly targeted the *foulard* despite the absence of any expressed intent to do so.[26] The law of 2004 also was an important step with respect to France's international legal commitments to human rights. Since November 1950 France has been a member of the European Convention of Human Rights, which confers rights of thought, conscience, religion, and public expression. But these rights are limited to the extent that they cause public disorder or attacks on the freedom of conscience of others.[27] To invoke this limitation, the national governing body of a member country must pass a law stating this. The French law arose from the contextual motivations for the French Parliament to protect the country from possible future, supranational headscarf cases brought by the ECHR against France.

In order to enforce the law, the French minister of education issued a circular (May 27, 2004) covering its various effects and specifying practical examples of "conspicuous" symbols. The law and circular gave headmasters the power to decide which particular attire is acceptable. The law does not apply to parents who come to school wearing a headscarf. According to regulations implemented by the ministry of education, primary and secondary school teachers are prohibited from advertising their religious and political beliefs while discharging their professional duties. The law does not cover civil servants or workers. However, observers note that since 2001, the Conseil d'Etat has rendered frequent legal rulings on an increasing number of cases concerning headscarved civil servants.

Designated as the very counter-symbol of *laïcité,* the headscarf now tends to be interpreted, in a context of growing Islamophobia, as bolstering fundamentalism among Muslim groups. Supporters of the law claimed that the law did not increase identity or religious tensions within French society, but, on the contrary, reduced the use of headscarves in public schools without any significant complaint.[28] Liberals raised slightly more balanced arguments and opinions about the impacts of the 2004 law: "Although the law banning the headscarf was passed for petty political reasons, an unintended benefit may result: French Muslims who do not want to impose the headscarf on their daughters may now be able to refer to the law to deflect criticisms of those in their communities and neighborhoods who feel they are being unfaithful to religious practices."[29]

Stereotypes of Women Who Wear Headscarves

The study of the 2004 law reveals a stereotypical approach to cultural and social identities that is also reflected in discussion of the West versus Islam and the French integration model versus other models. Gender issues, even if absent from the judicial framework, have also been part of the public debate since 1989. The main argument put forward by the supporters of the law is that girls who wear the headscarf suffer from the domination and authority of their fathers or their brothers.[30] During the debate on the 2004 law, only a few feminists initiated an important petition claiming "the women's rights argument is masking discrimination against women in the context of anti-scarf discourse."[31] It is striking that women with headscarves are presented as nonautonomous subjects. Throughout the debates on the headscarf issue, the voices of young Muslim women were seldom heard in the media. Newspapers continually published pictures of young women wearing headscarves, but never gave them an opportunity to speak for themselves. In keeping with Orientalist scholarly tradition, their essential truths are supposedly better explained by Western intellectuals or politicians, without even a semblance of dialogue with the targeted headscarf-wearing women. The researchers of the Stasi report, despite the commission's strong opinions on Muslim women's lives and social conditions, interviewed only two Muslim women.[32] Yet, the commission report insisted on the "regression of the situation of young veiled women" in French inner cities. "They are victims of the return of sexism under which they suffer verbal, physical and psychological violence. Young men force them to wear clothes that cover their bodies as well as not to look in the eyes of men."[33] This argument later was used in a court case against a Muslim woman who was working in an underwear shop. A French court held that she could be fired from her job because, according to her employer's opinion, she dressed too modestly, and she was not encouraging shoppers to buy, therefore her employer had the right to dismiss her. The court accepted this defense. Such a ruling creates stereotypes of Muslim women and encourages stereo-typing of women overall.[34]

Muslim girls with headscarves have more to their identities than this single and reductionist characterization. They have different motivations and choices. Gaspard and Khosrokhavar, in their book based on a survey, distinguished among those who wear the headscarf because it is traditional (e.g., their mothers and grandmothers wore it); those who want to avoid a conflict with their families' expectations, notably in relation to a father's obligation to defend his daughter's honor and virginity; those who use it in order not to be bothered by males in the neighborhood; and those who are more militant and use the hijab as a flag of revolt.[35]

Identity formation attracted the attention of many scholars in the face of issues of global mobilization such as multiculturalism, integration, toleration, inclusion, exclusion, and individualism versus belonging to groups. Moreover, individuals with multiple identifications and belongings make this issue even more complex. Scholars Anthony Appiah and Amy Gutmann, emphasizing these multiplicities, claim that individuals cannot be categorized by one single reference.[36] Thus the category of "Muslim girls" needs to be deconstructed for an understanding that currently eludes France's political class, committed intellectuals, and the media, who found it tempting to essentialize females who wear the headscarf rather than to examine their cases one by one.[37]

Voices of French Feminists

Well-known female artists and academics, including many feminists, argued that the headscarf is a threat to women. These feminist voices were very influential in the headscarf debates. They argued that banning religious symbols in school would take pressure off Muslim girls who are forced to veil by their parents, by fundamental groups, or by peers who call them names and even threaten violence against girls who do not veil. Given that one of the key arguments for the ban relates to peer pressure, the exact number of girls wearing the veil to school is important. The French government's estimates show a constant decline in the total number of headscarves in school.[38] Yet, the argument that "because so many girls wear the headscarf, it puts tremendous pressure on nonveiled Muslim girls to wear headscarves" was used over and over in the Stasi report and in the decisions of the ECHR and Turkish courts. Is it necessary to limit religious expression in order to protect the several thousand schoolgirls who do not wear a headscarf from the thousand or so who do? The ECHR, in its ruling in the Leyla Sahin case, without having paid attention to the statistics that reveal who wears a headscarf and who does not, supported the argument and decided not to protect freedom of religion for headscarf users.[39]

The exclusion of young women who wear the headscarf from French society encouraged the creation of a separate women's section within Muslim organizations. The voices of young women claiming to be feminists became vocalized in public forums. They use the term "feminism," but they distinguish themselves from Westernized feminist movements, which they consider to be racist and paternalist.[40] Contrary to the arguments of headscarf opponents, these women are not always "manipulated" by their parents, their brothers, or Islamist activists. Some choose to wear the headscarf as a sign of their faith, while others adopt it to free themselves from the authority of their father or brothers. Indeed, by wearing the headscarf they can occupy public space more freely, without attracting the glances of men. They claim that they are no longer considered an object of seduction, capable of arousing male desire.[41]

3. The Impact of the 2004 Law on Muslim Women

Muslim women's responses to the headscarf ban in schools differed, due to demographic factors such as age and level of education. It is especially revealing that many immigrant women who grew up with the veil in their countries of origin abandoned it in France to be hired for work and to fit in. Many of them were cut off from family members. Religion, a communal affair in North Africa and other Muslim countries, became a more private affair in France.[42] Although all religion in France is supposed to be private, the cultural climate is conducive to practicing Catholicism but not very receptive to Islam.[43] Many older women who immigrated before the 1980s and 1990s and have lived in France for decades have learned to accommodate by redefining what it means to be a good Muslim woman. However, for their young, French-born daughters, the identification with their culture is a religion in itself, even if they do not live according to religious norms. This identification helps explain why many members of the second generation choose to oppose and criticize the compromises and adaptations of their parents.[44]

Contrary to the French government's argument, the impact of the headscarf ban on young Muslim girls is huge. A report—issued in January 2008 by the Islamic Human Rights Commission (IHRC) for submission to the committee of the United Nations Convention on the Elimination of All Forms of Discrimination Against Women (CEDAW)—concerning the violation of CEDAW by the ban on headscarves and other religious symbols in schools and the law's social impact on Muslim women across France provides significant testimony about the suffering experienced by young girls.[45] According to the IHRC report, between March 2004 and 2005, the law affected 806 young Muslim women and girls. For the same period, the French government produced figures showing that there were 639 cases that arose under the 2004 law.[46] The dispute over these figures causes concerns about how the effects of the ban are understood and monitored. The official cases do not indicate the full impact of the law, because many families do not want to endure the exposure and unpleasantness of a legal fight.

The French government acclaimed the ban as a success because it had "stemmed the Islamic fundamentalism tide and brought calm atmosphere to the nation's *lycées*."[47] Further, the ban on religious symbols that targeted the Islamic headscarf was primarily bound up with an ongoing debate regarding secularism and the French state, thereby ignoring embedded concerns about human rights and gender issues. For the French government to speak of the headscarf ban as implementing CEDAW is misleading. Such a claim is neither an accurate reflection of how the law came into being nor of the success of its implementation.[48]

The IHRC report includes interviews with young girls who left their education because of the headscarf ban. According to Muslim students, after the 2004 law, they "were set apart, alone in a room or sometimes in a mere corridor; they were not allowed any contact with their fellow-students. All the girls said they felt like plague victims in quarantine."[49] Based on school regulations, a "pedagogical follow-up" should theoretically be undertaken, but teachers have insisted they would in no way agree to give private lessons to those students who refused to comply with the ban.[50] The vast majority of Muslim girls who were keen on wearing the headscarf gave up covering their heads altogether. They opted for studying and accepted to forget about their beliefs for a while. Some tried to rebel by ceasing to respect their teachers; others spoke of covering their heads again to get expelled, and of giving up their studies. Further examination of cases three to four years after the ban showed that some girls were suffering from different forms of post-traumatic stress disorder, in some instances even manifesting schizophrenia.

Despite the significant impact of the ban on some girls' physical and emotional well-being, as well as the loss of educational opportunities, very few of the affected girls pursued a judicial remedy. Many of the cases ended up being negotiated, and conciliatory settlements were reached. School administrators encouraged students and their parents to leave school at their own will, because they would later be allowed to register with the National Center for Distance Learning, with registration fees waived. One student even received a new computer and a year of Internet access in addition to the free registration. Faced with the suffering of their daughters, many parents who were unaware of their rights accepted such proposals, which, in fact, were designed to deprive them of their right to take legal action.[51]

Wider Implications of the Law

The psychological impact of the 2004 law, even with its limited scope, is wider than its jurisdictional limits. The effect of the ban is felt in the public and private sectors and even at private schools and universities. For example, three female students wearing headscarves were recently expelled from the universities of Toulouse, Saint-Etienne, and Villetaneuse.[52] The social and legal implications of the ban not only include the interruption of education, but also cause interference with future employment opportunities. France long had a ban on the wearing of religious symbols by government employees;

the number of cases challenging this prohibition has risen since passage of the 2004 law. The reasoning behind the prohibition was based on secularism, and women's rights had never been treated as an issue. Despite consistent reassurance by governmental authorities that the headscarf ban is applicable only in middle and high schools, lower administrative courts have issued many decisions concerning the loss of government jobs because of the headscarf.[53]

The situation in the private sector is more confusing. No law or administrative regulation clearly prohibits an employee from wearing a headscarf, and legal rulings on the issue varied widely. Court cases based on similar facts produced different outcomes. Employers generally give reasons such as "business need" or "respect for disciplinary rules" to justify banning employees' headscarves. Societal hostility, reinforced by the school and public sector bans, touches on every aspect of women's lives, and anecdotal reports of discrimination increased, particularly after the 2004 law came into effect.[54] For instance, women wearing headscarves have been removed from juries, banned from kindergartens, banks, and even human rights organizations.[55] Moreover, women wishing to marry have been asked to remove their headscarves or else were denied entry to places of civil registration for marriage. IHRC also notes the trend in recent years of Muslim women being forced to unveil for the purposes of receiving an identity card. In 1997, a BBC documentary claimed that one woman who refused to remove her headscarf when asked to show her ID card had the words "fervent Muslim" added to the official notations on her card.[56]

Some women who wear the Islamic headscarf are prevented from becoming French citizens despite meeting residency and other criteria. The criteria for awarding citizenship turn out to be highly subjective, and no standard exists. For instance, one of the criteria is assimilation, defined as "similarities with the French in terms of mores and language." Bureaucrats have a lot of room to maneuver. Wearing a headscarf could be interpreted differently from one regional authority to another, depending on whether the headscarf is treated as evidence of a failure of assimilation. Currently, under the law and the jurisprudence of the Conseil d'Etat, wearing a headscarf does not constitute an assimilation deficiency. But, in certain regions of France, since the early 1990s, citizenship has been refused on the grounds that the applicant is wearing a headscarf.[57] A ruling by the Conseil d'Etat can be reversed if there is opposition to the naturalization of headscarf-wearing women.[58] For instance, in November 2005, Chetouani El Khamsa received a letter from a regional government official stating that her application for ten years residency had been turned down because she wore a hijab that was associated with "fundamentalist Islam." El Khamsa was employed and had four children, all born in France. Her husband had been granted a ten-year residence permit. One could easily infer that, according to French naturalization officials, wearing the hijab is not compatible with the condition of "assimilation."[59]

Dealing with mounting controversies associated with Islam, the French government set up a national institution, HALDE, to promote equality and combat discrimination. The role of this institution is questionable, however, when considered in the light of the prevailing legal culture with regard to discrimination cases in France. Of the 220,000 recorded discrimination cases in 2006, only 43 went to trial. The possibilities of a successful challenge in a French court by a litigant affected by the March 2004 ban are very low.[60] Several reasons explain why so few cases go to trial. For one, the prevailing culture within French law firms favors conciliation over litigation.[61] A closer inspection of HALDE's power, efficacy and imperative suggests that no overt judicial challenge is likely to be made through HALDE.[62] Such institutional attempts are helpful in the long run, especially if members of an immigrant society tend to believe that such government efforts are sincere and helpful rather than hypocritical. But if the French state fails to find concrete means to address structural problems concerning education, social security, and job opportunities that disproportionately and adversely affect Muslim immigrants and their children, these cosmetic efforts to mitigate the harm to immigrants seem destined to fail.

4. Beneath the Surface

Laïcité

The 2004 law's limited jurisdiction allows one to argue that the law was mainly designed to reinforce the principle of laïcité as the guardian of French identity rather than being aimed at young Muslim girls. This argument is subject to scrutiny, however, as laïcité requires a more comprehensive application than this law provides. Viewed in this way, the headscarf ban is more an outgrowth of political and social hysteria, designed to uphold the cultural side of Frenchness rather than to protect laïcité as claimed.

If the French law is serious about a danger posed by young Muslim women to laïcité, why does it not cover schools at all levels of education in France? Or, is the danger only in public schools? Under the French educational system, private schools are not free to create their own curricula, which are under the control of the minister of education. So, why are private schools given this latitude when it comes to religious significations? After the 2004 law many Muslim girls reportedly transferred to Catholic schools so they could wear a headscarf freely while receiving their education. Of course, not all of the headscarved girls went to schools run by Catholic nuns. Many who came from very conservative religious families were sent to private Islamic schools. It is not far-fetched to speculate that this was not the desired result of the 2004 law.

Secularism in French schools goes back to the mid-nineteenth century, when primary education was made compulsory for boys and girls, and when religion was no longer taught in the classroom by Catholic priests and nuns. Yet while "militantly *laïc* in theory, French schools were more flexible, allowing teaching about religion if only in recognition of the historic significance of Catholicism."[63] Some of this flexibility is seen in the way the French approached the headscarf ban. This may be the reason that headscarves were not banned in private schools. Even in public schools, inconsistent implementations suggest that *laïcité* has a margin of flexibility, depending on the political and cultural situation in French society.

One of the unintended consequences of the headscarf controversy was that it reintroduced strict secularism as a matter for debate in French society after a century of consensus. With the presence of Islam as a minority religion, the *laïcité* principle was interpreted more rigidly than previously. For instance, a French law of 1905 provides for the conduct of worship in public space: religious edifices are public, processions are conducted in public, chaplains carry out their activities in public places, and priestly dress are not prohibited in public spaces. It was only in 2004 that the administration banned such practices to avoid the perception that the prohibition of the headscarf was discriminatory.[64] The 1905 law was about limiting the power of the Catholic Church in Catholic France and did not really apply in cases involving minority religions. But the existence of the 1905 law served to initiate an anti-headscarf argument, and *laïcité* was the politically correct policy to rely on if the real goal was to remove Islamic symbols from the French scene.

The question of *laïcité* in France raises two additional problems: one is the identity and particularity of France, and the other is the relationship between Islam on one side and the French concept of secularization and democracy on the other. France is experiencing crises of identity, due in part to the presence of significant numbers of Muslims in the country. When *laïcité* was conceived, the main enemy of the French state was the Catholic Church, but not necessarily religion as such. Today, Islam seems to have taken the place of Catholicism.[65] But the hostility toward Islam is more aggressive than it was to its Christian counterpart. In Western understanding, and specifically in France, Islam raises a theological and societal challenge; that is, whether Islam is compatible with modernity and *laïcité*.[66]

It is important to note that prior to the new law, Christian crosses and Jewish kippot had generally been tolerated in French public schools. It has been rightly argued that "it is likely that the everyday signs of religious adherence to Christianity and Judaism have not been understood to threaten the foundations of the French nation because they are not associated with immigration or racial difference."[67] At one point during the headscarf affair of the 1990s, François Bayrou, the minister of education at that time, declared that "France is a Judeo-Christian country," despite the fact that *laïcité* was the argument for excluding Muslim girls from school. Critics thus assert that the addition of large crosses and Jewish kippot to the 2004 law was simply to discourage charges that the government was racist toward the law's real target: Muslims.[68]

Incidentally, not all of the *laïcité* debates were devoted to Islam.[69] However, Islam has a greater demographic weight than those other movements that helps account for its prominence. Islam was perceived as having the potential to produce a profound change in society. According to Roy, the prohibition of the headscarf and the issue of *halal* meat in school cafeterias were more of a territorial conquest by "others" than a defense of neutrality in relation to Judaism and evangelical Protestantism.[70] Any process of communitarianism in the *banlieues* could cause a profound imbalance in French society. In France two different concerns operate: the fear of an ethnic Islam (Arab, Middle Eastern) that would import the conflicts of the Middle Eastern region into France, and the fear of a nonethnic and supranational Islam that becomes specifically European.

Republicanism

Education in France has always played an important role in building and conserving French republicanism. Schools are charged with forging future citizens within a secular frame. In this sense, the French nation, unlike Germany, is not based on ethnic affiliation, but rather founded on the common use of the French language, and an acceptance of fundamental French values such as the principle of laicism in public life. Accordingly, those elements of coherence are widely seen as indispensable for preserving the identity of the French nation. These elements have an ideational, rather than a natural character. Schools must implant a French sensibility in each new generation. For these reasons, an individual's freedom of religion could be sacrificed in France for the sake of the "systematic consistency" that laicism entails.[71]

Moreover, the ban on the headscarf presupposed that French identity and loyalty to the French government required the subordination of religiosity. To allow "the tiny cross, the tiny star of David, but not the Orthodox garb of yarmulke, Sikh turban and *foulard* seemed to raise the national flag above faith."[72] The united front against Muslim schoolchildren was created by a combination of the ideology of French republicanism based on strict *laïcité*, the colonial past and memories of Algerian resistance, Islamic fundamentalism, the emergence of Islam as the second biggest religion in Europe, and, finally, the problematic features of Islam's approach to women's rights. When a society accepts differences without prejudices, then students and teachers will gradually get used to headscarves. It is likely that the headscarf would eventually lose some of its meaning and power as a symbol of an unassimilated minority or repressed women, or as an indication of terrorism in societies fearful of Islam.

After all, Muslim girls with headscarves are a small minority in France. Among 200,000 Muslim females, only 1,200 are subject to the 2004 law. Moreover, among the estimated Muslim population only 12 percent say that they go to a mosque every Friday. These figures indicate that, similar to the recent burqa debate, we are talking about a very small minority, and the sound bites they provoke are much too loud. Such figures are important, however, according to the philosopher Charles Taylor. If a difference makes sense for a large number of individuals over a long period, it should be respected. One might interpret this as an argument that consensus and length of time are essential dimensions. These yardsticks give culture a coherent view. It is important to understand what is acceptable and what is excluded in a given culture over a period of time.[73] From a legal perspective, a consistent pattern of implementation and recognition would give customary law legitimation.

The Fear Factor

Considering that the French cultural milieu exhibits a fear of Islam, the 2004 law can be understood as a precautionary action. The Stasi Commission openly denounced "political-religious militants, extremist political and religious trends, an activist minority, and organized groups testing the resistance of the Republic," all of which refer, more or less, to Al Qaeda in the popular imagination.[74] *Le Monde* pointed out that what the Stasi Commission had undertaken was a "psychoanalysis of the French conscience."[75] The Stasi

Commission reflected French fears of fanaticism, and associated fears of diluting French culture with a growing Islamic presence. Public reactions against the veil is a way to reassert national identity at a time when France is feeling threatened by globalization, the European Union, and immigration. As one French writer put it: "the defensive and punitive policies towards all visible signs of Islamity" are a response to fear of an "Arabo-Muslim menace."[76] A remark by Alexis de Tocqueville gives insight into such fear: "In politics, fear is passion which frequently increases at the expense of others. One easily fears anything when one no longer desires anything with fervor."[77] The French have experienced fear for their sense of national unity, arising from the existence of "dangerous others." In the twentieth century, plots against Frenchness were said to come from the Freemasons, the "yellow peril," "perfidious Albion," the communists, the delinquent youth of a postcolonial origin, and, now, Islamic fundamentalists.[78] The headscarf debate reveals that this fear is associated with Islamic culture more than with the Islamic terrorist in French society.

7

Germany

We kidded ourselves a while. We said: "They won't stay [after some time] they will be gone," but this isn't reality. And of course, the approach [to build] a multicultural [society] and to live side by side and to enjoy each other…has failed, utterly failed.

ANGELA MERKEL, CHANCELLOR OF GERMANY,
December 2010

Germany, the EU's largest and, arguably, most powerful member state, and home of the greatest number of Turkish Muslim migrants, has experienced a contentious headscarf debate (*Kopftuchstreit*) that has raged in all segments of German society and in the German media in the recent decade and is still ongoing.[1] Germany is an important case to consider because it is the EU member state where both antidiscrimination legislation and headscarf regulation are seen as relatively problematic. Moreover, the cultural and political attention paid to Germany's national socialist experience forms an ever-present backdrop to present-day social and political discussions about citizenship and the state. The threat of a return to fascism looms large in the German imagination, though where and how this threat is identified—whether in banning or allowing headscarves, in discrimination against minorities, or in state intrusion—is a subject of constant debate. The German case shows how race, religion, gender, and the role of the state go together but also diverge.[2]

Despite Germany's relatively less visible militant opposition to the headscarf, similar to its neighbor France, the German federal system has imposed wider and deeper legal barriers on its Muslim female teachers and civil servants. The German justification for a headscarf ban applicable to teachers is based on a legal argument not unlike the one relied on in France, which identifies the headscarf as a "political symbol" that puts social peace at risk. Yet there are important differences between the two countries in their treatment of the Islamic headscarf. German laws have targeted teachers and civil servants, as opposed to middle and high school students. Another difference is due to the differing administrative systems of the two countries. German laws are targeted at education and are therefore under the control of regional governments as opposed to the French centralized system. More important, German laws, in general, target Islam specifically with exemptions made for Christian symbols. In France, however, *laïcité* was the overt reasoning, and no exception was made for other religions. Germany has never claimed to be as secular as France. Germany's basic reason was the neutrality of the liberal state but also conveyed was the sense that "our neutrality is Christian."[3]

There are several explanations for these differences between the two countries. First, Germany has a different historical experience than France. It has a smaller Muslim population than France and has no colonial baggage. In France, there have been nearly two decades of political debate on Islam and whether and how to deal with Islam, while Germany has seen much less concern. Until its politicization by the headscarf laws, the accommodation of Islam had mostly been delegated to the German judicial system. And yet, Germany's significant population of guest workers, mostly Turks, have had a more difficult time adjusting to and melting into German society than their counterparts in France. Finally, France has a strong assimilationist identity based on "Frenchness," while Germany never wanted its minorities to become German. German policy is not based on assimilating Muslims or encouraging Turks to become German. In fact, one can read the German headscarf controversy as a battle over the meaning of the "German State": Is it a liberal state obliged to treat the adherents of all religious creeds equally, or is it an ethnic state where the "Christian-Occidental" majority has certain privileges that the Islamic minority do not enjoy?[4] The first position was taken by the German Constitutional Court (FCC) as a result of the "constitutional patriotism" specified by German philosopher Jürgen Habermas.[5] The second position was adopted by regional parliaments using their authority to legislate against the headscarf.

1. Islam in Germany

Germany has a total population of 82 million, mostly Christian. The ethnically homogeneous German society with its dark memory of the Nazi period had difficulty figuring out how to deal with an increasingly diverse population. Since the early 1960s, Germany has been home to many Muslim immigrants, predominantly Turkish guest workers (*Gastarbeiter*), who were invited by the German government in response to the shortage of unskilled workers that arose in the post–World War II period of rapid economic development. Since that time, the majority of the guest workers have settled permanently in Germany and have been joined by their families.[6] Germany now has a Muslim population of approximately 3.5 million, including approximately one million German citizens.[7] Many second- and third-generation Turks continue to perceive themselves as "Turks" or "foreigners," even if they hold German citizenship. Yet, this identification does not have a negative connotation. On the contrary, for instance, women who wear the headscarf in Germany have often stressed the "tolerant" and "liberal" character of German society, particularly compared with Turkey, where the headscarf is prohibited at schools and universities. This is particularly important because there is no legacy of colonialism to harden, embitter, or unduly politicize the stance of Muslims toward the German state. The Germans also have fairly positive feelings toward Turks, and Muslim political groups are not popular among Turkish minorities.[8] Turkish Islam has a unique presence in Germany based on Turkish nationalism in the European setting, apart from the Arabs. It is almost unconceivable that the majority of Turks in Germany and in Europe in general will become part of the global jihadist movement. Despite this, relations between Turks and Germans have never been free of problems. In the early 1990s, a series of attacks on Turks by neo-Nazi groups that resulted in the deaths of a Turkish woman and her two young children created tension and fear among Turks.[9]

Theoretically, the German state follows the neutrality principle to ensure that individuals can express and live out their religious convictions not just in private, but also in public. In practice, this result is difficult to achieve. Islam is the second largest religion in the country, after Christianity, yet no Muslim congregation has been recognized as a legal entity that would enjoy privileges under German law.[10] According to Christian Joppke, to the degree that the German state, unlike France, is identified as "Christian-Occidental," Islam has no place there. Moreover, "a Christian 'us' " is posited and the Islamic "them" is a substitute for the shattered idiom of ethnic nationhood."[11] In particular, a close relationship has existed between nation building and Protestantism.[12] These arguments have been used in one way or another as justifications for anti-headscarf laws. For example, a significant argument used against the headscarf was to decry a society without values: "A society without values is a worthless society. We are a society that has been marked by the Occident and by the Christian values."[13]

2. German Constitutional Order and the Headscarf Cases

Unlike in France, the German headscarf controversy was not manifested as a massive movement of veiled women supported by vigilant Islamic organizations. Instead, it was a top-down result of judicial politics, initiated by a single court case involving the clothing of public schoolteachers. Under Germany's federal government system, the state parliaments and courts of its sixteen states *(Länder)* enjoy substantial legislative and judicial autonomy. The laws and policies on the use of religious symbols in schools are the responsibility of each state and not matters for the federal government. The approach of the sixteen states toward the headscarf and other religious symbols has varied. At the same time, the states are bound by the German constitution (the Basic Law) and by rulings of the FCC.

The personal liberty and religious liberty clauses in articles 2 and 4 of the German Basic Law, which are universally granted to all individuals irrespective of their citizenship, have provided the key mechanisms for headscarf cases. The German Basic Law is one of the strongest constitutional orders in terms of protecting religious freedom. Article 4 protects freedom of religion without reservation.[14] This strictly enforced constitutional protection of the individual from the power of the state was, at first, a reaction to Germany's recent totalitarian past.[15] This long-established German approach contrasts sharply with the European Convention on Human Rights. As we have seen, the Convention expressly acknowledges that some limitations on freedom of religion may be necessary in a democratic society in the interests of public safety, public order, health, morals, and for the protection of the rights and freedom of others.[16] While the German judicial treatment of religious freedom is more permissive than the European Convention on Human Rights, the patterns of German judicial treatment of religious freedom cases are far from simple.

Apart from headscarf cases, the highly controversial classroom crucifix case, heard by the German Constitutional Court in 1995, marked the first shift in German jurisprudence toward an understanding of religious freedom that is in greater harmony with the jurisprudence of the European Court of Human Rights (ECHR). In this case, the FCC held that an existing law requiring that crucifixes be hung in all public elementary school classrooms was unconstitutional.[17] The Court declared that the Christian cross was "inherently religious," and therefore its installation in every Bavarian public classroom was unconstitutional because it "forced pupils to learn under the cross."[18] This violates pupils' and their parents' rights of religious liberty, interpreted to include the negative right not to be exposed to religious symbolism. The Court's holding in the crucifix case implied a possibility of further restrictions on religious freedom according to Article 9 (2) of the European Convention. The decision led to a huge public debate about religion, culture, and education in Germany. Due to the strong religious rights provisions in the German constitution, adhered to by Germany's higher courts, Christian elements were steadily withdrawn from German public schools until the challenge of Islam put the issue of religion back on the table.

A few court cases involving headscarf issues arose before the headscarf became politically controversial. Most of the early headscarf cases in Germany were about passports and identification pictures and did not interfere with women's wearing the headscarf. The first high-profile court cases occurred in the late 1990s and concerned teachers who wore headscarves in public schools. The timing of these cases coincided with the increased enrollment in German universities by Muslim women seeking work as teachers.

In an influential 1993 ruling, the Federal Administrative Court (FAC) decided that a twelve-year-old Turkish student had the right to abstain from co-ed sports on the grounds that, among other religiously forbidden things, she would face the risk of "losing" her headscarf and of being exposed to the boys because of "tightly cut of fitting sport dress."[19] In court, the girl's parents openly declared that they did not wish the "emancipation" of their daughter according to "Western standards."[20] Certainly, the religious rights of students and their parents had to be reconciled with the educational mandate of the state; in judicial terms, "a 'practical concordance' between both had to be reached."[21]

Another case, from the Upper Administrative Court of North Rhine-Westphalia, held that a Muslim girl in tenth grade had the right to abstain from the annual class retreat because of her "permanent fear" of violating her religious duties.[22] This decision received attention because it implicitly endorsed the so-called Camel Fatwa issued by a local cleric, according to whom Sharia law does not allow a female Muslim to travel more than eighty-one kilometers away from home, the distance a camel supposedly could walk in twenty-four hours, without a blood-related male chaperone.[23]

If a school failed to "exhaust all available organizational possibilities to accommodate Islamic precepts, then Muslim parents had a free hand to withdraw their children from inconvenient parts of the public school curriculum."[24]

In such a permissive setting, no one questioned the right of students to wear headscarves in the classroom.[25] In this multiculturalist atmosphere, German public schools depended on regional (*Länder*) decisions that mostly took the form of "Christian communal schools," which followed Christian cultural tradition.

Landmark Federal Constitutional Court Decision (2003)

Against this background, Ferestha Ludin, born in Afghanistan in 1972, who had lived in Germany since 1987, brought the most influential headscarf case to a German court in 2003. Ms. Ludin became a German citizen in 1995, and, following her university studies, she was accepted by the state preparatory service for grade schoolteachers in Baden-Wurttemberg. However, after passing the second state examination in 1998, she was not employed permanently as a public schoolteacher. In failing to hire Ms. Ludin, the school board could not—and did not intend to—suggest that she would misuse her teaching position for the purpose of Islamic indoctrination, or that she supported religiously motivated violence, or even that she would tacitly advocate a strict Islamic lifestyle within the classroom. Instead, the decisive factor for the school board was that she was unwilling to refrain from wearing a headscarf during instruction. Thus, she lacked the necessary "personal aptitude" and hence was considered unsuitable and unable to perform the duties of a public servant in accordance with the German Basic Law.[26] It was not disputed that she was fully qualified to work in this profession, and there had been no complaints by parents, children, or the school about her behavior during her preparatory service.

At the various levels of administrative jurisdiction, Ms. Ludin was unsuccessful in challenging the rejection of her application for permanent placement. The Federal Administrative Court, which sanctioned Ms. Ludin's loss of her job, justified its decision based on an interpretation of the neutrality principle in times of diversity: "In a plural society the state must pay respect to very diverse parental opinions, and it has to refrain from any religious indoctrination by teachers. Therefore, the neutrality mandate becomes more important with the increase of cultural and religious diversity, and this mandate is not, as the plaintiff holds it to be, loosened up in reference to the fact that cultural, ethnic and religious diversity in Germany is now shaping life in the school also."[27]

In September 2003, the FCC struck down the decision of the Federal Administrative Court, deciding that the denial of the right to wear a headscarf represents an undue restriction on the religious freedom of teachers unless it is based on an explicit legal prohibition. The Constitutional Court left no doubt that, within the traditional understanding of "open" neutrality, veiled teachers had to be tolerated, despite the fact that most of the Court's written decision is devoted to dispelling public fears and prejudices about the head-scarf.[28] Ms. Ludin achieved partial success before the FCC, Germany's highest court, and the outcome of her case had a profound impact on the headscarf issue in Germany. Yet the decision created a political backlash. For example, Gerhard Schröder, Germany's chancellor at the time, said in a 2003 interview that there was no room for headscarves in the German public service.[29]

Arguably, this was the most criticized decision ever made by the German Constitutional Court, which held that the political branches of the state, most importantly the democratic legislature and not the courts, should resolve such a socially and politically contested issue, i.e., how to manage religious and cultural differences. As indicated earlier, the Turkish Constitutional Court had taken the reverse approach, vesting control over the headscarf issue in the judiciary and thereby taking the decision-making power away from the democratically elected legislative body.

During the German legal proceedings, Ms. Ludin insisted that her head-scarf use was religiously motivated.[30] She also, predictably, defended herself by appealing to the German tradition of open neutrality, which would allow her to wear the headscarf for "personal" and "religious" reasons. While she categorically rejected any form of compromise, she simultaneously asked for tolerance from parents, children, and professional colleagues. During the lawsuit, Ms. Ludin began working for a private school belonging to the Islamic Federation in Berlin, an organization closely associated with the controversial Turco-Islamist group Millî Görüş.[31] Because the lawsuit was attracting a great deal of media attention, it was not a smart move, from a public relations point of view, to enter such an affiliation while the case was ongoing.

While the five to four majority decision created a sharp division within the Court between the liberal judges and the conservatives, in the end it represented a compromise between the two groups. After the judgment, the dilemma of regulating religious clothing shifted to the federal states. Immediately after the FCC's decision, eight of the sixteen states passed legislation that banned, to varying degrees, the wearing of headscarves by teachers and, in some states, by other public civil servants.

Immediately after the new laws came into effect, in states with bans, teachers were asked to remove their headscarves and were reprimanded, and in some instances dismissed, if they refused. Teachers, some employed for many years, were threatened with disciplinary action if they continued to wear a headscarf and were disciplined in North Rhine-Westphalia and Baden-Wurttemberg.[32] These restrictions have led some women to leave their home state or leave Germany altogether, to prolong maternity leave, and to take other leaves from their employment, or even to give up teaching despite years of study and investment in developing their pedagogical skills. The affected women were concerned about feeling alienated and excluded although they had lived in Germany for decades, or their entire lives, or were German-born converts to Islam.

The legal conflict over headscarf use by teachers highlighted two issues on Germany's agenda: anti-Western and anti-Islamic political sentiments, and the problem of integration of immigrants, in particular those from countries strongly shaped by Islam.[33] The *Ludin* decision had a lasting impact on German media and academic circles and led them to initiate public discourse about the problem of Islam symbolized by the headscarf controversy. In addition to the headscarf becoming a powerful religious symbol, the controversy over the headscarf became linked with wider culturally and politically charged concerns. The mere fact that a Muslim woman wears a headscarf is not in and of itself seen as religious symbolism. She is simply fulfilling an obligation stemming from her faith as she understands it. In this sense, the headscarf can be differentiated from a Christian cross worn on a necklace. The headscarf, however, gradually became symbolic as it became an instrument of intra-Islamic cultural struggle following the emergence of political Islam.[34]

Social and Political Arguments Concerning the Ludin *Decision*

Following the FCC's *Ludin* decision, proponents of headscarf restrictions initiated several arguments:

i. Women's rights and equality: Left-leaning German liberals, who generally otherwise support multiculturalism, displayed a certain discomfort with the way of life and political orientation associated with the headscarf. Feminists were joined by other advocates of emancipatory lifestyles, including Turkish writers and intellectuals living in Germany, who view the headscarf as an expression of gender-based social subordination, whereby women are oppressed, in violation of the constitutional principle of gender equality. From this perspective, restrictions on wearing the headscarf are viewed in a positive light, i.e., as upholding women's rights.[35] As we saw in Turkey, intervention by feminists in favor of the headscarf ban was considered a valuable contribution to the debate and put forward as the "authentic voice of Muslim women."

It was also argued that the ban offered a form of protection against possible compulsion and pressure to wear the headscarf on women and girls by their communities or families. Moreover, it was claimed that teachers wearing the headscarf would not be able to support girls fighting their families and communities to be allowed not to wear the headscarf.[36] Renate Schmidt, the German minister for women from 2002 until 2005, also spoke against the headscarf, as did a number of MPs of Turkish origin in the Bundestag.

By contrast, Marieluise Beck, Germany's commissioner for Migration, Refugees and Integration, spoke out against the headscarf restriction, together with other prominent women politicians.[37] Their support reflected a minority view of the headscarf among women's rights activists, and Beck was strongly criticized by feminists and, in particular, by a group of immigrant women from Muslim countries. In 2004, this group wrote an open letter to Beck that stressed that religion should be a private affair and that those who "under the influence of Islamists choose to wear the headscarf in public life should not be eligible for the civil service."[38]

Only postmodern feminists associated the headscarf with the desexualization of the social world, and thus welcomed it as obscuring sexual expression. They emphasized that a teacher with a headscarf who is integrated into modern professional life demonstrates the emancipation of women. A prohibition of headscarves for teachers, in this view, would lead Muslim women away from employment and solidify the stereotype of the "Anatolian housewife" in the diaspora, doomed to be forever isolated from normal social contact.[39]

ii. The neutrality of the state: Social Democratic Party (SPD) politicians in Berlin and Bremen, including Lale Akgun, a member of Parliament of Turkish descent, claimed that the law against the headscarf is designed to ensure the neutrality of the teaching environment and of public services, as well as to establish "political and religious peace" in the school and the state. Akgun argued that the wearing of headscarves by teachers must be prohibited to protect pupils from being confronted by a teacher who, while representing the state in the school, expresses alignment with a particular religion.[40]

iii. Islam: Some church representatives and some Christian Democrat politicians were vehemently opposed to the headscarf, warning that Islam is a cultural import into the "Christian Occident" and that it represents a threat to the Christian heritage that underpins German constitutional values.[41] These justify restrictions that privilege Christianity on the grounds that it is an integral part of German culture and the German value system. By this logic, Christian symbols are not considered a threat to the principles of the constitution because they are cultural rather than religious and therefore neutral. Right-wing nationalist parties, the Republican Party and the German People's Union (DVU), and the former communist leadership in Eastern Germany supported the secular orientation of the Federal Republic and together formed a coalition against headscarf use that arose from their antireligious motivations.[42] In addition to German proponents, some Turkish organizations in Germany, mainly secular feminists, joined proponents of the ban, seeking to raise public consciousness with the contention that the Islamic religious movement planned to challenge and even eliminate secular structures by stages. The acceptance of the headscarf was alleged to be the first step in this supposed insidious process, which would then be followed by escalating demands from Islamists.[43]

The secular Turkish community in Germany (TGD) and the Turkish Union in Berlin-Brandenburg (TBB) repeatedly warned against tolerating the headscarf. The TGD seeks the prohibition of all religious symbols in schools, and throughout the civil service, and has been critical of headscarf regulations that do not also prohibit Christian symbols, on the grounds that they discriminate against Muslim women.[44] It is astonishing to observe that the Turkish headscarf debate simply traveled from Turkey to Germany and thus inhabits a cross-border, cross-cultural environment. It is ironic also that secular Turks in Germany have fought against the headscarf while at the same time trying to organize opposition to ongoing discrimination and racism against Turks in Germany. It seems almost unimaginable that organizations established to fight against discrimination would join with their chief enemies, the right-wing nationalists and Christian Democrats. These intense anti-headscarf sentiments were deeply rooted in struggles going on in Turkey, their country of origin.

The Legal Arguments

The main sociopolitical arguments for and against headscarf use were also formulated as legal positions.

i. Teachers' religious freedom and nondiscriminatory access to public facilities: The German Basic Law, articles 3 and 4, paragraphs (1) and (2) guarantee the "freedom to have and cultivate a faith, to manifest it outwardly, and to live according to it, orient one's entire life toward religious doctrine."[45] The German Basic Law strongly formulates the importance of equality, repeatedly emphasizes the right to equal protection and equal enjoyment of rights and privileges. In wearing the headscarf, the believer is persuaded that she is fulfilling a religious obligation, and the headscarf is considered an expression of her religious beliefs. Yet, the schoolteacher appears as a public official. Therefore the freedom of religion she enjoys in her personal life can only be taken into limited consideration in the context of civil service. This kind of reasoning is hotly debated in Germany: from the total exclusion of fundamental rights as a result of a special status (in the military, prison, school, or civil service), to total inclusion in any state area. Within the current understanding, the interests of the public official cannot be a priori excluded. A civil-servant status brings with it an expectation of moderation that limits the exercise of fundamental rights to different degrees, depending on each sector of public service. For instance, the pedagogical sector allows greater discretion to the individual than the military or the judiciary allows.[46] Article 33 paragraphs (2) and (3) of the Basic Law provides teachers with comprehensive constitutional protection. These norms prohibit religious discrimination in regard to access to public office; placement must occur independently of religious affiliation, and adherence or nonadherence to religion should not be a disadvantage.

ii. Balancing the rights of parents and students: Unlike the international human rights principles on freedom of religion, the German Basic Law contains no statutory reservation. As a consequence, restrictions on religious freedom will only be deemed compatible with the law if they serve to directly protect other fundamental rights or similarly important objects of legal protection. Therefore, the teachers' constitutional rights must be weighed against the fundamental rights of parents as well as students. Freedom of religion positively protects the right to possess a faith and act accordingly, but it also protects negatively against being forced to practice a religion and against coercive confrontation with religion. Students are subject to compulsory education and thus cannot avoid the teacher's headscarf as a religious symbol. If negative freedom of religion protects students from having to "study beneath the cross," as the FCC forcefully formulated it,[47] then it also protects against any permanent, unavoidable, state-sponsored exposure to other religious symbols. This is true in particular when such symbols are not discreet and inconspicuous. Similarly, the Basic Law safeguards parents against objectionable religious influences on their children in public schools. Article 6 (2) of the Basic Law states that the care and upbringing of children is the natural right of parents.[48]

Against these arguments, the FCC pointed out that "not enough knowledge" existed with respect to the psychological effect of the headscarf on uniformed schoolchildren. In light of this, the restriction of a fundamental right to religion of the plaintiff was not warranted. In fact, one psychologist audited by the court opined that to the children the headscarf was at most "funny clothing," akin to what "grandmother wears in *Kasperletheater* [Punch and Judy shows]," and it certainly did not incite conscious emulation.[49]

iii. State neutrality: The state is the common home of all citizens and constitutionally may not identify itself with any specific religion. The FCC also decided that "state neutrality" in public schools could mean "open, inclusive neutrality" which permits all religions at school, enables the school to serve as a means of practicing mutual tolerance and, in this way, makes a contribution to the attempt to achieve integration; it could also mean "strict, distanced non-religious neutrality." Having said that, in order to evaluate state neutrality, one must analyze the separation between church and state. The German Basic Law has been interpreted with a "religion-friendly" understanding of neutrality and as a rejection of laicism as it operates in France. It should be kept in mind that the potential for conflict arising from the state's openness to the faiths of its citizens was lower when more than 90 percent of the German population belonged to one of the two main Christian churches. Today, Germany is different. Religious pluralism produces an altered conception of neutrality. Therefore, strict separation in the manner of the French model is not appropriate if the goal is to establish a friendly interaction between religious groups and the state.[50] The FCC made clear that permitting individual "religious" statements by teachers through their clothing should not necessarily be treated as an endorsement by the state. The Court made a subtle distinction between the "state" and the "teacher" acting in the state's name. To opponents of the veil, the teacher is the state, and thus should appear neutral. Headscarf opponents draw their view from the FCC's 1995 *Kruzifix* ruling, which equated a state-ordered crucifix on the school wall with a teacher's headscarf. However, as a legal critic commented, "the headscarf of a teacher is an expression of her individual beliefs, which cannot be attributed to the state."[51] In Germany, which officially declared itself "Christian Occidental," how is it possible that an individual teacher who wears a headscarf would be promoting Islam on behalf of the German state?

iv. "Multiplicity of motivations": The FCC argued that, considering the multiplicity of motivations for wearing it, the headscarf must not be reduced to a sign of the oppression of women," and that, in the case of genuine religious motivation, the act of veiling was protected by Article 4 of the Basic Law. Interestingly, the subsequent anti-headscarf laws issued by *Länders* drew the exact opposite conclusion from the basic argument of the "multiplicity of motivations."[52] Due to this multiplicity, the headscarf could be viewed as a political confirmation of the inequality of women, which violates the principles of the Basic Law and justifies banning the headscarf.

Opponents of the decision further argued that constitutional issues arise from the symbolic ambiguity of the headscarf.[53] The constitutional scholar

Hans Michael Heinig argues that the inherent relationship between the headscarf and political Islam in Iran and Turkey, as well as in European immigrant
circles, is considered to be an antidemocratic feature of political Islam; therefore, "the headscarf wanders into the hazy territory of unconstitutional symbols." A strong democracy can justifiably expect that its civil servants refrain
from wearing a symbolically ambiguous piece of clothing.[54] Heinig also raises
a similar argument in relation to gender equality: "Fundamentalist Islam
does not attribute the same participatory opportunities to the sexes, insisting instead on a traditional allocation of gender roles. The headscarf then is
supposed to reflect these beliefs visually."[55] The German Basic Law Article 3
requires the state to promote the equal rights of men and women.

The problem with these arguments is that they rely on an essentialist interpretation of political Islam, or invoke an image of a fixed, societal Islam that
exists in the Western mind. If a woman wears a headscarf, she is automatically associated with the most rigid understanding of Islam, and there is a
certainty that any uniform collective treatment will initially impose restrictions on genuine believers who are not political activists. More interesting,
German jurists put Iran and Turkey in the same basket without hesitation and
associate both of them with political Islam; they simply prohibit a teacher's
headscarf without taking into account any of the vast differences in national
circumstances. From the legal point of view, the Turkish judicial establishment has not acted very differently from the German courts, although it has
been somewhat more rigid and undoubtedly more secular.

Dissenting Opinions, Minority Decisions

Within the FCC, the *Ludin* decision was highly contested, and only five out
of nine justices supported it. The decision led to sharp criticisms from different points of view.

> 1. According to the minority decisions, the fundamental flaw of the
> majority was to "ignore the functional limitation of individual rights pro-
> tection for civil servants." Civil servants have essentially waived the consti-
> tutional rights that are incompatible with their office, and they are obliged
> to "temperance and professional neutrality."[56]
>
> 2. The teacher's headscarf violated the civil servant's duty to modera-
> tion. Regulations of civil service law were sufficient to justify the complain-
> ant's nonplacement. A separate headscarf provision was not necessary.[57]
>
> 3. Following the position of the FCC in the *Kruzifix* case, the Court
> should have ruled out an unconditional right on the part of the teacher

to express her religious identity. A proper interpretation of the Basic Law precludes an unconditional authorization of religious symbols within the realm of public service. Therefore, "for the sake of safeguarding the fundamental rights of third parties, a public schoolteacher can and must be required to refrain from wearing a headscarf or other religious garments in school in case of serious conflict, motivated by religion or worldview."[58]

Critics of the decision were not a sympathetic audience supporting Ludin's freedom of religion. They were criticizing the FCC because it did not go far enough. Thus, not only the FCC, but also its opponents, failed to show tolerance and protect minority religions in Germany.

Intended Consequences of the Decision

The German Court pronounced that "it is not the FCC, but the democratically elected legislature that is called on to make the general decision on the teacher's headscarf." The Court added that the headscarf did not represent a "concrete, constant endangerment of peaceful school operation."[59] Nevertheless, the FCC held that an "abstract danger" exists and the lawmakers would therefore have to conduct a comprehensive investigation to measure the degree of the threats. For this, the lawmaker may consider the objective appearance of the headscarf and its effect on third parties, and may also make a general assessment about the wearer's concrete motivation.[60] The FCC expressly permits the federal states "to arrive at varying outcomes, since the appropriate middle course may also incorporate school tradition, the denominational composition of the population and the degree to which it is religiously rooted."[61] The FCC thereby consciously acknowledges that different regulations might be adopted in the sixteen federal states. The FCC also pointed out, however, that any regulation, as well as its justification and the practice of enforcing it, must strictly treat all religions and religious communities equally in law and practice.[62]

In the aftermath of the *Ludin* case, legislators in half of Germany's states rushed in quickly to enact laws banning public schoolteachers from wearing religious symbols and clothing, with the actual target being headscarves in schools, and even extended this ban to other civil servants. The first group of states (Bavaria, Baden-Wurttenberg, Hesse, North Rhine–Westphalia, and Saarland) enacted laws prohibiting religious symbols and clothes that could be regarded as dangers to the state's neutrality, to the peace of the school, or to the principle of gender equality. These regulations are not only intended to ban Muslim headscarves but are also framed to allow the "exhibition of Christian-Occidental values and traditions." In April 2004, Baden-Wurttenberg was the first state to pass a law amending its School Act that regulates the wearing of religious clothing and symbols by teachers in public schools. Justifications for the exemption of Christian clothes were based on the reasoning that such clothing and symbols are in line with and preserve values expressed in the state constitution. Therefore such Christian symbols do not risk compromising the neutrality or peace of the school.[63] The Baden-Wurttenberg School Act states that "the respective exhibition of Christian and western educational and cultural values or traditions does not contradict a teacher's 'duty to behavior,' and corresponds to educational objectives."[64] By enacting this law, Baden-Wurttenberg intended to permit public school-teachers to continue to wear Judeo-Christian religious clothing and symbols such as the nun's habit, cross, and kippa.[65] In Saarland, a regulation, without hesitation, emphasized Christian values and traditions claiming that "The school has to teach and educate pupils on the basis of Christian educational and cultural values showing due respect for the feelings of differently minded pupils."[66]

The second group of states followed a strictly secular (laic) model, new to Germany but now practiced in three federal states, Bremen, Niedersachen and, especially, Berlin. In Berlin the ban is applied more widely, covering not only schools, but also some civil servants in the administration of justice and law enforcement. No exceptions are granted, and persons of all religions have to be treated equally. Those laws do not allow any visible religious signs, symbols, or clothing. Undoubtedly, in a liberal constitutional democracy, none of the laws banning religious symbols and dress explicitly target the headscarf. A third model is practiced in the other eight federal states, which have not yet passed new regulations, and therefore continue to address complaints through individual, case-by-case rulings.[67]

Prior to the enactment of the laws with explicit exceptions for Christian symbols, passed in five state legislatures, the major focus in parliamentary debates and explanatory documents was the headscarf, with an emphasis on the need to safeguard Western cultural traditions shaped by Christianity and Judaism.[68] The intention of the legislators is demonstrated in their accompanying explanations, providing that "the headscarf must not be allowed during teaching because at least a substantial part of its proponents link it to an inferior position of women in society, state and family or a fundamentalist statement for a theocratic political system in contradiction to the constitutional values."[69] Moreover, in several official hearings, the headscarf has been characterized as a "political symbol," and in the course of the anti-headscarf arguments, these hearings and parliamentary reports made reference to the jurisprudence of the ECHR.

The referral to the Court opened a Pandora's box of increasing human rights abuses and intolerance against Muslim women in Germany, a country that needs always to be careful about releasing hostile social feelings affecting minorities, considering its memories and menacing past experience. Apparently, hate crimes toward the Turkish minority by ultra-right-wing neo-Nazis are common in the states where most Muslim immigrants reside. The responsibility of legislators and judicial institutions is to provide firm limits on a society's abridgement of rights, even in cases of a seemingly trivial headscarf issue; this ban may be giving vent to a concealed racism and intolerance that could be a warning sign of a coming storm.

3. The Constitutionality of German Laws and Individual Challenges

The arguments arising from the FCC decision and its critics make it seem improbable that a total headscarf ban in public schools would be held constitutional in Germany. It is not yet clear what will happen when the FCC assesses the headscarf-related laws of the German federal states. To the degree that these laws specifically intend to privilege a Christian teaching staff, they appear to contradict judicial guidelines. It does not seem justifiable to explicitly forbid the wearing of a headscarf while permitting a teacher to visibly wear a cross. With these manifest discriminations against Islamic symbols in Germany, the ECHR's decisions in favor of headscarf bans in member states and the French law of 2004 likely gave a green light to Germany to relax some of its constitutional rules and ban the wearing of headscarves by students, although this is speculative. Apparently, German judicial decisions, rather than protecting freedom of religion under the neutrality principles, demonstrate the implementation of an unfriendly attitude toward Islam. Whether this is intentional or unintentional, the future will tell.

Since the introduction of the state laws, the vast majority of legal challenges have been unsuccessful.[70] Surprisingly, an official from the Bavarian Ministry of Education, who was interviewed by Human Rights Watch (HRW) researchers, said, "the absence of disputes involving teachers affected by the ban was evidence that the law achieved its aim and functions smoothly."[71] The French government raised a similarly absurd argument: the 2004 law banning religious symbols from schools was successful because there were not many applications to courts by individuals. Some of the cases in the various federal states are summarized here.

Baden-Wurttenberg

Doris Graber, a Muslim convert who served as a primary and secondary schoolteacher for more than thirty years at a school in Stuttgart, brought the first case. After the state law was passed in 2004, the local school board ordered her to remove her headscarf in the classroom or be dismissed from her post. Graber challenged the decision in an administrative court. In July 2006, the court ruled that the order for Graber to remove her headscarf constituted a violation of the principle of equal treatment, since nuns wearing habits were permitted to teach in a public school in Baden-Wurttenberg.[72] However, the state administrative court of Baden-Wurttenberg overruled the judgment in March 2008. The court held that the order was lawful. Wearing a headscarf during classes amounted to the display of a religious symbol contrary to the obligation to keep religious expression out of the classroom. According to the court, the decision to allow nuns to wear their habits was "a historic special case under a unique special contract basis… However, even if one would have to consider it an unequal implementation of the law, this would not entitle Graber to wear her religiously motivated headwear, as there is no entitlement to 'equal treatment in unjustness.'"[73] This reasoning seems very troubling in an attempt to find a justification for unequal treatment.

North Rhine-Westphalia

This region has seen the greatest number of cases challenging the ban, although many have been dismissed before litigation went forward. In a decision of the administrative court of Dusseldorf, issued in June 2007, a trainee teacher who refused to remove her headscarf was prohibited from becoming a teacher. (It is always easier to dismiss teachers with nonpermanent status.) The court's reasoning was very interesting. It held that while the exception clause of North Rhine-Westphalia cannot be a justification for Christian or Jewish clothes or symbols worn by teachers, the ban did not apply to nuns teaching in public schools in the state because these were rare exceptions and therefore did not constitute a "deficit of execution" of the law.[74] Another Dusseldorf court reached a similar conclusion in August 2007 in the case of Mariam Brigitte Weiss, determining that it did not make a difference that she wore her headscarf "Grace Kelly style" because she was still perceived as obviously manifesting her religion.[75]

In June 2007, a decision of the Labor Court of Dusseldorf drew a lot of public attention. A social worker specializing in education, who had worn a headscarf for some years while working in a school, replaced it with a rose-colored beret that fully covered her hair and ears following the new school act. The court judged that the function of the beret was the same as the function of a headscarf. In April 2008, the State Labor Court affirmed the lower court's ruling in the case, stating that the teacher expressed her religious belief by wearing the hat, thereby violating neutrality and the "negative" religious freedom of pupils. The teacher refused a proposed settlement whereby she would wear a wig instead.[76]

The style of the headscarf was an important consideration in Turkish headscarf cases. According to several judgments of administrative courts and university directives, the way in which students and civil servants wear their headscarves is considered "a symbol of political Islam" while "grandmothers' style" is considered "innocent." Nevertheless, school administrators in Turkey have not been as strict as Germany. It is possible for Turkish students or civil servants to wear a beret or hat, and in some situations to wear a wig on top of the headscarf. The religious importance of wearing a headscarf concerns modesty rather than the display of female hair in public. Wearing a wig is not modest, according to Islamic rules. Accommodation is an important consideration, but German courts and schools seem to have no interest in understanding the real motives for wearing the headscarf or in accommodating Muslim women in public spaces.

Bavaria

In January 2007, the Constitutional Court of Bavaria upheld the state's law restricting religious dress in school as compatible in principle with the Bavarian constitution. In other words, the legislature cannot allow certain symbols and clothing expressing religious or ideological belief, unless they are compatible with the basic values and educational goals of the constitution. This simply means in practice that only Western, Christian symbols are compatible with the basic values of the constitution.[77]

Hesse

Directly after the state of Hesse enacted its law banning religious symbols it was challenged by the *Landesanwaltin*, the lawyer responsible for verifying the constitutional compliance of all legislation enacted in the state. She argued that the ban violated one's freedom of religion and was discriminatory, and called for it to be lifted. On December 10, 2007, a six to five majority of the Constitutional Court of Hesse upheld the state's law restricting religious symbols as compatible with its constitution.[78]

Unlike the laws in the previous five states, Bremen's and Lower Saxony's do not contain explicit exceptions for the Christian faith or Western traditions and values. Therefore, no cases have been reported in these states. At present, eight states in Germany have no special legislation relating to religious clothing or symbols in employment. Five of the states that lack bans were part of the former German Democratic Republic. These states generally seek to avoid the issue of church-state relations because of their history of anti-Christian and antireligion indoctrination and attacks on religious freedom during the communist period. Also, many Muslim immigrants lived in East Germany, which partly explains the lack of disputes involving Muslim teachers who wear the headscarf.[79]

In each of the states, under existing public service law that allows for sanctions in well-founded cases, the wearing of religious symbols can be prohibited on a case-by-case basis if there is evidence that a person's actions contravene the neutrality of the school. No relevant court cases have been brought in any of the eight states that have no specific laws. For example, Hamburg has no specific restriction on religious clothes and symbols. Therefore, applications and expressions of interest from headscarf-wearing trainee teachers who wish to come to Hamburg from other parts of Germany increased in recent years. The school authority has had no problems to date with parents regarding trainee teachers who wish to wear a headscarf, with the exception of one Muslim parent who objected to a teacher wearing a headscarf. After a conversation with the parent, a solution was found.

The EU's Anti-Discriminatory Directives and Germany's Hesitation

In addition to constitutional protection, the EU's anti-discriminatory directives entail numerous provisions on equal access of women and men to employment and a prohibition of religious discrimination in occupations that would protect women with headscarves from losing their jobs.[80] Depending on its form, a headscarf ban for teachers may conflict with these legal guidelines and the anti-discrimination that is supposed to be a key feature of European integration.[81] With regard to the headscarf, the legal arguments overlap with several EU directives covering discrimination on the basis of race, religion, sexual orientation, disability, and age. The EU demands that all its member states implement enforceable anti-discrimination laws, both to ensure gender fairness and to protect racial, ethnic, religious, sexual, and other minority groups, whether indigenous or immigrant. These laws cover discrimination in civil society, such as housing, credit, and public facilities.

However, unlike other member countries, strong opposition to the EU's anti-discrimination directives emerged during the negotiation process of the directives in Germany. For example, large property-management companies argued, "they choose their renters carefully and personally to see if they are suitable neighbors."[82] The proposed anti-discrimination legislation meant that landlords could not refuse to rent to potential tenants because they were Muslim or homosexual.[83] Laws comparable to the anti-discrimination bill of 2004, easily passed in other EU states, were extremely controversial in Germany, and the law that finally passed in 2006 was significantly weaker compared with those passed in other EU countries. During the discussion of these laws, the headscarf debate never became an issue in relation to the anti-discrimination law. Ironically, no connection was drawn between the two. Especially, in the years from 2000 to 2005, during the EU anti-discrimination discussions the lack of protection for Muslim women's headscarves exhibited this anti-Muslim trend.

4. Impact of the Headscarf Ban on Women

The impact of German state laws on women is huge. Academics and representatives of women's groups and Muslim groups interviewed by Human Rights Watch (HRW) suggested that state headscarf bans and debates in Germany aggravated discrimination against women who wear the headscarf. Muslim women have difficulties obtaining jobs as trainee teachers, and trainee lawyers were denied employment following the successful completion of their educations if they failed to abide by the restriction. There have been cases in Berlin, Hesse, Lower Saxony and North Rhine-Westphalia where trainee lawyers wearing the headscarf had their access to court for training purposes restricted.[84] These women were excused from parts of the required education and training because they were not allowed to perform as the representative of the prosecution in session or sit at the judge's bench.[85] It appears that the headscarf ban debate has had a negative effect on employment of women who wear the headscarf as lay judges.[86] Even in states that have no law imposing a headscarf ban, or other employment sectors not covered by the law, Muslim women are experiencing social resistance when seeking a job because the series of laws are effectively implementing policies against the headscarf throughout Germany and creating a social stigma that penalizes women who wear a headscarf even in the absence of a legal ban. Some members of Parliament in Germany acknowledge that the danger of discrimination is real, especially because such restrictions on employment in the private sector would be completely unlawful.[87]

These regulations are not only abstract rules. They have a profound effect on human lives.[88] Women who spoke to HRW described how, after years or decades of working as teachers without disputes or disciplinary problems, their employment and qualifications were suddenly thrown into question. The broad scope of the bans and the debates surrounding them fuel a perception among Muslim women that they are suspect in the eyes of Germany and they have expressed feelings of alienation and exclusion.[89] One group of women interviewed by HRW noted that being declared "dangerous" was very difficult for them.[90] Women teachers are constantly asked to explain why they wear a headscarf. Their independence and views on women's equality are questioned.[91] Many of them have been accused of preaching Islam.[92] Women who wear a headscarf have felt that their personalities are "reduced to [a] headscarf." To avoid being dismissed from their jobs, some have moved to another state, where they could teach without giving up the headscarf. In interviews, many of them emphasized that they need their jobs due to financial difficulties and have almost no chance of returning to their country of origin.[93] Those who decided to take off their headscarves in order to keep their jobs, or to wear a wig that does not cover their ears and neck, described the upset and unease this caused them.[94]

Court cases and the accompanying media attention also put considerable pressure on women affected by the headscarf ban, as well as on their schools and families. This helps to explain why some avoid legal action,[95] aware that the important cases receive attention. Only the *Ludin* case resulted in the positioning of the headscarf issue as a matter of public debate in Germany. However, in the few cases brought to court, the claimants were women who had converted to Islam rather than immigrants. This suggests that immigrant women still do not feel comfortable formally challenging the rules and laws of their adopted country. During the interviews with HRW, Muslim women's groups particularly emphasized the issue of integration of Muslims in Germany and how the headscarf ban imposes on them how to behave and dress, in a discriminatory, paternalistic way. Such measures nourish their alienation and subordination by limiting their prospects for independent income and, instead of empowering women affected by the ban, contribute to the deterioration of their social position.[96]

To solve the series of social issues related to immigrant societies and native citizens and to enable the successful integration of immigrants, many

European states, including Germany, have established committees charged with producing policy recommendations. The *EU Directive 2002/73/EC* on anti-discrimination derived from an equal-treatment commission that recommended to member countries that they set up such institutions. An anti-racist organization, the Intercultural Council of Germany, established as the basis of this EU directive, is opposed to blanket bans on the wearing of the headscarf.[97] It advocates intercultural and interreligious dialogue in order to prevent the ethnic segregation of minorities, and it proposes that a case-by-case approach to the headscarf ban is the only acceptable solution.

Accommodation based on mutual respect is an important part of the solution. Many of the women interviewed by the HRW pointed out that they are ready to compromise by wearing hats and were willing to consider alternatives that comport with their religious obligations. The majority of women wearing the headscarf in Germany agree that it would be appropriate for states to impose restrictions on teachers wearing forms of Muslim dress that cover the face if it were shown to interfere with occupational requirements, such as children needing to learn language and other skills by imitating their teachers' facial expressions.[98] In Germany too, like France and Turkey, women who wear the headscarf have never been properly consulted, have never been included in any of the committees that would enable them to explain their exact positions and grievances, or, more simply, to understand better who they really are. For any solution to headscarf tension in Europe, women who wear the headscarf and suffer immensely from the societal tension must be included in the debate.

5. Beneath the Surface: Neutrality and German Identity

Germany legally defines itself as "neutral" but, in practice, does not always act with neutrality. The various state laws have undermined the federal constitutional principles of neutrality, equal treatment, and nondiscrimination. In the case of the headscarf, it was the compromising Federal Court decision in *Ludin* that paved the way to diverse types of regulations. The legal situation in Germany as a whole carries the disadvantages of either the "laic" or "the Christian-conservative" model.[99] Despite the fact that the ECHR has repeatedly stated that "the State has a duty to remain neutral and impartial to ensure the preservation of pluralism and the proper functioning of democracy," the German courts and some legislation often act against this principle. The ECHR does not act in conformity with its own principles when the headscarf becomes a source of tension. The Court has given "weak" interpretations of the right to manifest religious freedom, and these judgments give a wide margin of appreciation to the individual state. Following the neutrality principle, the role of the states in such circumstances should not be to remove the cause of tension by eliminating pluralism, but to ensure that the competing groups tolerate one other.

In the headscarf debate, not only the fundamental values and norms of liberal democracies are renegotiated, but also collective identities are reconstructed within the European negotiation process.[100] In Europe, politicians of all persuasions compete to stress the importance of a strong sense of national identity and belonging; the language of integration—once perceived as objectionable and nearly requiring assimilation—now dominates the debate. Muslim immigrants are especially called on to make it clear that they have opted for the values of their host society. At the same time, Muslim immigrants' pledges to the constitutions of their respective host countries are suspected of being insincere and hypocritical.

On the surface, the debates on the headscarf in European countries seem to be about the separation of religion and state. However, the headscarf controversy is part of a larger debate about the public space of Islam in European countries and how to reconcile it with various national identities. Moreover, it is a highly gendered debate. The headscarf debate not only reflects the struggle for a redefinition of the German nation but also reveals how the issue of gender equality is perversely used to work against the civic recognition of Muslims.[101] Within the society and the political system of Germany, actors are not used to behaving as if Germany were a "country of immigrants" because the normative acceptance of this fact has been denied for a long time.[102]

The conflict about teachers' headscarves is, from this point of view, less a conflict about religious clothing and the state's neutrality than a conflict about the rules and values of a reorganizing society and democracy under the new paradigm of Germany as an immigration society.[103] According to Berghahn and Rostock, at the end of the twentieth century, the German nation had to invent a new self-definition. Gender played a pivotal role in this process of redefining a "German identity." The formation process of a new identity finds the external border necessary for its self-definition in opposition to the Oriental and patriarchal "other." The perceived oppression of Muslim women, symbolized by the headscarf, serves as a strong signal that Islam in general and Muslims specifically are not (yet) part of German society.[104] The main argument put forward to prohibit the headscarf, and not other religious symbols, is that the headscarf is not a religious symbol but a political one that is rightly associated with the oppression of women in Islam.

In German public discourse, the division between the pro and con positions regarding the headscarf runs through the German society and even divides political parties, the Christian churches, and the women's movement. But gender equality is always situated at the center of the argument. The headscarf is either depicted as a symbol of the oppression of women or as a symbol that enables so-called Neo-Muslims to emancipate themselves from their parents and to participate in German society. The debate has created strange allies among various groups because the headscarf instrumentalizes gender and interferes with the civic recognition of Muslims. Both conservative opponents of the headscarf and certain German feminists and authors who have Turkish immigrant backgrounds cite the headscarf or veil as evidence of the incompatibility of Islam with German values of democracy and freedom.[105] This position ignores the complex intersections of racism and sexism in the context of growing anti-Islamism, religious fundamentalism, and continued violence against women.

A liberal treatment of the headscarf in Germany will not emerge without changes on the societal and discursive level. Although the society demands that Islam find its place within the German value system, it remains unclear where this place could be, especially because there is no societal consensus as to what "German values" are. Instead of trying to find a closed definition of "Germanness," the uncertainty as to what "German values" are should not be seen as a weakness but as one of the strengths of a pluralistic and open society.[106] It leaves room for changes in societal structures that are favorable to the inclusion of perceived others and also encourages a reformed self-perception of the community as a heterogeneous society. Accordingly, integration should not be understood as a demand on immigrants to achieve cultural assimilation, but as a process of exchange, in which both the majority and minority can converge in creating an endless multiplicity of identities—no one more legitimate or respected than any of the others.

8

The United States

FROM MELTING POT TO ISLAMOPHOBIA

> It is important for Western countries to avoid impeding
> Muslim citizens from practicing religion as they see fit,
> for instance, by dictating what clothes Muslim women
> should wear.
>
> U.S. PRESIDENT BARAK OBAMA, CAIRO, June 2009

In the United States, the headscarf debate has received less public attention than in Europe and Turkey. For the United States, these issues are embedded in a broader debate about the role of religion in public space generally and in public schools in particular.[1] Americans mostly view clothing styles dictated by religion and culture as a private matter, outside the realm of legitimate intervention by state or society. Moreover, the United States is probably the most religiously observant country among Western industrialized nations. Although the majority is Protestant, many religious practices are freely exercised and enjoy wide acceptance because the constitution contains a particularly liberal approach to religious freedom. Secularism in the United States is strikingly different in its applications than the French and Turkish models of *laïcité* and Germany's idea of the "Christian Occident."[2] In the United States, religion is fully entitled and expected to be a player in the public sphere.[3]

The First Amendment of the United States Constitution, in addition to ensuring freedom of speech, addresses religious activities by delineating the structural relationship between church and state as well as guaranteeing individual freedom from state coercion. The first part of the First Amendment sets forth the establishment clause ("Congress shall make no law respecting an establishment of religion") while the second ("or prohibiting the free exercise thereof") posits the free exercise clause. Both clauses together regulate the relationship between state and church on one hand and freedom of religion on the other. The constitution does not permit the state to favor one religion over another, and all religions, or the lack thereof, are equally protected under the law. The Constitution of the United States is a classical and relatively short text, which does not regulate behavior in explicit detail. However, the rulings of the U.S. Supreme Court during the lifetime of the nation have compensated for this abstractness. Other modern constitutions typically contain both provisions and tend to be more specific as to the scope of protection.[4]

The United States, although it is the most multicultural country in the world and an immigrant society, established strong connections with white, European, Judeo-Christian values. Most Americans believe that such values are superior and that everyone should adhere to them. Newcomers and foreigners should try to assimilate if they want to be part of American society and culture. In the 1970s, however, a global multiculturalism movement influenced American society, and the myth of the "melting pot" was largely abandoned. Since then, assimilationist policy is not openly promoted, as it was during the historical period of missionaries, yet it has become a tacit policy, hidden beneath the realities of a large-scale immigration and naturalization process. Comparatively speaking, Muslims have encountered more welcoming behavior in the United States than in Europe.

In recent years, influenced by the development of multiculturalism, the postcolonial movement, emerging Muslim identity at the global level, and a civil rights movement at the national level, American Muslims have created a fairly strong and distinct identity in the United States. On one hand, Muslim and/or Arab society is marginalized, subordinated, and discriminated against by the dominant American culture; on the other hand, it has developed its own independent cultural environment. Although there were some intrinsic tensions between the heterogeneous, Judeo-Christian dominated American religious culture and the Islamic presence, it did not cause widespread concern until recently.

The relatively positive interaction was significantly damaged following the 9/11 attacks, and "Islam" has been used as a common denominator to establish a new, inflammatory racial category. Contrary to general belief, however, Muslims in the United States were subject to discriminatory behavior before the terrorist attacks of 9/11. Over the years, various national and international policies and events paved the way for post-9/11 discrimination and anti-Muslim behavior on the social, political, and legal fronts, and those sentiments quickly came to the surface. Before considering the constitutional and legal issues of the headscarf controversy in the United States, it is useful to examine the nature of American Islam in relation to the immigration laws, social structure, political events, and racialization processes that increasingly impact Muslims in America.

1. American Muslims

Islam, as it is in Europe, is the fastest growing religion in the United States. Although it is difficult to estimate the precise number of Muslims currently living in the United States because the U.S. Census Bureau's survey forms do not ask about a person's religion, the estimated figures range widely—from two million in one study to as many as seven million.[5] When Muslims in the United States exceed the Jewish population (of approximately seven million) it will be second only to Christianity in size. Because of this large population in the United States, for example, there are more Muslims in America than in Kuwait, Qatar, or Libya. The American Muslim minority comes from diverse national backgrounds, originating from as many as sixty-five countries.[6] American Islam is a mosaic of many ethnic, racial, and national groups. They speak a wide variety of languages and represent a range of cultural, economic, educational, sectarian, and ideological perspectives.[7] Unlike in Europe, Muslims in the United States are divided into two major categories: immigrants and native-born Americans.

Muslim Immigrants

Early signs of prejudices against Muslims, Arabs, and Middle Easterners can best be detected by looking at various immigration policies. These policies are clear indicators of the existing discrimination against Muslims, Arabs, and Middle Easterners based on race, the Islamic religion, international politics, and the media. Many of the earliest immigration law cases, however, were not specific to Islam as a minority religion or to Arabs and/or Middle Easterners as ethnically non-European immigrants. Arabs and Muslims faced discriminatory attitudes similar to fellow non-European, non-Christian immigrants. The dominant sentiment was that the United States was founded by white European immigrants. This phenomenon is related to episodes of racism in American history. Despite the rhetoric of a country founded on the backs of immigrants that serves as a melting pot for all races and ethnic identities, Muslims often encountered anti-Muslim and anti-Arab prejudice, complicated by the fact that their darker skin subjected them to additional forms of racial prejudice. In many cases, such designators as "sand nigger" or "raghead" were used as epithets.[8]

Considerable literature, legislation, and court records reveal that early immigration policies were indications of a hierarchical social order and ideals of citizenship, but, surprisingly, the consequences of the debates about citizenship of Muslims were not discussed in the standard works on immigration.[9] The renowned scholar, the late Edward Said, was one of the early Arab-American intellectuals who conceptualized racial discrimination in these early years.[10] Despite ongoing reforms, a strong "assimilation" policy existed in the U.S. immigration system as late as the 1990s. For example, in 1997 the report of the Commission on Immigration Reform called for the "Americanization" of new immigrants and the importance of conforming to white, Christian, Western European norms, especially with respect to the adoption of English as their primary language.[11]

After 9/11, immigration laws were the most effective tools with which to attack Muslim and Arab immigrants.[12] The government used immigration courts in terror-related cases because they provided fewer legal protections for the accused and did not give an immigrant the right of access to an attorney. The governmental authority may detain immigrants even after a judge has ordered them freed on bond. Using such legal remedies, U.S. authorities severely punished minor violations by Muslims and Arabs, while ignoring millions of other immigrants who violated laws to a similar extent. The approach is basically "to target the Muslims and Arab community with a kind of zero-tolerance enforcement."[13] Authorities have even taken the unusual step of stripping some immigrants of U.S. citizenship. Officials are also using immigration charges to pressure people to provide information about Muslim organizations.

African American Muslims

A large segment of the Muslim population in the United States is part of the native population. The figures for African American Muslims vary significantly from one to two million. During the post–World War II period, when several African nation-states achieved independence, black nationalism became influential in the United States. Africa became a symbol of liberation and a model for black Americans, especially of the younger generation, in their attempts to deal with daily problems arising within America. Christianity increasingly came under fire from black activists as a racist, "clan" religion of white people, and such criticism added to the longing of black Americans for a new religious vision.[14]

In recent years, a good deal of recruiting to Islam was done in jails and prisons, which have become major centers of Muslim reflection and identity.

Malcolm X was undoubtedly the most famous black Muslim prison convert.[15] Such converts are an important locus of Islam's appeal to African Americans. While there are no statistics available on the number of converts or the scope and effectiveness of conversion in the penal system, some scholars estimate that by 2020 the majority of African American males in prisons will have converted to Islam.[16] The emergence of this large African American Muslim population in prisons deserves special attention but is well beyond the scope of this chapter.

The conversion of African Americans to Islam has been both an inspiration and a challenge to the immigrant Muslim community. Immigrants are generally prosperous, educated, and middle class. They separate themselves from the experiences of the black Muslim community, which overwhelmingly consists of individuals from more humble socioeconomic backgrounds. Initially, African Americans paid special attention to the cultural aspects of Islam, for example, by taking Islamic names and wearing Islamic dress. Then others told them that the adoption of local cultural practices is not integral to Islam. Many African Americans grew tired of hearing various immigrant groups insist that their way was the only Islamic way.[17] Although the majority of American converts to Islam are the product of African American, rather than immigrant, missionary activities, immigrants persist in regarding themselves as more authoritative on issues relating to conversion and do not consult with African Americans. Immigrants are also ethically bound to and concerned with issues of injustices and suffering in the communities from which they emigrated, often completely disregarding comparable problems in America.[18] Tension between African American Muslims and the immigrant Muslim community is a continuing and important reality. Immigrant Muslims are accused of innate racism by Muslims belonging to non-white minorities, allegedly preferring the conversion of whites to Islam and totally disregarding the plight and outlook of African Americans, Hispanic Americans, and Native Americans.[19]

2. Unique Features of the American Headscarf Controversy

Against this background, the headscarf controversy has had a rather different momentum in the United States than in European countries and Turkey. The special position of American society with respect to the headscarf debate, and the wider controversy about Islam generally, gives the concern a particular character. On one hand, with the most liberal constitutional order and arguably the most religious-friendly secularism, the United States starts from its own vantage point. Moreover, the United States as an immigrant society has vast experience with multiculturalism and diversity. On the other hand, the headscarf dispute reflects not only larger debates about tolerance, pluralism, and the role of religious extremism, but also the sentiment of the American public, especially in the aftermath of 9/11. An ultraconservative media that has the support of a highly receptive political constituency bombards the American public by constantly emphasizing the difference between the Western and Islamic worlds. The discourse often centers on the status of women in Islam—veiling practices, sex discrimination, segregation between men and women, arranged marriages, and cruel and inhumane punishment, especially for adultery. In the aftermath of 9/11, the Bush administration launched a propaganda campaign to justify the wars in Afghanistan and then in Iraq and used as one argument that an American goal was to liberate Muslim women.[20] Increasingly, the American public has identified the headscarf or burqa with Islamic militancy, extremism, jihadism, and the oppression of women. As a result, in the eyes of ordinary Americans, Muslim women wearing headscarves are considered symbols of antidemocratic and antisecular feelings. The headscarf served as a synecdoche for extremism and the oppression of women in the name of religion, even though most American Muslim women do not wear a headscarf, and many who do wear it consider themselves protected by constitutional guarantees of religious freedom.[21]

"Muslim Woman" as a New American Identity

According to recent studies, the role of Muslim institutions in the United States, specifically mosques, has had a positive impact on American Muslim identity and particularly on the headscarf debate—a difference from the countries previously discussed. Mosques have the capacity to increase individual levels of political knowledge and civic skills that construct identity. A number of studies have indicated that, especially in the post-9/11 period, some American Muslim women wear the headscarf because of the influential role of Islamic institutions, and many have analyzed this phenomenon in relation to gender role attitudes and the politics of identity.[22] Moreover, according to Kathleen Moore, Muslim groups, in a similar way to U.S. religious groups such as Christian evangelicals and Catholics, are conducting litigation and prelitigation campaigns, sponsoring court cases, writing amicus briefs, and using the threat of litigation to expand accommodation of religious expression in schools, prisons, the workplace, neighborhoods, and the armed services.[23] For Christians and Muslims alike, the mobilization of the law through lawsuits and media campaigns serves a larger purpose: the mobilization of a specific "identity." Thus, the law discursively produces a particular kind of Muslim identity by increasing the public space in which wearing a headscarf is officially authorized. While most Muslim women in the United States choose not to wear the headscarf, the visibility of the head-scarf serves as a focal point for a controversy that influences the American perception about what constitutes Islam. In this view, the headscarf is not only a volatile emblem that can be viewed as a symbol of male oppression or of female modesty and religious and cultural identity, but it is also inter-twined with discussions about the assimilability of Muslims in Western societies.[24]

Similarly, a recent study conducted by the influential writer Yvonne Yazbeck Haddad argues that a process of re-Islamization has accelerated in the aftermath of 9/11, as an increasing number of adolescents and young adults assume a public Islamic identity by wearing headscarves. As Islamophobia took hold in the public domain as a consequence of propaganda or the war on terrorism—sidelining political correctness in regard to Arabs, Muslims, and Islam—the phenomenon became an important factor in the re-Islamization of Muslim youth.[25] Drawing on two decades of research on American Muslim communities and on in-depth interviews with American Muslim youth, the study finds that the hijab (headscarf) has become a symbol of American Islamic identity, authenticity, and pride—arising as a public affirmation of trust in the American system, to the extent that freedom of religion and speech are upheld.[26] Earlier, the headscarf was seen as an integral part of revo-lutionary and anticolonial struggle, illustrated most vividly in Algeria in the 1950s and in Iran in the 1970s. From this perspective, the reappropriation of the headscarf in North America can be seen as an expression of solidarity, as well as resistance to an effort to eradicate Islam in an American environment that is increasingly perceived to be anti-Islamic.[27]

Liberating Muslim Women

As in Europe, the American focus on the headscarf was perceived by many Muslims as the reemergence of a centuries-old Western effort to liberate Muslim women from Islam. For hundreds of years, Muslims and Westerners have engaged in endless debates over whether the veil should be vilified or defended. For every criticism raised in the West, a counterargument was developed in defense of Muslim womanhood. According to Haddad, the most prominent feature of twentieth-century Islamic literature on women is its dialogical and/or apologetic nature, regardless of the gender or ideological orientation of the author.[28] Most of the discourse appears beholden to ever-changing Western values and norms. It mirrors Western discourse in upholding the importance of women's empowerment. At the same time, it refutes Western norms that debase woman by treating them as sex objects and argues that Islam liberates women and elevates their status. With each encounter, the veil has acquired new meaning and significance as it is appropriated as a symbol of identity threatened by ruthless enemies.[29]

American feminist scholars initially tended to be defenders of modernity, secularism, and the demise of colonialism and examined women's issues through the prism of development. Especially after the Iranian revolution, many Muslim women academics started to write critically about Islam. The political forces hostile to Muslims used those scholars and their writings to feed a growing antipathy toward Islam in the United States.[30]

Western literature is notoriously biased against the status of women in Islam. Beginning in the eighteenth century, the depiction and construction of the "Muslim as Other," in a whole body of Orientalist art and literature, reflected this bias. In the nineteenth century, the focus of interest shifted to the representation of Muslim and Eastern characters as possessed of bizarre and sexually perverse promiscuity. European men projected the Victorian view of female inferiority on Muslim women. What the European could not say about European women could be said about Eastern women.[31] This image of the subjugated Muslim woman in need of rescue was used during the colonial French and British empires, and provided part of the American justification for the Barbary wars.[32]

The legacy of the colonial period of Orientalism evolved over the years, responding to new changing political realities. Secular American feminists, it appears, joined with their European sisters to seek the "empowerment" of Muslim women.[33] American feminists think that Muslim women need liberation to obtain more sexual freedom. They believe American culture and values should be deemed universal and must be made available, coercively if necessary, to all people throughout the world. The excesses of the feminist movement in the United States during the 1960s are highly relevant to defining Islamic civilization as countering Western culture, which is viewed as degenerate.[34] Many Arab Americans countervailed by joining the National Organization for Women (NOW) and began to engage the American public in an attempt to alter the image of the Muslim woman and the veil. Over these political issues, American feminists and Muslim women organizations antagonized one another. Muslim feminists openly complained that they did not need to be further victimized by the West.[35]

Post-9/11: The Headscarf as a Symbol of the Enemy

In the aftermath of 9/11, many Americans, traumatized by the attacks, began to identify the headscarf as a symbol of the enemy. Some Muslim women who had worn the headscarf prior to 9/11 removed it, as a precaution to avoid harassment. Others became convinced that wearing a headscarf is not prescribed in the Quran. Some continued to wear it, or choose to wear it to bear witness to their pride in being Muslim. Muslim women who wore the headscarf endured the consequences of blatant stereotyping. They became the objects of both harassment and pity, as Americans began to wonder what kind of women would "participate in their own oppression." The harassment restricted their freedoms and stripped them of their anonymity. Public cat-calls of "I hate you," "Go home," "America is for Americans," and "Death to Muslims" had devastating effects. Many Muslim women stayed home to avoid public defamation.[36]

According to Haddad's research, the events of 9/11 and their aftermath had an important impact on the role of the mosque in women's lives. Living in fear and apprehension, they saw the mosque as a shelter, providing a safe space where one could find comfort and companionship.[37] This is a uniquely American experience. One aspect of this phenomenon is its connection with American religiosity. Unlike Europeans, Americans are churchgoers. Especially in small towns, churches are often the biggest part of a person's social life. Muslim Americans, influenced by their fellow Americans, started to establish their own religious institutions. Traditionally, mosques in Muslim countries are not places where women can gather for religious or social pur-poses. Mosques generally belong to men, and women either pray at home, or, if they go to a mosque, have special places set aside, typically in an invisible part of the building. By contrast, in the United States mosques became social centers. They provide a Muslim space in a non-Muslim country, a refuge for Muslim friends who share the same values, where one can be Muslim with-out outsiders criticizing, accusing, condemning, threatening, and prescrib-ing what they ought to be doing. In finding this security within the mosque, many have had to put up with more conservative interpretations of Islam. This might be interpreted as an unintended consequence of the isolation of Muslims as a community.[38] This observation helps us to understand the recent controversy about mosques in the United States and to consider the empowerment of mosques as institution-building, which is foreign to some Muslim countries, such as Turkey.

For all of these reasons, the American headscarf debate has different features from the debate in Europe. In the United States, there has never been a systematic rejection of headscarf use, or any attempt to ban the headscarf in schools or workplaces. The protection of religious dress and First Amendment rights gives Muslim Americans strong legal protection. Apart from individual incidences and disguised, or thinly disguised, discrimination against Muslims and Islamic practices, the general public discussion has never openly targeted headscarf use in any way that resembles what is happening in many European countries.

3. The Legal Front: An Accommodationist Model

The accommodationist model of the United States offers a wide range of processes, operating at many levels and sites, regarding issues of social and cultural differences. "Accommodation" refers to the practices through which the law or social actors take into account and make room for values and meanings that differ from their own.

As some might expect, implementing the abstract principles of the First Amendment does not strongly protect the right to wear religiously inspired attire.[39] First, no decision of the highest national court has ever considered a case that bears directly on issues of religious dress, in general or in relation to schools.[40] Secondly, the U.S. Supreme Court doctrine with regard to the religion clauses of the constitution has fluctuated over time, implementing a variety of standards from rational choice to strict scrutiny.[41] To add to the confusion, legal experts disagree about likely outcomes. At this time, no lower court cases about the headscarf have reached the Supreme Court. In fact, only a handful of cases have reached the lower courts. Moreover, the executive branch of the federal government has interpreted the law differently in successive presidential regimes. State legal practices add a further layer of confusion and complexity to the American approach.[42]

Although the Supreme Court has not been asked to address the constitutionality of headscarf use, it has been asked to review decisions that concern the constitutionality of obligatory uniforms for school children, for public employees, and for members of the U.S. armed forces. There are only a few cases in U.S. law that deal with religious garments worn by students in public schools because, normally, no compelling state interests can be invoked to restrict a student from wearing a Muslim headscarf, a skullcap (kippa), or a Christian cross. Rarely is a mandatory school uniform policy required to address disciplinary problems. So far, there are no cases in which the duty to wear a school uniform poses a challenge to an individual's religious beliefs.[43] However, religious garments might exceptionally be restricted if they posed a danger to safety or public order.

Taking account of the absence of relevant cases in the American judicial system, a few comparable cases addressing hairstyles, school uniforms, and choice of clothing give some idea whether U.S. courts would be willing to accommodate Muslim headscarves. Generally speaking, in cases related to other religious and ethnic minorities in the United States, courts have given a sympathetic interpretation to religious customs. I examine these cases to shed light on how American courts would likely handle a future headscarf controversy. Obviously, these hypothetical speculations have limited predictive value.

Relevant Cases Applicable to Students in Public Schools

There is no doubt that religious freedom in relation to education is a difficult challenge for any legal system. Almost all of the interests involved are fundamental, and the resulting legal and political debates are heated in almost every country. Despite the widespread belief that the U.S. Constitution protects the right to wear religious symbols in school, in reality, revealed in practice, the situation is far more complex. In general, personal religious statements are protected in schools, yet students currently do not have a right to wear religious dress that is prohibited for other rational reasons. According to U.S. constitutional law, "neither students nor teachers, even in their function as public employees, are deprived of their First Amendment freedoms when they enter schools."[44] The mere discomfort of other students, or the unpopularity of the speaker's views, are not sufficient to overcome a student's right to express or hear ideas, even ideas associated with the exercise of religious belief. Some cases that have arisen concerning public schools provide examples.

Hairstyles

In the 1970s, many public high schools adopted strict hairstyle codes in response to the popularization of long hair among entertainers, college students, and hippies. On a number of occasions, the federal courts addressed the question of whether schoolchildren are constitutionally entitled to wear their hair in styles prohibited by school administrators. Similar questions arose in relation to the hairstyles of public employees. The Third Circuit Court of

Appeals recognized that "the length and style of one's hair is implicit in the liberty assurance of the due process clause of the Fourteenth Amendment, except as applied to shop classes, where safety was an apparent issue."[45] However, in *Kelly v. Johnson*, the Supreme Court refused to invalidate hair-length regulations promulgated by a police department.[46]

The Jewish Kippa

In *Menora v. Illinois High School Association* (1981–1983), several support-ers of the Jewish faith filed a class action against the Illinois High School Association, which prohibited wearing headwear, including yarmulkes, dur-ing basketball games. The district court found that the plaintiffs had a sincere religious belief that led them to wear a head covering even while playing bas-ketball. As the no-headwear rule would force them to choose between observ-ing their religious beliefs or participating in interscholastic basketball games, the students were considered to be burdened in the free exercise of their reli-gious beliefs. The district court could not find a compelling safety interest that was invoked in such a manner to overcome First Amendment rights.[47] The judgment was vacated by the court of appeals. Despite sharp criticism of this decision, the U.S. Supreme Court denied the petition. The *Menora* case remains a rare example of judicial approval of a restriction that interfered with religious dress codes. U.S. law generally exempts religious garments from no-hat rules in schools as well as other public institutions.

The Sikh Kirpan

In *Chema v. Thompson*, the U.S. Court of Appeals for the Ninth Circuit had to decide whether three young Khalsa Sikh boys could be permitted to wear a ceremonial knife in school for religious reasons.[48] The court concluded: "We simply cannot allow young children to carry long, wieldable knives to school. Period."[49] The court actually considered the possibility of allowing Sikh boys to wear a fake knife in class, which could not hurt anyone, but the applicants did not compromise. This case proves that an American court is willing to accommodate religious needs to a certain extent, but within reasonable limits. The case raises the question whether strict religious rules that are fundamen-tal to the believers can be accommodated at all, and more important, whether the courts are entitled to take into consideration a compromise solution.

African Headgear

In *Shermia Isaacs v. Board of Education of Howard County* (1999), an eighth-grade girl was prohibited from wearing an African head-wrap rising several inches above the top of her head. Shermia Isaac wished to wear that head-gear even in class because she wanted "to celebrate her African-Caribbean heritage."[50] This was incompatible with the school's "no hat rule" that banned hats from school except religious headgear, such as yarmulkes and the Muslim headscarf, including nonreligious headscarves. Hats were considered to cause conflicts in the hallways, obscure the teachers' view of the students and the students' view of the blackboard, and foster a "less respectful climate" for learning. Shermia lost her court battle to wear an ethnically inspired head-dress to school.[51] Shermia Isaac's case suggests that head coverings not dictated by religion or cultural traditions of modesty need not receive the legal defer-ence that a religious schoolgirl's headscarf would receive. Because the consti-tution does not mention cultural identity, the court found no entitlement to special consideration for cultural, nonreligious claims. However, in a case involving the claim by male members of the American Indian movement that their culture and tradition barred them from cutting their hair as required by school rules, the court regarded the practice as entitled to First Amendment protection whether it was regarded as a religious duty or cultural tradition.[52]

Catholic Rosaries

In *Chalifoux v. New Caney Independent School District*, students were told they could not wear Catholic rosaries because the school had identified rosaries as "gang-related apparel." For this reason their display on campus was prohib-ited. The students sued, claiming that such a restrictive dress code constituted an infringement upon their free exercise rights as well as free speech. The court decided that there were only three instances of alleged gang members wearing rosaries as a gang identifier, and only one of those incidents occurred on campus. The contested evidence at trial demonstrated that plaintiffs wore their rosaries with the intent to communicate their Catholic faith to others. According to the court, evidence is crucial in determining whether a restric-tive dress code will actually serve the interests claimed, and here the evidence was insufficient, placing "undue burden" on the plaintiff students.[53]

Armbands

In *Tinker v. Des Moines Independent Community School District*, the Supreme Court held that "the wearing of an armband for the purpose of protesting the Vietnam War was protected as free speech."[54] After noting that "students and teachers do not shed their constitutional rights at the schoolhouse gate," the Court held that the symbolic act of wearing an armband in protest "could not be circumscribed where there is no finding and no showing that engaging in the forbidden conduct would materially and substantially interfere with the requirements of appropriate discipline in the operation of the school." The court also noted, "Undifferentiated fear or apprehension of disturbance is not enough to overcome the right of a freedom of expression."[55]

Cases Related to Muslims in Public Schools

The generally tolerant and accommodating attitude toward religious garments in U.S. courts has changed somewhat in the post-9/11 era. Public schools in the United States have discretion to impose a uniform standard of dress. However, in practice only about 3 percent of all public schools require students to wear a uniform. Many school districts prohibit students from wearing hats and head coverings in school, ostensibly to disallow gang insignias and to teach proper behavior. Several religions require that a devout adherent cover his or her head, providing fertile ground for controversy. These controversies have become more frequent with the growing diversity of religious and ethnic groups in the United States and the demand for recognition by several minority groups. In the wake of the 9/11 attacks, the federal government reported an increase in incidents of harassment against Arabs, Muslims, Sikh, and Jewish students.[56]

The Nashala Hearn Case

One of the victims during this period was the eleven-year-old Nashala Hearn, who was suspended from school in Oklahoma for wearing a Muslim headscarf in early 2004.[57]

Nashala Hearn, an African American whose father had converted to Islam, began to wear a headscarf in July 2003. Under the Muskogee school district's policy, students were banned from wearing hats, caps, bandannas, or jacket hoods inside school buildings; Hearn's headscarf was classified as a "bandanna." Hearn had actually worn a headscarf to school with permission from her homeroom teacher from August 18, 2003, until September 10, 2003. On September 11, 2003, the same homeroom teacher, after discussing the 9/11 attacks with a colleague, told Hearn that she should not wear a headscarf and sent her to the principal's office. The principal concluded that the headscarf violated the school's rule "barring hats," and asked Nashala to remove her headscarf or leave the building. The school district's dress code was created in part to maintain the school as a "religion-free zone," in an effort to comply with 1998 federal regulations.[58] Students had been permitted to wear crucifixes and shirts with Christian messages; moreover, there was no indication that Hearn's headscarf threatened the preservation of safety and discipline, which underlies the policy. In settling the suit in May 2004, the assistant attorney general for civil rights of the Department of Justice stated that the department would "not tolerate discrimination against Muslims or any other religious group. As the President and the Attorney General have made clear repeatedly, such intolerance is un-American, and is morally despicable. Thus, the state will not tolerate discrimination and equates intolerance with being un-American. We may assume that part of the impetus for this stance was to create space for Christian practice; while purportedly secular, the United States by no means follows the *laïcité* of France."[59]

The United States Justice Department's Office of Civil Rights supported Nashala's claim that accused the school district of violating the equal protection clause of the Fourteenth Amendment to the constitution. She had been singled out for discipline because of her particular faith, arguing that the school had allowed girls who had lost hair after chemotherapy to cover their heads. Moreover, the federal government took the position that Nashala's symbolic speech could not be restricted under the *Tinker* test because she had not disrupted the school or interfered with the rights of others.[60] Eventually, the case was settled in a friendly way.

The Council on American-Islamic Relations Report

Although there are no reported cases in U.S. courts involving the right to wear the headscarf in public schools, in several states Muslim girls have been excluded for dress code violations until outside intervention prompted settlements. On one occasion, a teacher in Louisiana ripped a headscarf off a student's head during class. In another instance, a middle school student missed a week of school before the Department of Justice intervened in her case, leading to a settlement and her return to school.[61] Another student barred from school for wearing a headscarf was able to return only after the Washington, DC–based Council on American-Islamic Relations (CAIR) intervened on her behalf. As pointed out earlier, post-9/11 sentiments have had a negative impact on existing anti-immigrant laws in the United States, and several discriminatory cases have emerged that included headscarf use. CAIR, the largest American Muslim civil rights and advocacy organization, has collected several discriminatory cases relating to the headscarf. According to a CAIR report published in 2005, after airports, schools were among the top five places where incidents of discrimination occurred.[62] The report also acknowledged that some identifying Islamic features, such as the headscarf, instigated most acts of anti-Muslim discrimination. In fact, the hijab was the second most common feature to trigger mistreatment.[63] Examples of growing misunderstanding about the headscarf, whether religiously, culturally, or politically motivated, are becoming more common.[64] According to CAIR's investigation, discrimination based on wearing the headscarf in schools is escalating. In one example, a New York high school prohibited two Muslim girls from attending their 2004 graduation because they refused to remove their headscarves.[65] Another Muslim student who was visiting the United States on a State Department foreign exchange program was prohibited from wearing the headscarf to school in California.

After 9/11 certain rights-advocacy groups such as CAIR and the ACLU took up the cause of opposing anti-Muslim backlash discrimination. In June 2004, the Nebraska chapter of the ACLU filed a civil rights lawsuit against the City of Omaha on behalf of Lubna Hussein, who was told she would have to take off her headscarf and encompassing cloak if she wanted to accompany her children to the municipal swimming pool.[66] In February 2005, the City of Omaha and the Nebraska ACLU announced a settlement, according to which the dress code was amended to accommodate religious and/or medical needs. Ms. Hussein was elated by the news. "I am so pleased at this change in policy," she said. "My little girls have been waiting for a chance to try out the water slides, and they'll finally get the opportunity this summer. We're happy to feel like part of the community again."[67]

In 2005 the Florida office of CAIR intervened with officials of an Amateur Athletic Union tournament because they had cited NCAA rules prohibiting head coverings. After being contacted by CAIR, the officials agreed to allow the Muslim headscarf if it was tucked into the player's uniform. In a similar vein, a University of South Florida basketball player, a Muslim convert, said she had left the team and lost her athletic scholarship because the head coach refused to allow her to wear long pants, a shirt with long sleeves, and a headscarf during competition. The Muslim student later left school and returned to Christianity.[68]

In sum, the constitutionality of dress codes and school uniform requirements do not necessitate a legal option to ban the headscarf or religious attire. To have such an option, it must be shown that the First and Fourteenth amendments permit a substantial interference with religious liberty. Based on the above-mentioned court decisions, the evidence in the *Hearn* case and the public reaction to it, it is unlikely that a federal court would sustain a school dress code or uniform requirement that did not make an exception for bona fide religious garb or clothing worn for cultural modesty.

The courts distinguish schools from the military, a limited context where requirements of appearance have been held to trump the right of religious expression.[69] Uniformity in the military and law enforcement has been accepted as a legitimate, compelling state interest. The argument for uniformity in school is far less persuasive. The needs of schools, police departments, and the military differ sufficiently to warrant constitutionally different approaches to religious or cultural claims for special treatment. Schoolboys and girls who wear head coverings inherently offend no legitimate state interest, such as school discipline or safety. A categorical ban on religious or cultural headgear in schools is viewed as legally incompatible with proper respect for the religious and expressive freedom of children and their families.[70]

The Rights of Parents

In the United States, the issue of schoolchildren and religious symbols is also framed by a line of cases that emphasize the right of parents to control their children's upbringing and to indoctrinate their children in their belief systems.[71] In 2000 the Supreme Court upheld the "fundamental right of parents to make decisions concerning the care, custody and control of their children."[72] These cases are particularly significant for contemporary discussions of religious and cultural minorities because the early "parents' rights" cases had their origins in disputes over the use of public schools to "Americanize" immigrant children.[73]

Nevertheless, when parents entrust their children to a public school system, they are not entitled to have the school system bend its regulations to suit their preferences in matters of curriculum.[74] Because parents have the right to remove their children from the public school system, the classic response to parental curricular complaints has been to inform the unhappy parents of their option to remove the child from the public school system at their discretion and send him or her to a private school or to homeschool the child. This response can mean that some parents remove their children from public schools and place them in learning environments that offer less exposure to diverse views.[75] Obviously this result is not satisfactory, especially if it were to lead to the exclusion and isolation of minority cultures.

The current state of the law governing the freedom of religious exercise for individuals is constantly changing, creating significant confusion for local school authorities. Despite the rhetoric affirming that the constitution supports diversity of belief and cultures, the law in the United States fails to provide protection to children and parents whose minority beliefs or cultures require a unique and symbolic form of dress or appearance. Instead, tolerance and accommodation depend on the goodwill of local officials in each of the more than 94,000 public schools spread among the roughly 16,850 school districts in the United States.[76] This "individualized accommodation model" places a heavy burden on the individual student and his or her family who make choices about dress or appearance that school officials may regard as privileges rather than rights.[77] To promote diversity and respect for minority beliefs, the law should impose an affirmative obligation on school systems to accommodate displays of religious views, even though current Supreme Court jurisprudence does not require such accommodation.[78]

The accommodationist model of U.S. doctrine has been the subject of criticism from two very different directions.[79] The first set of criticisms argues that "pervasive secularism" in public school creates "hostility to religious expression in the public square."[80] The second line of criticism, found in more theoretical discussions of children's rights, contends that the United States gives too little weight to the right of children to explore options about these matters and make their own choices, independent of their parents.[81]

The accommodationist model is not free from danger. The most vigorous advocates of this view are conservative Christians, who seek a larger role for religion in public life. Ironically, progressives who normally champion individual First Amendment liberties tend to be wary about the accommodation of religious practices of minorities, fearing that it could ultimately play into the hands of those who wish to restore Christian prayer in the public schools.[82] Groups with Islamophobic tendencies could also manipulate this model to influence local administrators against the Islamic headscarf.

Religious Garb and Public School Teachers

The compatibility of religious dress with the role of public schoolteachers is an old issue in U.S. law, which assumed importance in the period from the late nineteenth until the middle of the twentieth centuries.[83] The earliest cases dealt with the garb worn by Catholic nuns. The tension was between a Protestant religious majority and the Catholic Church on one side, and the effort by the secular elite to reduce clerical influence in state institutions on the other. The varied resolutions of these tensions helps explain the inconsistent pattern of court decisions. While some states (Pennsylvania and Oregon) enacted statutes prohibiting religious dress, other states did not; some even explicitly allowed teachers to wear religious garb in public schools. Accordingly, some of the cases were decided on the grounds of a specific statute or regulation, whereas other judgments were based on general constitutional or statutory provisions prohibiting "sectarianism" in public schools.[84] In the mid-1980s when multiculturalism gained wide acceptance, a series of new cases concerning religious dress came before U.S. courts.

Sikh Attire

Cooper v. Eugene School District (1985) concerned a public schoolteacher who converted to the Sikh religion after marrying a Sikh man. She then decided to wear white clothes and a white turban in the classroom. The Court of Appeals of Oregon held that Ms. Cooper had violated the Oregon Garb Statute.[85] Attributing to her a "dual role," the court described the teacher both as an individual entitled to express her belief and, at the same time, as an agent of the state who represents its authority to her students. The Court of Appeals also addressed the question of whether Cooper's Sikh attire would "let the school district appear to support her religion" or whether everyone (including her youngest students) would think that she was acting as an individual. The court avoided giving an answer by relying on the disproportionate action taken by the school by way of dismissing the teacher from her job.

The Supreme Court of Oregon when vacating this judgment in 1986 pointed out that there was a legitimate concern that a teacher's appearance in religious dress may leave a conscious or unconscious impression among young people (and their parents) that the school endorses the particular religious commitment of the person to whom it has assigned the public role of teacher. This underlying concern was assumed to make the otherwise privileged display of a teacher's religious commitment incompatible with an "atmosphere of religious neutrality." Some of the concepts that the Supreme Court relied upon in this decision are critical. For example, the court stressed "a degree of commitment beyond the choice to wear common decorations, such as a small cross or Star of David." This means the decision defers to majority culture and religion and accepts Judeo-Christian symbols. It is highly difficult to find comparable symbols in Islam or the Sikh religion. Cooper appealed the decision to the U.S. Supreme Court, but the case was dismissed.[86]

The Muslim Headscarf

In *U.S.A. v. Board of Education for the School District of Philadelphia* (1990) the U.S. Court of Appeals for the Third Circuit decided on the constitutionality of Pennsylvania's Garb Statute of 1895.[87] The case concerned Alma Delores Reardon, a substitute teacher who was dismissed from her job. Later in her life, Reardon became a devout Muslim and began to wear clothes that covered her entire body except her face and hands. The federal Court of Appeals had to decide whether the Board of Education had violated Title VII of the Civil Rights Act of 1964.[88] According to this provision, there is no ground for deferring to "religion" if the accommodation of religious practices would cause "undue hardship" to the employer. As the U.S. Supreme Court held in *Trans World Airlines v. Hardison* (1977), concerning an employee who refused to work on Saturdays for religious reasons, it is an undue hardship to require the employer to bear more than a *de minimis* cost. However, "cost" need not necessarily be measured in dollars.[89]

Viewing the concern of preserving an "atmosphere of religious neutrality" and also considering that the Pennsylvania statute is almost identical to the Oregon statute, the U.S. Court of Appeals concluded that the summary disposition by the U.S. Supreme Court in *Cooper* had precedential value: if the Oregon Garb Statute was narrowly tailored to a compelling state interest, they could not treat the Pennsylvania statute differently.[90] This holding was attacked by one concurring judge and also was sharply criticized in publications.[91]

African Headgear

In *McGlothin v. Jackson Municipal Separate School District* (1992), a former teacher's aide sued a Mississippi school district for unfair termination in violation of her rights under Title VII of the Civil Rights Act of 1964 and the First Amendment.[92] Ms. McGlothin was blamed by her employer for willful failure to conform to the dress code of the school. Over the years she had worn either red berets or African style head-wraps in class. She let her hair grow and refused to wash it for months in order to keep it natural. Respecting the fact that Ms. McGlothin had to teach a course in elementary school entitled "Keeping Healthy" (how personal hygiene affects one's mental, social, and psychological health) she was given notice by the school board several times that her appearance was not appropriate and that her head-wrap violated the school dress code. When she was asked about her reasons for covering her head, she originally responded that she needed to wear the head covering to keep from getting cold and to uphold her Afro-American heritage. It was only after her termination due to insubordination that she invoked her religious belief. She named her religion as "the original Hebrew Israelites from Ethiopia," and cited teachings from various religions including Rastafarianism. Ms. McGlothin described her religion as her "way of life," her "spiritual lifestyle," her culture, and also her personal preference. The court was not convinced that she had a "religious belief." Although it conceded that the U.S. Supreme Court had not defined precisely what constituted a religious belief and that such belief need not recognize a supreme being, it pointed out that merely the assertion of one's personal preference was not considered sufficient in American constitutional jurisprudence.[93] As Ms. McGlothin had not communicated her beliefs sufficiently to the employer, she was denied the protection of the religion clauses.[94] The court, not surprisingly, failed to consider intersectionality. Obviously, Ms. McGlothin should also have been protected against racial discrimination. As she pointed out, her "Afro-American heritage" was part of her appearance, and her appearance was not appropriate for her employer, who sought to "imitate the dress style and hair characteristics of the majority race in this country." Moreover, making a connection between her teaching of "Keeping Healthy" and her appearance is a typical form of stereotyping, and, likely, would have been considered racial discrimination by the court.[95]

Discrimination against Muslim Women in the Workplace

As seen in the cases of teachers, Title VII of the Civil Rights Act of 1964 prohibits employers from discriminating against individuals because of their religion, in hiring, firing, and other terms and conditions of employment. Employers must reasonably accommodate employees' sincerely held religious beliefs or practices unless doing so would impose an undue hardship on the employer.[96] Discrimination against Muslim women who wear the headscarf in the workplace has been well documented by the Muslim civil rights organization CAIR. Shortly after 9/11, the Equal Employment Opportunity Commission (EEOC) also encouraged victims of anti–Arab-Muslim harassment and discrimination in workplaces to come forward with complaints, so that the agency could investigate and resolve them. Between September 11, 2001, and May 7, 2002, in just the nine months following the terrorist attacks, the EEOC received nearly five hundred charges of discrimination on the basis of Muslim religion, many of which were headscarf related. During a comparable period a year earlier, only 193 complaints had been filed.[97]

Some of the 2001 complaints were solved through settlements before going to court, and some ended up in courts.[98] The latest documented opinion was issued in 2007. A gay African American in New York claimed he had been fired because his hospital employer thought he was Muslim.[99] While black Muslims are included in the statistics of employment discrimination cases, the majority of cases have involved Muslim plaintiffs from the Middle East, especially in recent years. The most remarkable thing about these cases is the exponential growth of Muslim employment discrimination cases after 2001.[100] Similarly, a *Forbes* magazine article reported on recent labor unrest in Nebraska arising from an employer's refusal to allow prayer breaks for its unionized Somali employees. Religious discrimination complaints by Muslims doubled in the last ten years, from 221 in 1996 to 594 in 2006.[101]

Data collected by the International Assessment and Strategy Center (IASC) indicates that a portion of this growth is explained by changes in available remedies. Prior to 1987, although the courts recognized religious discrimination, it was unclear whether Arabs could claim racial discrimination in the United States, based on the theory that Arabs were Caucasian and therefore not a racial minority. In May 1987, the Supreme Court established that Arabs were an ethnic minority for purposes of the federal anti-discrimination laws.[102] The growing demography of Muslim immigrants, the increased number of Muslim employees in the past two decades, and political concerns may also have been responsible for this result. For example, Muslim employment discrimination claims accelerated following the first World Trade Center attacks in 1993. At the time, the American media was also preoccupied by the Palestine-Israel conflict. Through the end of the decade, there were several more Islamic attacks on U.S. interests abroad and the entity Al Qaida began to be known to many Americans. Following the 9/11 attacks, emerging Islamophobia contributed to the skyrocketing employment discrimination.

While the discrimination cases are increasing, the result rate of cases won by Muslim employees is not. Muslim employees have succeeded in showing redressable religious employment discrimination in a total of only twelve cases in American legal history. In contrast, a total of 196 claims have been dismissed by the courts as lacking in legal merit.[103] Increasingly, Muslim employment-discrimination claims are also being advanced by white-collar employees, because most recent Muslim immigrants are professionals. The cases involve Muslim university professors, doctors, engineers, and government employees fired from their jobs, including some Muslim employees in national defense agencies. At the same time, Muslim asylum cases in the American courts are proliferating. It seems reasonable to conclude that the judicial rulings have not been very generous to Muslim employees, and reflect some racist and Islamophobic tendencies. Obviously, Islamic terrorism and meritless Muslim employment-discrimination claims have grown hand in hand. One should not, however, ignore that the Title VII rules concerning employment discrimination are inadequate. As a result, employees with valid complaints are commonly rejected by the courts because of procedural obstacles and evidentiary burdens.

Three cases that were highly publicized in the American media were specifically related to Islamic headscarf use. Two of them concerned headscarves and one was about niqab, a face-covering practice.

Karen Crisco

Karen Crisco converted to Islam on September 9, 2001. She had worked in North Carolina as a licensed practical nurse for over three years. Shortly after her conversion, which took place shortly before 9/11, Crisco had worn a headscarf to work, where she was promptly told to remove it because she had frightened a number of patients. Complaining of a work environment hostile to her religion and her romantic relationship with a Muslim man, Crisco reported derogatory remarks and verbal harassment on the job. The EEOC investigated the charges and reached a prelitigation settlement with the employer.[104]

Bilan Nur

On September 30, 2002, the EEOC sued Alamo Rent-a-Car because Bilan Nur, a customer service representative in its Phoenix office, was denied permission to cover her head with a scarf during the Muslim holy month of Ramadan. Alamo had previously granted Ms. Nur permission to cover her head, during Ramadan in 1999 and 2000, but in December 2001 the company refused to allow her to observe her religious practice. Alamo subsequently disciplined, suspended, and fired Ms. Nur for failure to remove her scarf. This case went to court after the EEOC had exhausted avenues for a pretrial settlement. Later, a Phoenix jury awarded Ms. Nur more than $287,000 in a religious discrimination suit.[105] This case received public attention as a result of opposition to the partial victory of the plaintiff. A court ruling in 1997 had relaxed the requirement for employers to accommodate the religious needs of employees under Title VII. Every year since 1997, legislation known as the "Workplace Religious Freedom Act" (WRFA) has been introduced in Congress to reinstate protections for religiously observant workers by requiring employers to accommodate the religious needs of their employees, provided it would not result in "significant difficulty or expense." Some advocates of this legislation cite Bilan Nur's case against Alamo as an argument for its necessity. Opponents cite the same case, arguing that the proposed legislation could harm the civil rights of co-workers, patients, and clients whose interests would not be served if employers were required to accommodate all religious practices and beliefs.[106]

Sultaana Freeman

The third case is an example of a controversy emerging from the practice of face covering and the response of a U.S. government agency. Sultaana Freeman, a Muslim woman from Florida, wished to have her driver's license issued either without her photo or with a photo of her wearing a dress that covered her entire body except for her eyes.[107] A former evangelist who converted to Islam in 1990s, Ms. Freeman had been permitted to wear the niqab in the photo for her Florida driver's license issued in February 2001. However, following a check of its drivers' license database prompted by the 9/11 terrorist attacks, the Florida Department of Motor Vehicles sent Ms. Freeman a letter stating that her existing license was suspended; she was asked to present herself for a new photograph without her niqab. Ms. Freeman refused and sued the state. Since the filing of the suit, Internet bulletin boards have been lighting up with postings from supporters and critics of her actions. Citing security concerns after 9/11, the State of Florida insisted that she needed to reveal her identity more fully. Ms. Freeman, along with the ACLU, believed that her license had been revoked unnecessarily because she was practicing the Muslim tradition of niqab, and that hindering this practice resulted in a restraint on her free practice of religion. The judge agreed with the state, writing in her ruling that while Freeman "most likely poses no threat to national security, there likely are people who would be willing to use a ruling permitting the wearing of full-face cloaks in driver's license photos by pretending to ascribe to religious beliefs in order to carry out activities that would threaten lives."[108] A Florida appellate court affirmed the trial court judge's ruling, stating that while "we recognize the tension created as a result of choosing between following the dictates of one's religion and the mandates of secular law... as long as the law is neutral and generally applicable to the citizenry, they must be obeyed."[109] Both sides presented expert witnesses on Islamic law to determine whether face covering is part of a religious mandate. The expert witness for the state averred that exceptions to the practice of hijab are made because of necessity, and that even in Saudi Arabia women are required to have full-face photos on their passports and for exam taking.[110] On Freeman's behalf, another expert witness testified the opposite, based on an interpretation of Quranic verses. The state also argued that, because the primary purpose of the hijab is to avoid sexual enticement, and because the state had made efforts to accommodate the appellant by having a female photographer and no males present when the photo was taken, the necessity providing security warranted an exception to the Islamic practice. In her ruling, the circuit court judge Janet Thorpe asserted that she would not choose between contending interpretations of Sharia provisions and agreed with state officials that letting people show only their eyes would compromise efforts to stop terrorists.[111]

This case was a clear example of the choice between national security and preserving personal religious freedom—national security prevailed. This decision also comports with the constitutional principles formulated by the

Supreme Court in *Church of Lukumi Babalu Aye, Inc. v. City of Hialeah*[112] and the *Department of Human Resources of Oregon v. Smith*.[113] The three cases occurred in different time periods and social climates, and concerned entirely different situations, yet all involved religious practices. In the *Freeman* case, the trial and appellate courts agreed with the state that giving priority to religious practices over a substantial legitimate public need would undermine the secular principles on which the government is based. Does freedom to observe one's religious beliefs compel freedom from the operation of the law? These are the kind of difficult questions facing America now and for many years to come, and will likely remain a topic of scholarly debate.

Modesty Law

Many might interpret the wearing of a headscarf in Islam as "modesty." This concept would give a devout Muslim woman another legal protection in relation to U.S. modesty laws. Modesty law refers to a dispersed set of legal norms that allow adults to cover their bodies, for the sake of chastity, humility, decency, or morality.[114] The leading historical example of such a rule is the Supreme Court decision in *Union Pacific Railroad v. Botsford*, in which the Court recognized the "right to be let alone."[115] The legal modesty battles in the United States mainly involve women seeking the freedom to dress less modestly than others expect, and only occasionally women who seek the freedom to be more modest than expected.[116] For instance, tavern dancers went to the Supreme Court seeking a right to perform totally nude but were not successful.[117] Extending such legal understanding to a hypothetical headscarf case, "in a country in which states attempt to impose a symbolic vestige of modesty on its female citizens to such an absurd degree, it is unlikely that women and girls exhibiting greater than average modesty would ever be required to remove modesty garments, solely for the sake of uniformity or cultural assimilation."[118] Moreover, in a nudity case, Judge Richard Posner's dissenting opinion invokes "Judeo-Christian modesty," which could easily encompass Islamic modesty, because, for many, the headscarf can be interpreted as a form of modesty that Islam requires for women. Therefore, according to some scholars, a national ban on the headscarf would be unconstitutional and virtually unthinkable in the United States, where religious expression and voluntary modesty are greatly valued.[119]

However, the temporary removal of a headscarf, especially a veil that covers the face or niqab, should not be considered unconstitutional. As seen above in *Freeman*, the required removal of a veil for the purpose of taking photos to obtain a driver's license or passport, or to go through airport security screening by a female professional in a secluded area is a reasonable requirement imposed to protect public safety and security. However, in the post-9/11 era, hostile acts against Muslims have significantly increased. The headscarf became a symbol of not only Islam but of terrorism in general. Traveling in the United States while wearing the headscarf is a nightmare for many Muslim women due to this hostile atmosphere, although this is a matter of societal attitudes, not legal constraints.[120] One can argue that societal attitudes often are a precursor of judicial tendencies. Therefore despite a strong judicial tradition against such limitations, it is possible that future political events might inhibit such tendencies, even in the United States.

4. Is a Legal Headscarf Ban for Public Schools Possible in the United States? A Hypothetical Argument

First Amendment Challenges

Considering these relevant court decisions and the post-9/11 public sentiments against Islam and Islamic practices, it is an open-ended question whether a government body in the United States might enact a ban on religious dress in public schools similar to the French law of 2004 and is unlikely to be answered definitively. First, in the United States, the federal government leaves the regulation of education to the states. However, a state regulation will not be upheld if it is regarded as a violation of the federal constitution. Therefore, such a law, if ever enacted, would likely be challenged on First Amendment grounds, primarily by reference to the free exercise clause, and secondarily in relation to the free speech clause. Some states, such as Oregon, Pennsylvania, and Nebraska, have laws prohibiting teachers from wearing religious symbols or dress. As a counterexample, the state of Missouri has proactively passed statutes expressly allowing students to wear religious insignia or emblems as long as they do not promote disruptive behavior.[121]

The hypothetical headscarf ban would be assessed by the Supreme Court's test for determining whether government action violates the free exercise clause and subject to strict scrutiny, because the clause treats religiously affiliated signs differently than nonreligious signs.[122] Therefore, the regulation must be narrowly tailored to achieve a "compelling government interest."[123] The requirement of a compelling government interest is very difficult to satisfy generally, and specifically it is almost impossible in the United States to claim that "protection of secularism" is a compelling government interest, as was plausible in France and Turkey. However, this interpretative method changed after *Smith* in 1990.[124] In *Smith*, the court held that if a law is "neutral" toward religion and of general application, even if it incidentally burdens religious exercise, it does not offend the First Amendment. There is a significant debate among constitutional law scholars about cases involving the freedom of religion and, more specifically, the free exercise clause. The general view is after the *Smith* decision the jurisprudence of the Supreme Court became more religion friendly.

Proponents of a hypothetical law to prohibit religious symbols would argue that such a law does not violate the constitution's free exercise clause because it is neutral, being applicable to all religious symbols. Therefore, they would argue that although the law has a disproportionate effect on religion, its purpose is not to burden the practice of religion.[125] Opponents of the law would likely raise a hybrid claim asserting that two fundamental rights, free exercise and freedom of speech, are at stake in this legal attempt to prohibit the display of religious symbols.[126] This means that a lowered threshold for interpreting the right of free exercise will be elevated to a stricter scrutiny in the case of free speech.

Public Order and Public Health

Proponents are unlikely to ground a strong argument on appeals to "public order" or "public health," or to narrow down the restriction of religious signs to headscarves only, limited to particular schools or specific conditions, which would enable such a law to survive. But if the hypothetical ban were limited to the headscarf and no other religious symbols, it would run up against another landmark principle of the Fourteenth Amendment to the constitution. As discussed earlier, some states already have laws prohibiting public schoolteachers from wearing religious clothing in the classroom, and numerous public schools throughout the United States have implemented student dress codes.[127] These strict dress codes may be an indication that public schools are now accepted as religiously neutral zones, which may "create a roadblock to students who wish to challenge dress codes that restrict their rights to wear religious clothing and symbols to school."[128] The question of teachers' dress is treated differently from that of other employees or students, due to the possibility that a public schoolteacher's religious dress might be perceived as a public endorsement of religion, with a potential proselytizing influence on students.

The cases cited indicate that a ban on religious dress in public schools would have a very difficult time surviving a free speech challenge. A headscarf, a yarmulke, Chalifoux's rosary and Tinker's armband are protected under the free exercise and/or free speech clauses.[129] As the court mandated in *Tinker*: "The government should set forth concrete evidence showing that the wearing of such religious garb would materially and substantially interfere with the requirements of appropriate discipline in the operation of the schools" or "impinge upon the rights of the other students."

Minority Religious Practices

While religious belief is guaranteed absolutely, the free exercise of religion may, however, be regulated to some extent by law. The United States federal courts have shown that they are capable of permitting bans on minority group practices disliked by or threatening to the majority.[130] For example, the late nineteenth-century decision *Reynolds v. United States* upheld a law applicable to the U.S. territories that banned the practice of polygamy among Mormons.[131] The Supreme Court held that "the right of free exercise is a right to believe what one wishes, not a right to do what one wishes when what one wishes to do violates laws of general application."[132]

A similar legal approach was repeated many years later in *Employment Division of Human Resources of Oregon v. Smith* (1990).[133] In that case, members of a Native American church lost their social service jobs due to their admitted use of sacramental peyote, an illegal drug. The court held that the First Amendment did not require that the use of sacramental peyote be treated any differently from the use of other illegal drugs. The court asserted: "The state interest in protecting the public from the dangers associated with drug use is a weighty one."[134]

These two Supreme Court decisions indicate that minority religious practices are subject to limitation, rather than protection, if there is a strong public interest in protecting majority views and values. If wearing a headscarf, or any religious dress for that matter, were considered a "minority religious practice," it could well be subject to legislative limitation that would be upheld if constitutionally challenged.

5. From Multiculturalism to Islamophobia

From the civil rights movement in the 1960s to the arrival of multiculturalism in the1980s, the United States has gained comprehensive experience in reaching a better solution than those adopted in Europe—one that aims at the accommodation of different racial, ethnic, and religious minorities.

Nevertheless, the recent controversy over plans for an Islamic center near the World Trade Center in New York City indicates that the United States is not completely immune from the xenophobia considered more common in Europe than in the United States. Post-9/11, the Islamophobia in the United States is becoming for Muslims what anti-Semitism was for Jews. Rooted in hostility and intolerance toward religious and cultural beliefs and a religious or racial group, it threatens the democratic fabric of American societies. Many examples illustrate that the social cancer of Islamophobia is spreading across the United States.[135]

The campaign against the Islamic center in New York was sponsored by groups and individuals with long histories of promoting anti-Islam sentiment. It quickly became a cause célèbre, as if establishing the center would be an outrageous action, harming the sentiments of the families of 9/11 victims. It has been the focal point for a fierce national debate about religious freedom and the legacy of 9/11. The center's opponents claim that all mosques are "monuments to terrorism" and "house-embedded [terrorist] cells."[136] The controversy has become a political issue, not only locally, but also nationally, and internationally.[137] Shortly after the New York City Islamic center debate, Hamburg, Germany saw a similar controversy, when authorities shut down the Masjid Taiba, a mosque where several of the 9/11 hijackers had met, asserting that it remained a source of radicalization nearly a decade later. According to law enforcement officials, "indoctrinating young people with a form of Islam that encouraged violence demonstrated the challenges faced by Western democracies like Germany in controlling extremism without impinging on civil rights and religious freedom."[138]

Politicians use fear of Islam as a political material. Former Speaker of the U.S. House of Representatives Newt Gingrich warned of the danger of Sharia law taking over American courts. Republican Rex Duncan, an Oklahoma state senator, declared that there is a "war for the survival of America" to keep Sharia from creeping into the American court system. Even the newly appointed Supreme Court Justice Elena Kagan is being accused of being "Justice Sharia" because she had once taught Islamic law. North Carolina Congresswoman Sue Myrick and Georgia Congressman Paul Broun have recklessly charged that Muslim student interns in Congress were part of a secret infiltration of Muslim spies into key national security committees on Capitol Hill.[139]

At the same time, an international coalition of right-wing politicians against Islam is emerging. For instance, controversial Dutch politician Geert Wilders recently said he is forming an international "freedom alliance" to amplify his anti-Muslim message across the West. The aim of the alliance is to end immigration of people from Muslim nations to the West. He identi-fied five nations (the United States, Canada, France, Germany, and Britain) as "ripe" for his message, as they already have large populations of Muslim immigrants and face the threat of Islamic terrorism. Surprisingly, this anti-Muslim politician, who has campaigned for a tax on headscarves and a ban on the Quran, seemed poised to emerge as a prominent player in a new minority government in the Netherlands. According to the news, while the outspoken and populist Wilders would not gain a ministerial appointment, the proposed formation of the government would make him one of the most influential politicians in the Netherlands.[140] As a result of politicians stimulating anti-Islam sentiment, hate crimes against Muslims are on the rise across the West.

Despite major polls by Gallup and the Pew Research Center showing that American Muslims are well integrated economically and politically, a Gallup Center for Muslim Studies report of January 2010 found that 43 percent of Americans admit to feeling at least "a little" prejudice toward Muslims—more than twice the number who say the same about Christians (18 percent), Jews (15 percent), and Buddhists (14 percent). Further, 9 percent of Americans admitted feeling "a great deal" of prejudice toward Muslims, while 20 percent admitted feeling "some" prejudice. Surprisingly, the Gallup data revealed a link between anti-Semitism and Islamophobia: contempt for Jews makes a person "about 32 times as likely to report the same level of prejudice toward Muslims."[141]

According to renowned Islamic scholar John L. Esposito, "there is no lack of hate speech in the media and in print to empower Islamophobia." Often, the primary focus in the media is not on balanced reporting or coverage of posi-tive news about Muslims, but instead on highlighting acts and statements of political and religious extremists. Political and religious commentators write and speak out publicly about Islam and Muslims, using with impunity slurs that would never appear in mainstream broadcast or print media about Jews, Christians, and other established religious groups. Esposito argues that if one takes out the word "Muslim" and substitutes "Jew" or "Catholic" in many of the articles targeting Muslims, the public outcry would be monumental.[142]

As a result, all Muslims have been reduced to stereotypes representing Islam against the West; Islam's war with modernity; and Muslim rage, extrem-ism, fanaticism, and terrorism. The rhetoric and hatred of a violent minor-ity has been equated with the "anti-Americanism or anti-Westernism of a peaceful, mainstream majority, all lumped together in the question of 'why do they hate us?'" Esposito warns that not only the small minority of Muslim extremists and terrorists but also Muslims at large are cast as the peculiar and demonized "other" within Islamophobic discourse, with serious international and domestic consequences.[143] Esposito further claims that Islamophobia, like anti-Semitism, will not be eradicated easily or soon. Islamophobic campaigns force even the most moderate and open-minded Muslims to question the value of integrating into the larger society, when the leaders of that society look at all Muslims with suspicion and prejudice. This is not reconcilable either with Judeo-Christian ethics or the civic moral values of America and Europe. "Islamophobia and its culture of hate is not only a threat to the civil liberties of Muslims, but also to the very fabric of who we are and what we stand for, the principles and values embodied in our Constitution which have historically made our democracy strong."[144]

The election of President Barak Obama opened a new page on multiculturalism in the United States. His connection with Islam became a liability during the election process. He had to drop his middle name Hussein, and, in one of his Chicago meetings with voters, his aides had to clear the podium so women wearing headscarves would not appear in photos with Obama. His campaign organizers were very careful not to create unnecessary antagonism. Thanks to some reactionary media, as of August 2010, 24 percent of Americans mistakenly believed that the president was Muslim.[145] President Obama's first overseas visit after his election was to the Middle East. Obama's famous "Cairo speech" sent an important message to the Muslim world. His motive was to correct the negative sentiments that had formed throughout the Muslim world against U.S. policies during the presidency of George W. Bush, which had led to U.S. engagement in two wars in the Muslim world. In the speech, Obama also mentioned the headscarf controversy.[146] His message, directed to Europe and the West, pledged tolerance on this issue. Yet, after Cairo, the president gave another speech in Europe in which he did not urge Europeans to be more tolerant toward Islam and Islamic practices. He also did not touch on issues of Muslim dress and the headscarf controversy in a speech in Istanbul, shortly before Cairo, perhaps due to his awareness of the delicate political controversy over the headscarf in Turkey and the knowledge that his words would be unwelcome to hardcore secularists.

Racism and Islamophobia

President Obama's close ties with Islam through his Kenyan father raised another close connection between racism and Islamophobia among reactionaries. As indicated earlier, Islamophobia is not unique to the United States. Europe is also suffering severe Islamophobia of its own. It is an interesting comparison that goes beyond the limits of this book: the way in which different European countries such as England, Germany, Netherlands, and even Northern Europeans deal with their own Muslim citizens and immigrants vis-à-vis the United States. There are lessons to be taken from how Europe handles or, more pessimistically, cannot handle the "multiculturalism" and Muslim presence that gradually became very problematic after 9/11, and the Madrid and London bombings.[147]

What is unique in the United States is examining Islamophobia in the context of the racialized nature of this particular bigotry. While internal and external factors were converging to create anti-Muslim sentiment, the American media had convinced American people that Muslims and Arabs are different, antidemocratic, and incompatible with American culture. From TV programs, to comic books, video games, and Hollywood movies, one after another outlet repeated the same themes: Islam is a violent religion, Arabs and Middle Easterners are primitive and backward. On this front, nineteenth-century European "Orientalists" were helpful sources. They rationalized colonialism during the colonial period for the British Empire. Learning from Orientalists, a new generation of intellectuals and pseudo-intellectuals are working on influencing American people to believe that Islam is incompatible with democracy, secularism, human rights, and particularly women's rights.

Efforts to distort the teaching of Islam, to discredit and defame Islamic organizations, and to marginalize and impugn the religion itself are widespread in reactionary American society. Islamophobia both results from and contributes to the racial ideology of the United States; an ideology based on socially constructed categories of phenotypical characteristics, or on how individuals physically appear.[148] In other words, wearing a hijab, headscarf, or turban; having certain skin tones; or speaking with certain accents are all physical markers that are enough to create a vulnerability to Islamophobia in the United States. As a result of this racialized process, Islamophobia affects Christians, Muslims, and Sikhs from all backgrounds and, in particular, people who have ancestry in Middle East, North Africa, as well as in Western and South Asia. In fact, Islamophobia affects a wide range of individuals who identify with many different ethnicities, nationalities, and religions. The vivid example of this occurred in Arizona right after the 9/11 terror attack, when Balbir Singh Sodhi was shot and killed by man who shouted "I stand for America all the way" as he was arrested.[149] Sodhi wore a turban in accordance with his Sikh faith, and he was killed in a deliberate hate crime explained only by his supposedly "Muslim like or Muslim-looking" appearance. Contemporary scholarship about Islamophobia often fails to examine critically the racialized nature of this particular bigotry.[150]

The category of "Muslim" in the United States is as problematic as any other racial or ethnic categories, if not more so because of significant intra-group differences. What is distinct in this new category is the fact that this group is not based on ethnic, linguistic, national, or geographical similarities, but is based on a common religion. In many recent studies, the group affected by Islamophobia is described as simply "Muslims" or "Muslims and Arabs." However, the "Muslim/Arab" category includes a significant number of non-Muslims. The majority of Arabs in the United States are not Muslims but Christians. Moreover, most Muslim Americans in the United States are not Arabs. Furthermore, unlike other groups, the category of Muslim in the United States covers not only immigrant communities but also includes a significant number of African Americans.[151] Racial categorization is not just a policy based on pure racism but it also incorporates various hidden ideological, economic, and geopolitical ambitions that help to dominate "others." In this context, Muslims are not the first example of such racialization. Historically, this kind of discrimination happened to Jews and Catholics too.[152]

In sum, Muslims, like any other religious group, are protected by the First Amendment. In other words, they can freely practice their religion. The problem is the implicit or explicit denial of their political, social, and economic rights based on their identity or perceived religious identity as Muslims.

9

Conclusion

It is not our differences that divide us. It is our inability
to recognize, accept, and celebrate those differences.
AUDRE LORDE, AMERICAN POET, Teacher, and Activist

Conceptual Confusion

In its multiple dimensions, the global headscarf controversy touches on fundamental issues of our time. Beyond questions of secularism and freedom of religion, vigorously invoked by both sides of the argument, the implications of the debate go well beyond posing a problem for Muslim pious women. The headscarf controversy has a profound symbolic value in its connotations for various conceptual issues such as patriarchy, feminism, gender equality, women's rights, multiculturalism, racism, cultural relativism, religion's place in democratic societies, modernity, secularism, liberalism, and constitutionalism.

Decision makers are influenced by these concepts and the societal stereotypes and political events of their particular countries. Therefore, very often, women's specific conditions are undermined when state interests prevail. Global politics, state interests, constitutional values and the philosophy of a nation-state become stumbling blocks for women. A woman becomes an entity released from her particularity, no matter which country she lives in and whether she is a student at an elementary school or university, or a civil servant or teacher. As the significance and relevance of her subjectivity are lost on decision makers, these issues are often concealed behind one another, and the headscarf controversy ends up in the hands of the legal system. Judiciary or legislative bodies make decisions about women's acceptability in schools or workplaces based on what they wear. This is itself enough to raise questions of gender inequality, injustice, and discrimination against Muslim women who chose to wear headscarves in democratic societies during the twenty-first century. Is a legal system the right venue for making such an important decision? This question has been raised throughout this book, and each country has its own response to it.

It is remarkable that the real victim of this legal and sociopolitical battle, the woman who chooses to wear a headscarf or is allegedly forced to wear a headscarf, has kept pretty much silent throughout the ongoing controversy. Decisions, either for or against her, are made on her behalf, and policies that affect her are discussed without her participation. This is true in countries where the headscarf debate is taking place. Male and female politicians, scholars, intellectuals, and national elites play the roles of debater, decision maker, or player, while headscarf-wearing women have for the most part occupied the role of silent victims in this debate. This furnishes enough support for the view that there is a fundamental injustice about this debate, no matter what kind of policy is enacted or will be enacted in various countries in the future.

Taken together, domestic policies, legislation, and court decisions on the Muslim headscarf in different countries, including the jurisprudence of the ECHR, raise important questions about religious exposure in constitutional democracies. Moreover, considering the interaction between national courts and international tribunals on one hand and the policies of individual countries on the other, the headscarf controversy reflects a strong connection with the political conditions existing in any given country. Even though each country has very different political, sociological, cultural, and legal responses to the headscarf controversy, this study indicates that there is a global trend: the headscarf controversy seemingly and gradually is heading in the same direction throughout the West, while subject to some insignificant variations. Unfortunately, this trend does not offer much hope of achieving peaceful coexistence and tolerance among the citizens of today's multicultural societies. Rather, the trend exhibits tendencies toward a new sort of racism, segregation, and intolerance, especially in Europe and the United States, and even to a degree in Turkey. Let us consider some forecasts for the future of the headscarf controversy.

Turkey: A Relaxing Headscarf Policy and Secularist Fears for the Future

Turkey, an overwhelmingly Muslim country, went through a unique modernization process in the twentieth century, importing a European legal system and French *laïcité*, yet it remains a traditional and religious society. Turkey's strict anti-headscarf policy went beyond the imagination and beyond the state's borders. It became a model for anti-headscarf tendencies and gained influence on European jurisprudence through the supranational European Court of Human Rights. However, unlike in Western countries, where the headscarf debate is a symbolic issue for questioning the place of Islam in a multicultural society, in Turkey the headscarf debate has a fundamental impact on the majority of its peoples' daily lives. It occupies the fault line of a society that is beginning to divide on the desire for modernization and Europeanization on the one hand and preserving religiosity and an Islamic identity on the other.

Historically, the headscarf controversy has been a tool for soul searching that casts its shadow across matters of national identity and state formation. Today, after nearly a century, the headscarf debate is becoming more complex than ever, as it is directly connected with an ongoing political struggle in the country. When the headscarf controversy reached its highest point in the early 2000s, a strictly secular Turkish government, empowered by the ECHR's judgments, did not hesitate to exclude women who wear headscarves from enjoying the basic human rights of the individual. There seemed to be almost no prominent role in the future for religious Muslim women in Turkish society because of the strict implementation of the headscarf ban. However, the current Turkish government with its religion-friendly outlook is disposed to correct this strict headscarf ban, a policy based on reasoning that was almost unimaginable for outsiders to understand in the first place. One can understand European countries' unease with Muslim immigrants and the expression of Islam, considering the historical animosities and political developments of recent years. However, it is not easy to understand why previous Turkish governments were so ready to harass their own citizens, especially considering that more than half of Turkish female citizens wear the headscarf. The only sensible interpretation of the Turkish headscarf controversy is that it operates as code for the power struggle between the old, Kemalist, Republican elite and the AKP, the new socially conservative, yet economically liberal, populist party.

The AKP, during its second period of governing the country, continually asked the Turkish Parliament to enact a new constitution to redress such grievances. The secular judicial establishment, represented by the Constitutional Court and other high courts, closed all doors and tied the hands of Parliament with unreasonable judicial decisions that blocked the process of constitutional reform. Finally, in September 2010, the AKP government put the proposed constitutional reforms to a referendum, to gain permission and support from

Turkish citizens. The opposition fiercely claimed that the constitutional referendum was nothing but a vehicle for Islamic forces to consolidate political power and to displace the secular establishment. On the contrary, the recent referendum was the necessary first step to initiate reforms of judicial institutions that empower civilian courts while reducing the jurisdiction of military courts. A reformed constitution would enhance economic and social rights and individual freedoms; strengthen gender equality and the protection of children, the elderly, veterans, and the disabled; would improve privacy rights and access to government records; expand collective bargaining rights; and, most important, remove immunities long afforded to those responsible for the 1980 military coup.[1] The constitutional changes are also aimed at bringing Turkey's constitution into compliance with the standards of the European Union. Fifty-eight percent of voters accepted the constitutional reforms. Undoubtedly, the future constitution will aim to solve the issue of the headscarf ban, which has been forcefully, yet inconsistently, implemented during the last four decades based on the decisions of the Constitutional Court and reinforced by the 2005 *Sahin* decision of the ECHR.

Since the AKP government came to power in 2002, the political atmosphere in Turkey has been slowly but firmly moving in the direction of a relaxed policy toward the headscarf. Indicative of this change is that even the intensely secular opposition party CHP is willing to cooperate with the AKP to lift the headscarf ban in universities. This seems to reflect the party's understanding that the political pendulum has swing in favor of lifting the headscarf ban. Despite these developments, the headscarf debate has never lost its prominence in Turkey because it has always been far more than a legal issue. As soon as the discussion of lifting the headscarf ban began in the postreferendum atmosphere, a new debate arose whether the headscarf ban should be lifted in universities only or in more comprehensive manner. A concern raised by the opponents of lifting the ban is if the headscarf ban is lifted in higher education, what will happen to secondary and high school students, teachers, doctors, lawyers, judges, and all civil servants? What limits, if any, should apply to headscarf use? It seems this argument is likely to continue for a few decades, even if the Turkish government's constitutional reforms are able to lift the headscarf ban in universities in the near future.

One should keep in mind that the headscarf controversy is very much entwined with the Turkish political structure. In the future, if opposition political parties dominated by secular Kemalists return to power, the first step will be to revive the old rules, bring back the headscarf ban, and again push religious women out of public spaces. This would be a social tragedy, and it is difficult to predict the political effects of such a reversal on societal peace in Turkey. The secular side of Turkish society cherishes a constant fear that allowing headscarves in universities goes too far, and the eventual extension to other places will result in peer pressure or, more seriously, political pressure that would threaten freedom of religion and the secular lifestyle. These fears are part of an internalized Orientalist view: that Islam and democracy cannot go together, and, as a result, secular Turkish women will lose their rights. Bad models in the region make this fear a reasonable one. At the same time, it is not reasonable to put religious women in a position where they fear that they will be forced to sacrifice. The idea of multiple modernities and multiple secularisms would afford protection for citizens' lifestyles. All we need to do is trust the Turkish democratic system and hope for the best, instead of sacrificing one large part of society.

The Empowerment of Women?

While Turkish politicians continue to devote their energies to the pros and cons of the headscarf ban, they must also focus on addressing gender inequality and women's empowerment. According to the World Economic Forum, in Turkey female participation in the labor force has fallen from 34 percent to 26 percent since 1989.[2] Very limited participation by women in some sectors is even more disturbing than these figures suggest. For instance, women make up only 9 percent of parliamentary deputies. The highest portion of these belong to the pro-Kurdish Peace and Democracy Party (BDP); the only party that has a quota (40 percent) for women deputies. Unfortunately, in 2009, the Turkish Constitutional Court closed this party because of its alleged separatist ideologies.

Turkey, despite being listed among countries that showed "high human development," still ranks 83rd out of 169 countries, behind all European Union member countries, other EU candidates, and below the average level of countries belonging to the Organization for Economic Cooperation and Development (OECD). The Human Development Index (HDI) by the United Nations Development Programme (UNDP) offers an alternative calculation to countries' GNP, considering individual economic prosperity in the light of education levels and life expectancy. The most recently released HDI reveals that many countries, such as Bulgaria, Latvia, and Romania, have lower per capita GNP levels than Turkey, but are ranked higher in the index as a result of better schooling and life expectancy rates.[3]

With a 112 percent increase in national income in the past thirty years, Turkey has made noteworthy gains in economic growth. However, a gender inequality index within the report shows the disadvantages of women in reproductive health, empowerment, and economic activity. Turkey's ranking in this index, 77 out of 138 countries, put it behind its neighbors.[4] These international reports and national surveys indicate that successful economic policy does not necessarily correlate with transforming the lives of citizens to attain equal and just living conditions. After almost a century of reforms bearing on women's rights, Turkish women are still far behind Turkish men, economically and socially; they also lag behind women in neighboring countries. As of 2010, participation in the labor force by females sixteen and older is only 21.6 percent; a figure that has gradually decreased over the past twenty years. These indicators demonstrate that there is something wrong with gender policy in Turkey. This regressive picture cannot be explained by the few years of AKP rule, as the secular opposition constantly alleges, claiming that the conservative social policies of the AKP government are responsible for the setbacks recently experienced by Turkish women.

These rather surprising international and national indicators induced the World Bank, with the collaboration of the Turkish State Planning Organization (SPO), to conduct research to evaluate the reasons behind the decline of the female labor force in the past two decades in Turkey.[5] According to their report, social attitudes toward working women have changed for the better: Turkish women are becoming more educated, they are getting married at a later age, and fertility rates are declining. It is thus surprising that the proportion of women who have or are seeking jobs should have decreased significantly. While the World Bank and the SPO have been trying to solve this so-called "Turkish puzzle," they have never even considered the relevance of the ongoing headscarf problem in Turkey as it evolved since the early 1980s, or its undoubted impact on the female labor force during the past twenty years. Instead, the major reasons for the decrease of women in the Turkish labor force cited in the report are urbanization, a decline in agricultural employment, and the cultural and economic barriers facing poorly educated women in urban areas. Women who wear headscarves are 60 to 72 percent of the female population in Turkey, and although the headscarf ban *de jure* was implemented only in relation to higher education institutions and government jobs, a spillover factor has had a tremendous impact on women's employment opportunities in the last two decades. No significant research is underway to assess the impact of the headscarf issue on social and economic conditions throughout Turkish society.

A recent study conducted by Turkish scholar Dilek Cindoglu attempts to fill this gap, connecting the headscarf ban with the decreasing employment of women during the last twenty years in Turkey as compared with OECD member countries and Muslim countries.[6] Her interviews with highly educated Turkish professional women offer a clear understanding of their frustrations with living in a society where they are constantly reminded that they are not fully accepted as participants. Moreover, according to the interviews, social resistance against women who wear headscarves does not only come from the secular section of Turkish society, but also from traditional, conservative social and business circles, which have their own resistance and reluctance to include these women in the public sphere. The headscarf controversy remains a fundamental question within Turkish society, and no fair and just solution can be envisioned for the near future.

Setting the Agenda in Europe: The Role of the Courts

The headscarf provides a litmus test for the Islamic presence and Islamic practices in the West, as each society determines whether it should be tolerated, recognized, accepted, and to varying degrees, regulated. Moreover, the headscarf controversy opened fresh discussions in France and Germany about the principles of secularism, state neutrality, and the limits of freedom of religion. Several questions have arisen: What would be the limits of secular principles in societies that gradually become more multiethnic and multicultural than they had been in the past? To what extent is Islam compatible with the value systems and lifestyles of Europeans? To what extent can the secularism principle be implemented to justify the removal of Islamic expressions from schools and public places? How do we approach a cultural heritage that is predominantly based on Christianity? Can we protect a cultural identity from non-European, public signs and still remain democratic, neutral, and secular? Philosophers, legal scholars, and politicians fiercely debated these questions when France created its 2004 law banning religious symbols from public schools, and when German *Länders* legislated headscarf bans for teachers after receiving indirect permission from the German Constitutional Court.

As long as immigration, multiculturalism, and religious and ethnic diversity pose challenges in the globally interconnected, twenty-first century world, matters related to cultural and religious expressions and their interpretations by judicial institutions will remain important. Whenever courts reach a judgment on a universal issue, it will have far reaching consequences. These consequences will cross geographic boundaries and have cross-cultural impact. The ECHR has had a significant impact on a wider environment through decisions that extend beyond the court's jurisdictional limits. Several countries in

Europe, specifically Belgium and the Netherlands, closely followed the decisions of the ECHR and member countries' high courts in seeking guidance for managing their own "problem." The *Sahin* case set a precedent of great relevance to other European countries. The court discreetly interpreted the "European consensus" on Islam in general and specifically on the headscarf issue in Europe. For many strictly secular Europeans and Turks who are fearful of Islam, the *Sahin* decision set just the "right tone." Only a few liberal human-rights organizations and scholars have offered criticism, noting the harmful impact of the court decision on human rights and secularism.

Immediate developments in member countries following the decision indicate that *Sahin* "succeeded" in paving the way for many regulatory arrangements in other European countries. For instance, the Danish Court's decisions on headscarf cases have not been very encouraging. In 2008, the Danish People's Party, a right-wing political party, began a campaign against Muslim female judges wearing the headscarf in Danish courts. The campaign resulted in the Danish Parliament debating a bill prohibiting judges from displaying any types of religious and political symbols. In 2009, "the headscarf bill" was submitted to the Danish Parliament reinforced by the claim that judges should be neutral and objective, and all religious and political symbols should be prohibited. Despite the objections of some politicians, the bill received support across the political spectrum and from the general public. Several legal institutions have criticized the bill, and the Danish Human Rights Institute has argued that it is redundant, since there are already laws in the Danish legal system that ensure a citizen's right to complain about a judge's objectivity. The critics further argue that the bill was directed mainly against the Muslim women's headscarf, and is therefore discriminatory, given that religious symbols such as the cross have not been an issue of contention in the past. The bill will have a negative impact on Muslim women in the legal profession in Denmark, including female Muslim law students.[7]

Moreover, after *Sahin*, the ECHR followed its own established jurisprudence on headscarf conflicts. Although the ECHR is supposed to consider each case in its particular context, as well as provide a "margin of appreciation" with respect to the legal arguments set forth by the country from which the case originated, the *Sahin* precedent made the principle of secularism a priority to justify interference with Article 9 of the European Convention on Human Rights, which guarantees freedom of religion. European countries interpreted the decision not only as a ruling on secularism or the Turkish headscarf controversy, but also as a guide for the treatment of Islamic practices in Europe and for dealing with gradually increasing Muslim immigrant populations in their country.

The Court Creates Its Own Standards for Christian Symbols

In 2009, the ECHR was confronted with another Article 9 case, this time a controversy concerning Christianity. In *Lautsi v. Italy* the lower chamber of the court decided that displaying the crucifix in Italian public schools was a violation of the Convention.[8] The children of a Finnish woman, Soile Lautsi, were taught in classrooms where a crucifix was displayed, but they were not required to attend Catholic religious ceremonies and could withdraw if they wished from religious education classes. When Ms. Lautsi's application to have the crucifixes removed was rejected by the school, she took her case to a local court. The Italian court decided that the crucifix was not merely a symbol of Christianity, it was also a ' "symbol of Italian history and culture, and consequently of Italian identity." She claimed that the presence of the crucifix contravened Article 9 (freedom of religion) and Article 2 of the First Protocol of the Convention (right to education).[9]

The court in this case had to deal with challenging problems of state neutrality, religious minorities, secularism, the question of collective identities within Europe, and the parameters of uniformity and diversity of states.[10] In keeping with its strong, secularly oriented jurisprudence, and to the distress of a majority of member countries, the court's lower chamber protected the secularism principle in its decision that the mere presence of a crucifix in the classroom constituted an "imposition" of a religious belief, and therefore breached articles 2 and 9 of the European Convention on Human Rights. The decision was considered "astonishing," in view of the past case law of the ECHR, and especially by not applying its "margin of appreciation" principle as in the headscarf decisions *Sahin v. Turkey* (2005), *Dogru v. France* (2008), and *Kervanci v. France* (2008). Some European legal scholars criticized the court for not implementing the margin of appreciation principle to give the decision power to the state in cases regarding the display of a religious symbol. These scholars blamed the court for imposing on the whole of Europe the French concept of compulsory state secularism in education, arguing that the decision would have stark consequences as a "distinctive part of Italian life and culture will have been brought to an end in order to satisfy the personal views of one individual and of a foreign court."[11]

The court declared that governments are also prevented from indirectly imposing certain beliefs, and that the presence of a crucifix in a classroom goes beyond the use of symbols in a given historical context.[12] The Italian government insisted, "there is no European consensus on how to effectively interpret the concept of secularism, so that states should have a wider discretion in the matter."[13]

On January 28, 2010, the Italian government, supported by twenty other European governments and the Orthodox Church of Greece lodged an appeal to the Grand Chamber of the ECHR. On March 18, 2011, the Grand Chamber overruled the lower chamber by fifteen votes to two, and granted that "by prescribing the presence of crucifixes in State-schools classrooms—a sign which, whether or not it is accorded a secular symbolic value in addition, undoubtedly refers to Christianity—the regulations confer on the country's majority religion preponderant visibility in the school environment."[14] But it declared: "A crucifix on a wall is an essentially passive symbol and…cannot be deemed to have an influence on pupils comparable to that of didactic speech or participation in religious activities."[15] Although the decision deserves to be evaluated carefully, it is safe to say that the ECHR was not able to keep its strong secular jurisprudence against the majority Christian culture in Europe.

Those who criticize the lower chamber's decision might be right about the necessity of a democratic decision-process and the importance of a public discussion before removing all religious symbols from schools in Europe, and may agree with concerns about the wider impact of court decisions regarding deep cultural and religious issues. What is disturbing in this argument, however, is why these critics were not equally sensitive to headscarf decisions when the court was freely making up its own mind, despite the fact that all of the headscarf cases involved different countries (Switzerland, France, and Turkey), each with different stances on religious freedom and secularism. The court's decisions on the headscarf and on the closure of an Islamic party in Turkey were based on almost identical "one size fits all" arguments.

As the crucifix is, in fact, important in defining Euro-Christian culture, and the court's secularism annoyed Europeans, why did the court's strong argument for secularity in the Turkish headscarf cases not bother Europeans? In an overwhelmingly Muslim country, the court's lecture on secularism and its almost political argument about the "peculiarity of Turkey's position" seems to have been acceptable to many legal scholars in Europe.

To give credit to the lower chamber of the ECHR, due to its earlier decisions, the court was constrained by how to interpret Article 9 and secularism without injuring its image of neutrality and impartiality. Therefore, the court had to follow its earlier approach, despite the fact that the case concerned

Christianity rather than Islam. It is easier to make a controversial court decision about Islam when its consequences will be experienced predominantly in non-Muslim countries. However, it is hard to go against the Christian culture in Europe without receiving significant criticism as an expression of societal disfavor.

The delicate issue in this situation is how to find the reasonable balance that is necessary for coexistence between majority and minority rights. In the Lautsi case, the court expressed its concern that it is not clear how the presence of a religious symbol linked to the culture shared by the majority of the population would ensure pluralism, which requires safeguarding in today's democratic society.[16] The court had failed completely to elaborate this assumption in previous cases when it decided on limitations on the rights of students who belong to minority religions. In *Lautsi*, the rights of children had been deliberately suppressed in the name of protecting and respecting the "national identity."[17] In headscarf cases, the rights of religious students had been denied in the name of protecting the "secular state."

Considering these cases, it is fair to say that the ECHR is chiefly a secular institution, despite its obligation to protect freedom of religion, one of the important individual rights set out in the Convention that gave birth to the court. The court preferred to rely on the margin of appreciation when a state's secularity principle makes it helpful, as in the cases arising in France and Turkey. In the lower chamber's judgment in the crucifix case, where secularity is not the country's main priority and therefore is not helpful, the court acted on its own jurisprudence rather than implementing the margin of appreciation This interpretation is more convincing than to insist that the court is biased against Islam, an accusation certainly deflected by the court's decision in the *Lautsi* case. The secular circles of Europe found the Grand Chamber's decision "highly regrettable." stating that, "It is to be hoped that the judges were not yielding to the huge political pressure put on them by Italy and what looked like a 'Holy Alliance' of Catholic and Orthodox states that backed its appeal and by the Vatican, the Greek Orthodox Church and other reactionary religious interests whose fears of losing influence in an increasingly secular Europe will have been abated by this judgment."[18] The European critics of the court in the *Lautsi* case should consider the wider picture of the European sensibility on judicial treatment of religion in the twenty-first century, rather than simply justify the presence or absence of a classroom crucifix on the grounds that it is a core European religious and cultural symbol. What if a Muslim girl with a headscarf were to attend this Italian school under the crucifix? Should the headscarf not be permitted, according to the ECHR's principles, because a headscarf is not a European cultural symbol?

From Headscarf to Burqa: What Is the Limit?

Apart from Turkey's headscarf ban in universities, which is likely to be eased in the near future, it is reasonable to conclude that the upcoming controversy in the West will focus on more excessive forms of religious dress, such as the *burqa/chador* or some form of face covering (*niqab*). In July 2010, for example, the generally tolerant Catalonian assembly in Spain narrowly rejected a proposed ban on the burqa in all public places. Yet, in France and Belgium, recent, similar proposals are becoming law with the support of parliamentary majorities.

The proposed French law imposes a fine of up to 750 Euros on anyone appearing in public "with their face entirely masked"; exemptions permit the wearing of masks on "traditional, festive occasions," such as carnivals. Stricter punishments are reserved for men who "force" their wives or daughters to wear full-body veils. The underlying idea is that the burqa, or niqab, is contrary to French traditions of freedom and women's rights laws. In the words of a French politician: "We can measure the modernity of a society by the way it treats and respects women."[19] Thus, the new legislation is intended to protect the dignity and security of women and to prevent the subjection of women to the most ruthless male domination. Unlike the 2004 headscarf ban law, *laïcité* is no longer the rationale. Instead, the proposed law directly attacks cultural differences on the one hand, and underestimates women's agency on the other. It does not even try to suggest a relatively acceptable argument for public safety and health.

Behind these arguments, French President Nicolas Sarkozy's statement is revealing: "A sign of subjugation...of debasement that is not welcome on French territory...In a secular country like France, the veil intimidates and alienates non-Muslims." Eminent European philosopher Slavoj Zizek rightly observes in his strongly critical statement: "One cannot but note how the allegedly universalist attack on the *burqa* on behalf of human rights and women's dignity ends up as a defense of the particular French way of life."[20] Moreover, Muslim women's sentiment and discomfort either against the burqa or in favor of it, is not even a matter of concern. Even more unspeakable statements come from the Swiss Justice Minister.[21] The minister Eveline Widmer-Schlumpf wants to ban facial veils, but exempts lavish-spending

Gulf tourists, as Switzerland is notorious for keeping the wealth of people regardless of regulatory constraints.

The discussion of the burqa is far from resolved at this point, as French deputies called the burqa a "veritable walking prison."[22] When protecting the comfort of the majority in a democratic society, the question is where to draw the line when considering the rights of minorities as well. It seems that Muslim women should be allowed to be full citizens and to participate in public life wearing religious dress if they wish, as long as this does not impose unnecessary burdens on others. When peace and safety are at stake, or the equal rights of others, some reasonable limits can be imposed on what people do in the name of religion.

In a recent article, Martha Nussbaum responds to arguments commonly made in favor of the proposed burqa bans that helps us understand whether Europeans treat all citizens with equal respect.[23] She claims that face coverings do not bother Europeans per se, but Muslim coverings cause havoc.[24] The security argument is not necessarily acceptable because of the many exceptions, inconsistent implementation, and highly sophisticated new security technologies that use eye recognition and fingerprints that are more accurate than face recognition.[25] However, the ECHR still uses this argument to deny equal access for Muslim women to public spaces.[26] Several national court decisions in Europe indicate that security and public health reasons are often used to deny Muslim women access to public spaces or to justify dismissals from jobs. The European courts, unlike the U.S. courts, are not interested in accommodating security needs and offering alternatives to Muslim women.

A widely used argument against the burqa is that it is considered a symbol of male domination that connotes the objectification of women. As Martha Nussbaum eloquently put it: "Society is suffused with symbols of male supremacy that treat women as objects. Sex magazines, nude photos, tight jeans—all of these products, arguably, treat women as objects, as do so many aspects of our media culture. And what about the 'degrading prison' of plastic surgery? Every time I undress in the locker room of my gym, I see women bearing the scars of liposuction, tummy tucks, breast implants. Isn't much of this done in order to conform to a male norm of female beauty that casts women as sex objects? Proponents of the *burqa* ban do not propose to ban all these objectifying practices. Indeed, they often participate in them."[27]

According to Nussbaum, the argument for banning the burqa to protect women from violence and promote equality of the sexes flatly ignores women's agency in Muslim society while knowing nothing of the cultural circumstances. This view is merely a restatement of the traditional, sexually discriminatory belief that women are incapable of making important decisions. Allowing that some Muslim women may be forced to wear a headscarf, to exclude all Muslim women wearing headscarves from public spaces, educational and employment opportunities is neither a necessary nor proportionate means of promoting sexual equality among Muslim women. Such policies may force them to remain at home, and ensure their continued dependence on male family members.

Unfortunately, European courts and the ECHR promote the popular Western assumption that the Muslim veil exhibits a woman's acceptance of or coercion into submission. The Chamber's judgment in *Sahin* proceeds on this assumption when referring to the ways in which women have been subjected to forced veiling in Iran and Afghanistan. Such a viewpoint indicates that the court saw the headscarf as an imposition by men as well as by religion, indicating submission and oppression, which would run counter to the idea of gender equality.[28]

The supposed coerciveness of veiling and the burqa extends to violence against women. All forms of violence and physical coercion in domestic spaces are already outlawed by domestic and international law, and should be enforced vigorously. It is a well-known fact that domestic violence does not only occur in Muslim societies, although Western media continually imply the opposite.[29] According to the U.S. Bureau of Justice Statistics, intimate partner violence made up 20 percent of all nonfatal violent crime experienced by women living in the United States during 2001. The National Violence Against Women Survey reports that 52 percent of surveyed women said they were physically assaulted as a child by an adult caretaker and/or as an adult by any type of perpetrator.[30] There is no evidence that Muslim families experience greater familiar violence. Given the strong association between domestic violence and the abuse of alcohol, it seems at least plausible that observant Muslim families will have less violence at home. Moreover, crimes like child prostitution and the trafficking of women are traditionally far lower in Muslim societies.

Nussbaum further asked, even if there were evidence that the burqa was strongly associated, statistically, with violence against women, could a government legitimately ban it on those grounds? Her analogy is the banning of college fraternities by some universities because fraternities are strongly associated with violence against women. A total governmental ban on a male drinking club would certainly be a bizarre restriction of associational liberty. She noted, "What is most important, however, is that anyone proposing to ban the *burqa* must consider it together with these other cases, weigh the evidence, and take the consequences for their own cherished hobbies."[31]

The arguments raised by Martha Nussbaum with regard to the burqa are even more persuasively applicable to the headscarf ban. Similar arguments were relied upon to justify a headscarf ban in several court cases. The real problem is not over the proper, legally permissible limits to body, head, or face coverings for Muslim women. The correct concern is how to accommodate, tolerate, and give equal citizenship rights to Muslim women. In the end, no matter which kind of veiling is the focus, the arguments are the same. If the true objective is the protection of women, is it not it better, as Nussbaum rightly put it, to give women decent education and employment opportunities that create genuine exit options from any home situation oppressive to women? Let's create ample opportunities, enforce laws that make primary and secondary education compulsory, accept and encourage women to seek higher education, and then see what women actually do. We must see them as persons with dignity, not as objects hidden beneath headscarves or more extensive veiling.

How to Live Well Together

In 2003, the late, renowned French-Algerian philosopher Jacques Derrida gave one of his last public speeches at the University of California, Santa Barbara.[32] While Derrida is perhaps best known among continental philosophers and literary theorists in the United States, his work on questions of religion has received growing critical attention in the past decade. Derrida's writings on religion address and question many of the fundamental concepts that inform the three Abrahamic religions and their cultures. His writings attempt to rethink the logic of religious difference and elucidate its significance for contemporary culture and society. As Derrida's work strongly suggests, such a rethinking today would need especially to address—beyond the assertions of ecumenism and mutual understanding—the wounds of irreconcilable differences. It is only through the avowal of such wounds that "living together," as Derrida asserts, might go beyond mere necessity and reach the space of a "living well together." The irreconcilable differences among the three monotheistic religions, as well other religious traditions, need to be articulated and clarified in order to yield the promises and chances of "living well together" today. There is no more appropriate ending to this inquiry, as our neighbors constantly remind us, that we have different values, different upbringings, different lifestyles, and different religions. Yet, as human beings, we share a common destiny and common DNA. We ought to learn to live well together, not only to tolerate or accept the "others" as coexistent, but celebrate the differences, even protect the "others" from dangers. Minorities are always vulnerable in times of political, social, or economic hardships. Muslims living in the West, like other minorities such as Christians in Muslim countries, Jews and Roma at different times in history, are in constant danger.

Today's menace of Islamophobia in the West is a culmination of racism and fear that creates more fear on both sides in a vicious cycle: "Kill them, including the children," is the way one official involved in U.S. homeland security described her understanding of Muslims' motives after a speech by Walid Shoebat at an antiterrorism training in Las Vegas in October 2010.[33] It is frightening that some public officials can easily accept such fear and hatred of Muslims. It is more frightening that a personality like Shoebat, an extreme anti-Islamic bigot and fearmonger, could be part of a training program for law enforcement officials and antiterrorism agents.

In 2011, as the tenth anniversary of the 9/11 terrorist attacks approached, reactionary groups in the United States agitated negative public sentiments against Islam. When Terry Jones, the pastor of a small church in Florida, threatened to burn a Quran, he drew national attention because the consequences of his act would cause potential danger to American soldiers in Muslim countries. The White House was able to stop him for a while, but on March 20, 2011, at the Dove World Outreach Center in Gainesville, Fla., he burned a Quran in a ceremony following a mock trial. Such a medieval act received a medieval response: thousands of miles away from Gainesville in northern Afghanistan, where thousands of demonstrators, angered by the burning of a Quran, mobbed a United Nations office in Mazar-i-Sharif and killed more than a dozen foreign workers.[34] The next day, nine people were killed and eighty-one injured in Kandahar as violent protests continued. In a global world, we all are in danger from fundamentalist acts, no matter where or who they are, or where and who we are. It is vitally important to speak up against hatred and injustices, especially vital if we do not belong to one of the minorities faced with immediate danger. German Pastor Martin Niemoller's famous statement against Nazi atrocities during World War II is still illuminating: "First they come for the communists, I did not speak out because I was not a communist. Then they come for the trade unionist, and I did not speak out because I was not a trade unionist. Then they came for the Jews, and I did not speak out because I was not a Jew. Then they came for me, and there was no one left to speak out for me."

Notes

CHAPTER I

1 Among many others, Fouad Adjami and Bernard Lewis are prominent writers who claim that the ideals of Islam and democracy are not easily compatible. For alternative views, see writings by John L. Esposito and Fred Dallmayer.

2 For a comprehensive comparison of headscarf debates in several European countries, see Dominic McGoldrick, *Human Rights and Religion: The Islamic Headscarf Debate in Europe* (UK: Hart Publishing, 2006).

3 For an example of religious human rights in various countries, see Johan D. Van der Vyver and John Witte, Jr., eds., *Religious Human Rights in Global Perspective: Legal Perspective* (The Hague, The Netherlands: Martinus Nijhoff Publishers, 1996).

4 For secularism in Turkey see Niyazi Berkes, *The Development of Secularism in Turkey* (New York: Routledge, 1998); and Andrew Davison, *Secularism and Revivalism in Turkey: A Hermeneutic Reconsideration* (New Haven, CT: Yale University Press, 1998).

5 As an example, French President Nicolas Sarkozy met with Pope Benedict in September 2008 and discussed how the strict *laïcité* of France is incompatible with the Christian identity of the country.

6 John R. Bowen, *Why the French Don't Like Headscarves; Islam, the State and Public Space* (Princeton, NJ: Princeton University Press, 2007).

7 Non-derogability needs further elaboration, especially in relation to this specific subject matter, because freedom of religion and belief, like any other rights, are potentially subject to restrictions for exceptional reasons.

8 On emerging Islamophopia in Europe, see Bruce Bower, *While Europe Slept: How Radical Islam is Destroying the West from Within* (New York: Doubleday, 2006); Ian Buruma, *Murder in Amsterdam: The Death of Theo Van Gogh and the Limits of Tolerance* (New York: Penguin Press, 2006).

9 Moustafa Bayoumi, "How Does It Feel to Be a Problem?" *Amerasia Journal* 69 (2001–02): 72–73.

10 Post-9/11 identification has a particular dimension that converges in this racialization "as the legitimacy of racial profiling, redeployment of old Orientalist tropes, and the relationship between citizenship, nation and identity." See Leti Volp, "The Citizen and the Terrorist," *UCLA L. Rev.* 49 no. 1575 (2002).

11 Krista Hunt and Kim Rygiel, eds., *(En)Gendering the War on Terror* (Aldershot, UK: Ashgate Press, 2006).

12 *Leyla Sahin v Turkey,* Application No 44774/98, Chamber, Fourth Section (2005) 41 8, [2004].

13 See Christopher McCrudden, "Human Rights and Judicial Use of Comparative Law," in *Judicial Comparativism in Human Rights Cases,* ed. Esin Orucu (London: The United Kingdom National Committee of Comparative Law, 2003), 1–22. The court's decisions that upheld a ban on a religiously oriented political party in Turkey call for a closer investigation of the objectivity of the judicial assessment: see *Refah Partisi (Welfare Party) and Others v. Turkey* Judgment, (Applications nos. 41340/98, 41342/98, 41343/98 and 41344/98)ECHR Grand Chamber; 13 February 2003.

14 Carolyn Evans, *Freedom of Religion Under the European Convention on Human Rights* (Oxford: Oxford University Press, 2001), 3.

CHAPTER 2

1 Director of the Austrian Cultural Forum, New York, May 2009, "It's Not About the Veil, It's About Us," http://www.acfny.org/fileadmin/useruploads/fdfx_image/Press_Texts/Veil/Director_Andreas_Stadler_-_Catalog_Text.pdf.

2 The military enacted a law specifying the clothing and appearance requirements of civil servants, male and female, at public institutions in a military-like fashion, ruling that female civil servants' heads must be uncovered. These regulations are still in force, yet neither observed nor enforced. See Mustafa Sentop, "The Headscarf Ban: A Quest for Solutions," SETA Foundation Policy Brief, No. 8, March 2008, http://www.setav.org. Unless otherwise noted, all translations are my own.

3 According to the TESEV (Turkish Economic and Social Studies Foundation) Report, 62 percent of Turkish women wear a headscarf. See Ali Carkoglu and Binnaz Toprak, "Degisen Türkiye'de Din, Toplum ve Siyaset" 2006, Istanbul [hereafter TESEV Report 2006] http://research.sabanciuniv.edu/5851/1/DegisenTRdeDin-Toplum-Siyaset.pdf. This figure went up to 69.4 percent according to the *Milliyet* daily newspaper's poll of March 12, 2007.

4 Addendum No. 16 to Higher Education Statute No. 2547, Article 44: "In institutions of higher education, laboratories, clinics, polyclinics, and corridors, contemporary dress style will be obligatory. It is only acceptable to cover the neck and head or wear a turban for religious reasons." See Statute No. 3511, *Official Gazette,* December 28, 1988.

5 E.1989/I, K. 1989/12, T. 7.3.1989, JCC 1991 at 25. The Court in its decision annulled the Higher Education Statute No. 2547, Article 44.

6 Ibid.

7 Below, I will discuss this decision, and its influence on decisions of both French courts and the European Court of Human Rights in relation to the headscarf decisions. See ch.3, 64–67.

8 Statute No. 3670, addendum to Higher Education Law, addendum 17, *Official Gazette*, Nr. 20679, Oct. 28, 1990.

9 This approach, by way of "interpretative refusal," has not normally been recognized in the Turkish constitutional system. See The Judgment 09/04/1991, E.1999/36, K. 1991/8, in AYMKD, 27, V. 1 Ankara 1993, at 285–323; or RG 31/07/1991, at 20946.

10 Article 13 of the well-known decision of the National Security Council (MGK) decrees that "Clothing practices that emerged against the laws and will direct Turkey to an outdated appearance must be prevented, and the laws and the decision of the constitutional court in this regard must be diligently observed." http://www.mgk.gov.tr/Turkce/kanun.html [Webpage discontinued].

11 Sevinc M., *Milli Guvenlik Kurulu ve 1997 Sureci* [National Security Council and the Period of 1997] (Istanbul: Birikim Yayinlari, 2000), 131.

12 E. 1997/I, K.1998/I, T.1.16.1998, JCC 1999 at 31.

13 Istanbul Regional Administrative Court, T. 19.08. 1998, E. 1998/47.

14 *Basortusu Raporu* [Headscarf Report], Insan Haklari ve Mazlumlar icin Dayanisma Dernegi, Ankara (2007), http://www.mazlumder.org/ing/. [Hereafter Mazlum Der, Report 2007.]

15 *Turkish Daily News*, Feb. 11, 2000.

16 See *Lamia Karabulut and Senay Karaduman v. Turkish Government*, Admissibility Decision on App. No. 18783/91, May 3, 1993.

17 See *Yanasik v. Turkey* (Jan.6, 1993, DR 74, at 14–28).

18 ECHR, *Sahin v. Turkey*, App. No. 44774/98, June 29, 2004 (chamber), and Grand Chamber Judgment of November 10, 2005.

19 *Sahin v. Turkey*, para.109.

20 AKP is the acronym of the party's Turkish name Adalet ve Kalkinma Partisi.

21 It is a good example of such irony that when the chief prosecutor applied to the Constitutional Court to dismantle the AKP, one of his complaints against Prime Minister Erdogan was the observation that his two daughters were not able to attend universities in Turkey due to the anti-headscarf characters of Turkish secularism.

22 The rallies were organized in 2007 by the Association of Ataturk's Thoughts (Ataturkcu Dusunce Dernegi) under the leadership of General Sener Eruygur, who was later found to have participated in the planning of several abortive coups against the AKP government (see the Ergenekon Affair section in this chapter).

23 The 2006 survey conducted by TESEV, a secular research institution, indicated that while 71.5 percent of the 64 percent of Turkish women who wear the headscarf do so because of a sense of religious duty, only 1.1 percent indicated that they wear it due to pressure from their male relatives. Approximately 90 percent of those women responded that even if women in their immediate environment gave up the

headscarf they would continue to wear it. In other words, the majority of women wearing headscarves do so out of conviction, with their own voices and their own desires. They are individually as well as politically independent. See Carkoglu and Toprak, TESEV Report 2006.

24 See Mustafa Akyol, "Islamization of Turkey: Not What You Would Think," *Turkish Daily News*, March 15, 2008. The suspicions range from extravagant conspiracy theories about the "hidden Taliban-like face of the AKP," or "the gradual Islamization of our daily lives" to the more reasonable concerns about the rise of moral conservatism in public life.

25 The recent court decision, arising from a complaint by an Alevi Turkish citizen to the ECHR, contended that religious education in Turkey does not give equal space to Islamic schools outside of the dominant Sunni tradition.

26 See Hilal Elver, "Lawfare and Wearfare in Turkey," *Middle East Report Online*, April 2008, www.merip.org/mero/interventions.

27 After the constitutional amendment, the division between university administrators and academics became harsher. Some university professors gave interviews to TV stations that even if students with headscarves were admitted to classrooms, they would submit failing grades regardless of their academic performance. Adnan Kucuk, "Rektorun Basortusunu Yasaklama Yetkisi Yok" October 15, 2010. See http://www.stratejikboyut.com/yazi/rektorun-basortusunu-yasaklama-yetkisi-yok-1072.html.

28 Warfare waged by using the law and legal institutions as weapons.

29 In February 19, 2008, the 110 members of the CHP applied to the Constitutional Court opposing the law (No. 5737, dated February 9, 2008) that amends Article 10 and Article 42 of the Turkish constitution. The reasoning contended several violations of the constitution, including the preamble. Articles 1, 2, 3, 4, 6, 7, 8, 9, 24, 42, 138, 153, and 174.

30 Mustafa Akyol, "The Empire Strikes Back via Juristocracy," *Turkish Daily News*, Jan. 24, 2008.

31 The majority of the judges, six out of eleven, voted in favor of closing, but the constitution requires a two-thirds vote for party closures. Moreover, ten of the eleven judges (except the Chief Justice Hasim Kilic, appointed by the President Abdullah Gul) found the AKP guilty of being a focus for antisecular activities. This resulted in a penalty taking the form of reduced public financial support, according to Article 69 (8) of the constitution.

32 Sabrina Tavernese and Sebnem Arsu, "Turkish Constitutional Court Calls Ruling Party Constitutional" *New York Times*, July 31, 2008.

33 For legal ramification of the decision see Hilal Elver, "The Headscarf as an Instrument of Political Suicide in Turkey," *Today's Zaman*, Nov.19, 2008.

34 There is an extensive literature on the emblematic significance of the headscarf debate in the Turkish political context, particularly in light of developments in 2008. Some of them can be found in a blog on secularism hosted by the Social Science Research Council, www.ssrc.org/blogs/immanent_frame.

35 "Come Without Headscarf," *Yeni Safak*, Nov. 7, 2003.

36 *Sex and Power in Turkey: Feminism, Islam and the Maturing of Turkish Democracy* (Berlin Istanbul: ESI European Stability Initiative, 2007), http://www.esiweb.org/pdf/esi.

37 Serif Mardin, a well-known scholar, in the *Radikal* daily newspaper, on February 11, 2008, warned about peer pressure on non headscarved students. His comments created a hot debate. See Ates Altinordu, "The Debate on Neighborhood Pressure in Turkey," American Sociological Association, www.asanet.org/.

38 "This time he wanted to show me a reference from Hadis that headscarf is not necessary. I was very clear as to how to respond to this. I did not say anything. I just left the room. Of course, I did give up my registration to the university"; "As soon as they saw my picture, they took me the notorious persuasion room. They started telling me that it was a pity that I was already in third year, since I would not be able to graduate if I didn't take off my headscarf. My family will be very upset with me, but it will be waste of time and money if I leave school. I told them, 'the owner of life is God; he makes the rules, and I follow God's rules.'" Ferhat Kentel, "Bir Direnisin Anatomisi: Teorinin Raconunu Bozan Basortusu," in *Ortulemeyen Sorun Basorusu,* ed. Neslihan Akbulut (Istanbul: Akder Yayinlari, 2008), 45.

39 "On the first day of school, I went to school as usual. There was almost one police officer for every two students. These were the special police team for terrorism, facing the thirteen- to eighteen-year-old school children carrying their books, but with nothing in their bags. They acted violently against us, threatened, insulted, humiliated and took us to the detention center. This year was more serious than the year before. There was a violent spirit in the air." Student testimony from Imam Hatip School, ibid., 46.

40 Ibid., 46.

41 "I started to university in 1975, got married in 1978. In 1980 my son was born. In 1981 I was expelled from university. In 1995, due to the amnesty I was accepted to my school, and I was graduated. However, my diploma from Marmara University, my master degree on Islamic Economics and Banking that I earned outside of Turkey did not help me to get a job at all. I was not able to be hired because of my headscarf." Ibid., 43.

42 Ibid., 29–63; Mazlumder and Hazar Foundation have published several narratives of personal testimonies. Nazife Sisman and Cihan Aktas also have written excellent books and articles on personal experiences.

43 The concept of "public space" was predominantly discussed by political philosophers such as Hannah Arendt and more recently Jurgen Habermas. According to Habermas, public space is a different domain from state power and economic forums where citizens can discuss, argue, cooperate, and exchange ideas in a democratic society. It is open to all who will be affected by such discussions. For a comprehensive discussion see Jurgen Habermas, *Structural Transformation of Public Sphere* (Cambridge, MA: MIT Press, 1991).

44 Seyla Benhabib, "Models of Public Space: Hannah Arendt, the Liberal Tradition and Jurgen Habermas," in *Habermas and Public Sphere*, ed. Craig Calhoun (Cambridge, MA: MIT Press, 1993).

45 First Administrative Court of Istanbul, 23/12/2003, 2002/1666 E; the Supreme Administrative Court (Danistay) section 8, 7/2/2005, 2004/3421 E, 2995/460 K, Association for Liberal Thinking (Liberal Dusunce Toplulugu) www.liberal-dt.org.tr.

46 According to a survey by the Hazar Foundation on women who wear a headscarf: 32 percent of these women never worked; 20.8 percent were not able to work because of their headscarf; 17.1 percent worked only in secluded areas, behind closed doors; 17.1 percent were hired for jobs that were lower than their education levels; 12.7 percent of headscarf-wearing women earned lower wages than equivalent female workers. Only 1.4 percent of the women surveyed reported no problems in the workplace because of their headscarves. See *Turkiyenin Ortulu Gercegi* (Istanbul: Hazar Vakfi Yayini, 2008), 86, Table 7.

47 Because of unsympathetic and hostile attitudes of secular feminists toward women who wear headscarves, the few who have economic and social power established NGOs to present their views and claim their constitutional rights. They have organized meetings, invited academics that are sympathetic with their views on the headscarf problem, and conducted public surveys to present scientific evidence confirming their social trauma, all the while claiming equal rights and an entitlement to equal participation in their own society as normal citizens. For more information about these NGOs see: See Hazar Vakfi available at www.hazargrubu.org; Akder (Ayrimciliga Karsi Kadin Haklari Dernegi), available at www.ak-der.org.

48 Ministry of Justice circular, see No. 152, T. 3, 10, 2000, No. 149; See "Turban Exile for Judge," *Vakit*, Oct. 20, 1999.

49 *Turkiyenin Ortulu Gercegi*, 90.

50 Ali Bulac, *"AIHM ve Basortusu"* [The EHCR and Headscarf], *Umran Dergisi*, 129 (May 2005): 33.

51 Fatma Benli, "Assessment of the Women Condition in Turkey According to the Statistics and the General Impacts of the Ban on Women," (Istanbul: Organization for Women's Rights against Discrimination, AKDER, 2007).

52 Mehmer Agar, the leader of another political party (DYP) "Would It Hurt If We Win Women Wearing Headscarf?" *Zaman*, Oct. 1, 2004.

53 Ayse Guveli, "Turkiye'de Basortusu Yasaginin Kadinlar Uzerindeki Sosyal, Ekonomik ve Psikolojik Etkileri," in *Turkiye'nin Ortulu Gercegi* [Turkey's Covert Reality] (Istanbul: Hazar Vakfi, 2007), 79.

54 Carkoglu and Toprak, The First TESEV Report on Religion and Society, 1999; AKART Akademik Arastirmalar Merkezi (Academic Research Center) Report, 2002; SAM (Sosyal Arastirmalar Merkezi) Social Research Center, 1997; *Milliyet*, daily newspaper research, 2003; *Gercek Hayat Dergisi* [Real Life Journal], 2003; MODUS Research Center 1997; TUSES, Turkiye Sosyal Ekonomi Siyasal Arastirmalar Merkezi (Turkey Social Economic Political Research Center) Report, 2004.

55 Carkoglu and Toprak, TESEV Report 2006.

56 Guveli, "Turkiye'de Basortusu Yasaginin Kadinlar Uzerindeki Sosyal," 91.

57 According to the report commissioned by the HAZAR Foundation, 1,112 interviews conducted by the ANAR (Ankara Social Research Center) with snowball research method in nine big city centers. See *Turkiye'nin Ortulu Gercegi.*

58 The *Rapporteur* of the European Parliament Report Emine Bozkurt corrected this dismissal in her second report asking for an investigation of discrimination against women with headscarves in Turkey. Cited in Guveli, "Turkiye'de Basortusu Yasaginin Kadinlar Uzerindeki Sosyal," 90.

59 "Not to be able to enter my school, taken to persuasion rooms, testifying in courts, insulted and told by judges, 'if I want to wear a headscarf I should leave Turkey, find a new country for myself,' made me speechless. I cannot explain my feelings by writing." Kentel, "Bir Direnisin," 46.

60 "Because I was wearing modest clothes and a headscarf, my Air Force officer husband was under surveillance. They were controlling our private lives. They were putting pressure on officers who had come to social gatherings with their wives, and headscarved wives were not able to enter any military buildings. Therefore, several times my husband received disciplinary fines... One of the tactics of the military to learn whether officers are religious was asking him to drink alcohol. If you do not drink alcohol, then you are a religious fundamentalist... Finally they expelled him from his position." Ibid., 47.

61 A high school teacher sued the ministry of education because of his assignment being shifted to a remote city. The reason was his wife's headscarf. The couple was divorced before the new appointment. The wife also lost her position as a teacher. The high court found legitimate the administrative decision because despite the divorce, they were sharing religious books. Ibid.

62 One of the High Administrative Court's decisions is remarkable in its belief that a woman cannot make a decision on her own about whether she would wear a headscarf. See: T.C. Danistay 5th chamber, E: 1999/4212; K. 1999/4325.

63 Carkoglu and Toprak, TESEV Report 2006.

64 Nilufer Gole, Yesim Arat, and a few others deal with the headscarf controversy from an objective point of view. A majority of secular writers are implicitly or explicitly against lifting the headscarf ban.

65 For an example of this oversight, see Zehra F. Kabasakal Arat, ed., *Human Rights in Turkey* (Philadelphia: University of Pennsylvania Press, 2007).

66 *Being Different in Turkey: Religion Conservatism, and Otherization,* Research Group: Binnaz Toprak, Irfan Bozan, Tan Morgul, Nedim Sener (Istanbul: Open Society Foundation, 2009), http://www.aciktoplumvakfi.org.tr/pdf/tr_farkli_olmak.pdf. [Hereafter *Being Different.*]

67 "In almost all of the towns we visited, one of the most distinct complaints of male students was about reactions against their beards, long hair, and earrings. The general remarks on that: 'Are you boy or girl?'" Ibid., 62.

68 "One particular problem they speak of—and to express it may help its solution—is that of 'going out.' They cannot go out freely. Even if they do go out, there is no place outside their homes where they find comfort: 'You can't go out simply and walk around freely in small town in Anatolia. What is a natural for a man is not considered natural for a woman. They look at you if you are beautiful; they look at you if you are not beautiful, too…If you attempt to look around, you are immediately labeled as looking for a man. Covering oneself is as much a practical necessity in provincial areas as it is a religious requirement. The provinces devour their women. That is, they devour the weakest among those who go against their rules.…Anatolia at night was like a sum of all those dull, lightless, deeply silent streets of womanless cities where womanless men lived. After sunset, cities were no more like cities; they looked more like military camps run under the toughest discipline." For more telling stories about women in Anatolia, see an excellent article by Arzu Cur, "Kadinlar Tasranin Yurtsuzlari" [Homeless in Periphery, Women], in *Tasraya Bakmak*, ed. Tanil Bora (Istanbul: Iletisim, 2006), 124–6.

69 The suicides were women who immigrated, from towns and villages to the city of Batman in Eastern Anatolia. This was interpreted as a consequence of starting to behave too liberally in the city. They committed suicide when they were unable to handle the gap between their expectations and the reality of their lives. Cited in report *Being Different*, 56.

70 Ibid., 58.

71 Ibid., 60.

72 According to the report a university student from Sivas (a city in Eastern part of Turkey) complained that she found it hard to go out without wearing a headscarf because of harassment. She said, "they are a different race; I do not consider them as members of the human race." Another testimony from a woman in Trabzon underlined that not only unveiled women were harassed by men in the streets but also veiled women. As cited by Arzu Cur, women prefer to wear the headscarf for religious reasons, but also have the hope of escaping from harassment in those cities where they can't feel comfortable in public spaces. The report concluded that this phenomenon requires further research. For two important studies supporting the argument that women from conservative families cover themselves in order to participate in public space, see Nilufer Gole, *Modern Mahrem* [Forbidden Modern] (Istanbul: Metis, 1993); Yesim Arat, *Rethinking Islam and Liberal Democracy: Islamist Women in Turkish Politics* (Albany, NY: SUNY Press, 2005).

73 A *carsaf* is a black, bulky dress that loosely covers the entire body and head, and leaves only the face showing. In Turkey, this traditional clothing represents very religiously conservative, orthodox Muslims. Research shows that the number of women who wear the carsaf has become so small in Turkey that they do not show up on a sample of the whole population. See: Carkoglu and Toprak, TESEV Report, 2006.

74 See "Female Students Wearing a Full Face Veil Will Be Barred from Syrian University Campuses," BBC News, July 19, 2010, www.bbc.co.uk.

75 "Turkiye de Basortusu Sorunu Yok" [There Is No Headscarf Problem in Turkey], *Haber Vakti,* June 11, 2010, interview with Kilicdaroglu, the new leader of the opposition party CHP, http.www.habervakti.com.

CHAPTER 3

1 Asli Bali, "Cultural Revolution as Nation Building: Turkish State Formation and Its Enduring Pathologies" (unpublished essay, February 2009), 8.

2 I will limit the use of the concept of modernity to the context of legal reforms. Therefore, cultural, historical, and political meanings of modernity will be discussed only in relation to legal reforms and secularism.

3 See June Starr, *Law as Metaphor: From Islamic Courts to the Palace of Justice* (Albany, NY: SUNY Press, 1992).

4 For more information about the impact of European law on the Ottoman Empire see Esin Orucu, "The Impact of European Law on the Ottoman Empire and Turkey," in *European Expansion and Law: The Encounter of European and Indigenous Law in 19th- and 20th-Century Africa and Asia,* eds. W. J. Mommsen and J. A. De Moore (Oxford and New York: Berg, 1992), 39.

5 Ergun Ozsunay, "A Model of Modernization through 'Reception of Foreign Law': Some Remarks and Evaluation of Ataturk's Legal Revolution," in *Ataturk's Legal Revolution* (Istanbul: Comparative Law Institute Press, 1983), 14 [in Turkish].

6 The property law principles of the *Mecelle* are still operative in today's Israel and Palestinian territory, especially in the area of property law and public-private land ownership.

7 For some of the important writings on this theme, see Daniel Goffman, *The Ottoman Empire and Early Modern Europe* (Cambridge: Cambridge University Press, 2002); Halil Inalcik, *Turkey and Europe in History* (Istanbul: Yayincilik, 2006); Kemal Karpat, *The Ottoman States and Its Place in World History* (Leiden: Brill, 1974); Selim Deringil, *The Well Protected Domains: Ideology and Legitimation of Power in the Ottoman Empire: 1876–1909* (New York: I.B. Taurus, 1998).

8 For the details of on this debate see Tarik Zafer Tunaya, *Islamcilik Cereyani* (Istanbul: Cumhuriyet Yayinlari, 1962), 95.

9 Ibid.

10 Alan Watson; "Legal Transplants and European Private Law," *EJCL* 4, no. 4 (December 2000).

11 Perry Anderson, "Kemalism," *London Review of Books,* September 11, 2008, www.lrb.co.uk/v30.n17/andeo1_html.

12 Esin Orucu, "Critical Comparative Law: Considering Paradoxes for Legal Systems in Transition," *EJCL* 4, no. 1 (June 2000).

13 In the early years of the Turkish republic, Turkish legal scholars acquired most of their training in universities in the countries where the adopted laws originated. Language training and translations were extensive. Some prominent German-

Jewish academics were given sanctuary in Turkey before and during the Second World War. Their presence contributed significantly to the development of the new legal system.

14 For detailed information about Turkey and the EU relationship see Hilal Elver, "The European Union Enlargement Policy: Turkey versus Eastern European Countries" in *Memoriam to Haluk Konuralp* (Ankara: Bilkent University Press, 2009).

15 It was this aspect of the Kemalist understanding of reform that later prompted a number of its critics on the left to label it as "Ataturkism of the wardrobe" and its critics on the right as "aping the West." For a discussion of early republican reforms and their meaning for the project of modernity in Turkey, see Binnaz Toprak, *Islam and Political Development in Turkey* (Leiden: Brill, 1981), 35–58.

16 Bali, "Cultural Revolution as Nation Building," 10.

17 Ataturk's own words defending his new laws on dress is an example of the important role Orientalism has played in the construction of modern Turkish society. See Yael Navarro-Yashin, *Faces of the State: Secularism and Public Life in Turkey* (Princeton, NJ: Princeton University Press, 2002), 18.

18 In 1924 the law of education (*Tevhid-I Tedrisat Kanunu*) closed religious schools and brought all educational institutions "under the strict control of the state."

19 See a detailed discussion on Westernized public and private spheres in Feroz Ahmed, *The Making of Modern Turkey* (London & New York: Routledge, 1993).

20 For a detailed interpretation on this see Asli Cirakman, "From Tyranny to Despotism: The Enlightenment's Unenlightened Image of Turks," *International Journal of Middle Eastern Studies* 2003: 53; O. Burian, "Turkiye Hakkinda Dort Ingiliz Seyahatnamesi" [Four English Travel Books about Turkey] *Belleten* 15, no. 58 (1951).

21 During the reform period, the Minister of Justice Mahmut Esat's speech in the Turkish Parliament when introducing legal reforms is a good example of this attitude. See "The Rationale for the Draft Bill of the Turkish Civil Code," in *Secularism and Revivalism in Turkey*, ed. Andrew Davison (New Haven, CT: Yale University Press, 1998), 197.

22 "The objects of Orientalist knowledge fulfill its prophesies by embracing it. The modern Orient, in short, participates in its own Orientalizing." See Edward Said, *Orientalism* (New York: Vintage Press, 1979).

23 For example, the Renaissance, according to Said, perpetuated negative images; the Ottomans represented a constant threat and danger to Christian civilization and thus were portrayed as the cruel enemy. Other observations of the time depicted the Ottoman Empire as exotic, barbaric, corrupt, and, most importantly, weak in comparison to the West.

24 See Sibel Bozdogan and Resat Kasaba, eds., *Rethinking Modernity and National Identity in Turkey* (Seattle: University of Washington Press, 1997), 3.

25 Walter F. Weiker, *The Modernization of Turkey: From Ataturk to the Present Day* (Holmes and Maier, 1981).

26 For an excellent comparison between the Turkish and Japanese cases that criticizes the Turkish model as compared with the Japanese one, see Binnaz Toprak, "Economic Development versus Cultural Transformation: Project of Modernity in Japan and Turkey," *New Perspectives on Turkey* 35 (2006): 85–127.

27 Ihsan Yilmaz, "Non-recognition of Post-modern Turkish Socio-legal Reality and the Predicament of Women," *British Journal of Middle Eastern Studies* 30, no. 1 (2003): 26. [Hereafter Yilmaz, "Non-recognition."]

28 Gulnihal Bozkurt, "The Reception of Western European Law in Turkey from the Tanzimat to the Turkish Republic, 1839–1939," *Der Islam* 75 (1998): 295.

29 Ihsan Yilmaz, "Muslim Law in Britain: Reflections in the Socio-legal Sphere and Differential Legal Treatment," *Journal of Muslim Minority Affairs* 20, no. 2 (2002).

30 Yilmaz, "Non-recognition," 28.

31 Steve Bruce, *Religion and Modernity* (London: Routledge, 1992); Jose Casanova, *Public Religion in the Modern World* (Chicago: University of Chicago Press, 1994), cited in Wilfried Spoth, "Multiple Modernity, Nationalism and Religion: A Global Perspective," *Current Sociology* 51, nos. 3/4 (May/July 2003): 265–286.

32 David Martin, *A General Theory of Secularisation* (New York: Oxford University Press, 1987), cited in Spoth, "Multiple Modernity," 269.

33 "Instead of assuming a general evolutionary trend toward secular nationalism and national identity, nationalisms and national identities combine in varying forms of religious and secular components." Ibid., 271.

34 Ibid., 285.

35 Ibid., 286.

36 Serif Mardin, *Religion and Social Change in Modern Turkey* (New York: Oxford University Press, 1989).

37 Bozdogan and Kasaba, *Rethinking Modernity*, 58.

38 Daniel Lerner's *The Passing of Traditional Society* and Bernard Lewis's *The Emergence of Modern Turkey* became classic texts in the modernization literature.

39 For a very nationalistic-secularist view of the Turkish elite see Adrien Wing and Ozan Varol, "Is Secularism Possible in a Majority-Muslim Country? The Turkish Example," *Tex. Int'l L.J.* 42, no. 1 (2006).

40 See Serif Mardin, "Projects as Methodology: Some Thoughts on Modern Turkish Social Science," in *Rethinking Modernity*, Bozdogan and Kasaba, 64–80.

41 Ferhat Kentel, "Bir Direnisin Anatomisi: Teorinin Raconunu Bozan Basortusu," in *Ortulemeyen Sorun Basortusu*, ed. Neslihan Akbulut (Istanbul: AKDER Yayinlari, 2008), 35.

42 P. Bordieu, *Distinction: A Social Critique of the Judgment of Taste* (London: Routledge, 1985).

43 Alev Cinar, *Modernity, Islam and Secularism in Turkey* (Minneapolis: University of Minnesota Press, 2005), 3.

44 For more detailed arguments see Dominic Sachsenmaier and Jens Riedel with Shmuel N. Eisenstad, eds., *Reflections on Multiple Modernities: European, Chinese*

and Other Interpretations (Leiden, 2002); Fred Dallmyer, *Dialogue Among Civilizations* (New York: Palgrave, 2002). Dilip Parameshwar Gaonkar, "On Alternative Modernities," *Public Culture* 11, no.1 (1999):1–18; S. N. Eisenstadt, "The Reconstruction of Religious Arenas in the Framework of 'Multiple Modernities,'" in *Millennium* 29, no. 3 (2000).

45 "Non-western varieties of modernity are not simply an adaptation of non-western civilizations to western modernity, but an incorporation of western impacts and influences in non-western civilizational dynamics, programs of modernity, and modernization processes." See Eisenstadt and Schluchter, "Early Modernities," *Daedalus*, 127, No. 3, (Winter 2000).

46 S. N. Eisenstadt, *The Political System of Empires* (New Brunswick, NJ: Transaction, 1994).

47 An article by Sabrina Tavernese that appeared in the *New York Times*, October 13, 2008, described young Turkish women who represent a new Muslim elite, who fight for not only their rights but also to overcome other injustices. They established a group called Young Civilians.

48 "Islam is unique among world religions, and Turkey is unique within the Muslim world…Turkey is the exception within the exception." See Ernest Gellner, "The Turkish Option in Comparative Perspective," in *Rethinking Modernity*, Bozdogan and Kasaba, 233.

49 Susanna Dokupil, "The Separation of Mosque and State: Islam and Democracy in Modern Turkey," *W.Va. L.Rev.* 105, No. 53 (Fall 2002):58.

50 Mustafa Erdogan, "Religious Freedom in the Turkish Constitution" *The Muslim World,* no. 3–4 (July–October 1999): 377–388.

51 Article 2, titled "Characteristics of the Republic," declares, "The Republic of Turkey is a democratic, secular and social state governed by rule of law…and based on the fundamental tenets set forth in the Preamble." Article 4 declares that "the provision in Article 2 on the characteristics of the Republic…shall not be amended, nor shall their amendment be proposed."

52 http://www.byegm.gov [webpage discontinued].

53 Preamble: "No protection shall be accorded to an activity contrary to the principles, reforms and modernism of Ataturk and, as required by the principle of secularism, there shall be no interference whatsoever by sacred religious feelings in state affairs and politics." Article 13: "any restrictions imposed by law cannot be in conflict with the letter and spirit of the Constitution and the requirements of…the secular Republic."

54 These reform laws include the Acts on the Unification of the Educational System (*Tevhid-i Tedrisat*); the adoption of civil marriage within the Turkish Civil Code, according to which the marriage act shall be concluded in the presence of a competent official; the Adoption of International Numerals; the Adoption of the Turkish Alphabet; and the Prohibition of the Wearing of Certain Garments.

55 See Decision No. 2001/2, available at http://www.anayasa.gov [webpage discontinued].

56 Levent Gonenc, "1982 Anayasasindaki 2001 yili Degisikilikleri" [The 2001 Amendments to the 1982 Constitution of Turkey], *Ankara Law School Review* 1, no. 89 (2004).

57 Erdogan, "Religious Freedom in the Turkish Constitution," 381.

58 Ibid., 382.

59 Ibid.

60 Ibid., 381.

61 Omer Taspinar, "The Old Turks' Revolt: When Radical Secularism Endangers Democracy," *Foreign Affairs*, November–December 2007, 119.

62 Almost 5 percent of the annual state budget goes to religious affairs.

63 The most important Sufi orders are Naksibendi, Kadiri, Rifai, Nurcu, Suleymanci, Isik, Mevlevi, Bektasi and Alevi. The Nurcu movement has recently become an important religious group nationally and internationally under the leadership of Fetullah Gulen, who owns television channels, newspapers (*Zaman*), and more that two hundred middle and high schools in Central Asia. His followers are dispersed on all continents. A long court case against him for antisecular activities ended recently. For detailed research on the Gulen movement see John Esposito and Hakan Yavuz, eds., *Turkish Islam and the Secular State: The Gulen Movement* (Syracuse, NY: Syracuse University Press, 2003).

64 The Ottoman Millet System was one of the most advanced governing systems of its day, and was an early example of "multiculturalism" and a positive model of religious tolerance. See Miguel Angel Rivera, "Turkey, an Example of Religious Tolerance for 500 years," *VOANews.com*, Sept. 20, 2005, http://voanews.com/; Stanford J. Shaw, "Turkey and the Jews of Europe during World War II," http://www.sefarad.org/publication/lm/043/6.html.

65 Religious minorities in Turkey have problems acquiring property to expand religious institutions and obtaining permission to renovate religious buildings, conduct missionary activities, and train new clergy. See: Niyazi Öktem, "Religion in Turkey," Brigham Young University Law Review, Volume 2, Number. 2 (2002): 371–403.

66 New Foundation Act, No. 5735, February 27, 2008. See *Official Journal of the Turkish Republic*.

67 Article 24 states: "Education and instruction in religion and ethics shall be conducted under state supervision and control. Instruction in religious culture and moral education shall be compulsory in the curricula of primary and secondary schools."

68 The Alevis are a branch of Shi'a Islam, a subethnic and cultural community numbering in the tens of millions. Alevism is closely related to the lineage of Bektasi Sufi, a thirteenth-century saint. Alevism is also closely associated with Anatolian folk culture.

69 See *Hasan & Eylem Zengin v. Turkey*, The ECHR Chamber, App. No. 1448/04, No. 5735, February 27, 2008.

70 In the past twenty years, the Constitutional Court dissolved the National Order Party (Milli Nizam), the National Salvation Party (Milli Selamet), the Welfare Party (Refah), and the Virtue Party (Fazilet) because of their antisecular activities.

71 On the court's selective judicial activism, its conservative attitude, and the strategic alliance between the judiciary and the military, see Ceren Belge, "Friends of the Court: The Republican Alliance and Selective Activism of the Constitutional Court of Turkey," *Law and Society Review*, 40:652–92.

72 Turkey is the champion of dismantling political parties among democratic societies. Since 1963, the Constitutional Court has closed twenty-four political parties. These parties ranged ideologically from communist or socialist to ethnically oriented Kurdish, to predominantly Islamic.

73 In January 1998, the Turkish Constitutional Court closed the Islamic Welfare Party for violating the secular nature of the republic. Almost overnight, the Virtue Party replaced the Welfare Party, retaining its leader Necmettin Erbakan.

74 See *Refah Partisi and Others v. Turkey*, No. 41340/98 (Eur. Ct. H.R. Feb.13, 2003), http://www.echr.coe.int/.

75 For detailed information about party closure see Ergun Ozbudun, "European Criteria for Party Closure" *Today's Zaman*, May 4, 2008.

76 The Court dissolved the National Order Party (Milli Nizam Partisi, 1971) on the grounds that it advocated compulsory religious education and the abolishment of Article 163 of the Turkish Penal Code on limits of freedom of speech; the Tranquility Party (Huzur Partisi 1983) on the grounds that its program advocated the addition of a ninth vowel to the Turkish alphabet and that it rejected the notion that Turkey's secularism resembles that of socialist countries; the OZDEP Party (1993) because of its view that religious affairs should be removed from the structure of Turkey's general administration.

77 Many AKP members had formerly belonged to the Welfare and Virtue parties, both dissolved by the Constitutional Court for advocating change in the secular order of the republic. Accordingly, Turkish seculars view the AKP a successor to those parties; however, there are significant differences in the party programs.

78 This was a poem written by a defender of secularism and major political philosopher of the Ataturk period, who had been heavily influenced by his ideas, cited in Hilal Elver, "Reluctant Partner," *MERIP*, 2005.

79 Saban Kardas, "The Turkish Constitutional Court and Civil Liberties: Questions of Ideology and Accountability," *Today's Zaman*, June 5, 2008.

80 November 28, 1925, No. 671 "Sapka Iktizasi Hakkinda Kanun."

81 December 3, 1934, No. 2596 "Bazi Kisvelerin Giyilemiyecegine Dair Kanun."

82 See chap. II.

83 The Court's decisions in 1998 and 1991. See chap II. Also see Semih Gemalmaz, *Turk Kiyafet Hukuku ve Tuban* (Istanbul: Legal Yayincilik, 2005),1287.

84 Mustafa Sentop, "Universitelerde Basortusu Sorunu" [The Headscarf Problem in Universities], in *Hukuk Dunyasi Dergisi* (Istanbul, 1997), 69.

85 AYMT: 21.10.1971, E.5376, in AMKD (*Journal of Constitutional Court Decisions*), 10, nr.64; AYMT:7.3.1989, E:1/12, AMKD, No. 146, p. 25 Cited in Fatma Benli, "Hukuki ve Siyasal Boyutlariyla Turkiye'de Basortulu Kadinlara Yonelik Ayrimcilik Sorunu," in *Ortulemeyen Sorun Basortusu*, ed. Neslihan Akbulut (Istanbul: Akder Yayinlari, 2008), 169.

86 Ibid.

87 Bulent Aras and Sule Toktas, "War on Terror and Turkey," *Third World Quarterly* 28, no.5 (2007): 1033–1050.

88 Erdogan, "Religious Freedom in the Turkish Constitution."

CHAPTER 4

1 Winnifred Fallers Sullivan, *The Impossibility of Religious Freedom* (Princeton, NJ: Princeton University Press, 2005).

2 Cindy Skach, "Sahin v. Turkey," *Am. J. Int'l L.* 100, no. 196 (2006).

3 The European Convention for the Protection of Human Rights and Fundamental Freedoms entered into force September 3, 1953, 213 U.N.T.S. 222, Eur. T.S. No.5. It was opened for signature in 1950 within the Council of Europe, which at that time included ten member states. By February 2009, it has been ratified by forty-seven states.

4 For more detailed information and the court's jurisprudence on religious freedom see Carolyn Evans, *Freedom of Religion under the European Convention on Human Rights* (New York: Oxford University Press, 2001).

5 Andrew Drzemczweski, *European Human Rights Convention in Domestic Law: A Comparative Study* (New York: Clarendon Press, 1983); J. G. Merrills, *The Development of International Law by the European Court of Human Rights* (Manchester: Manchester University Press, 1988).

6 Laurence Helfer and Anne-Marie Slaughter, "Toward a Theory of Effective Supranational Adjudication" *Yale Law Journal* 107, no. 2 (1997): 273–391.

7 Andrew Moravcsik, "The Origins of Human Rights Regimes: Democratic Delegation in Postwar Europe," *International Organizations* 54, no. 2 (2000): 217–52.

8 Steven Greer, *The European Convention on Human Rights: Achievements, Problems and Prospects* (Cambridge: Cambridge University Press, 2006), 173.

9 See generally Evans, *Freedom of Religion under the European Convention on Human Rights*, 117–23; Paul Taylor, *Freedom of Religion: UN and Human Rights Law and Practice* (Cambridge: Cambridge University Press, 2005), which criticizes the ECHR's lack of a global approach to religious issues and its consequent difficulty in dealing appropriately with minority religions. Cited in Carolyn Evans, "The 'Islamic Scarf' in the European Court of Human Rights," 7 *Melbourne Journal of International Law*, 52 (2006).

10 Isabella Rorive, "Religious Symbols in the Public Space: In Search of a European Answer," 2672, *Cardozo Law Review* 30, no. 6 (2009): 2669–98.

11 Julie Ringelheim, "Rights, Religion and the Public Sphere: The European Court of Human Rights in Search of a Theory?" in *Is There a Conflict Between Religion and the Secular State,* eds. L. Zucca and C. Ungureanu (2009) cited in Rorive, "Religious Symbols," 2673.

12 For the names of the cases, see Rorive, "Religious Symbols," 2676.

13 Ibid.

14 *El Morsli v. France,* App. No. 1558.06 (ECHR 2008). Non-admissibility decision.

15 *Dahlab v. Switzerland,* App. No. 42393/98, (ECHR, 2001).

16 Ibid., 456.

17 Despite ultimately finding against the applicant, the domestic court gave a far more detailed and thoughtful consideration to the issues than the ECHR. The summary of the Swiss judgments is significantly longer that the operative part of the ECHR's reasoning. Cited in Evans, "The 'Islamic Scarf' in the European Court of Human Rights," 59.

18 The ECHR's reference to the vulnerability of children in the early years of school gives rise to several questions. While the court focuses on this issue as evidence that a teacher's headscarf might have a proselytizing effect, it seems relevant to ask what message is being sent to curious and vulnerable children when their teacher is dismissed for wearing Muslim clothing. Such children might well ask where their teacher has gone and what she had done wrong. Ibid., 64.

19 The general case law of the ECHR with respect to far more overt forms of proselytism underlines the weakness of the ECHR's use of proselytism to support its decision in *Dahlab.* Dahlab did not even tell her students she was Muslim. A prominent case in this area is *Kokkinakis v. Greece,* an appeal by a couple who were Jehovah Witnesses charged with proselytism by the Greek government. The ECHR held that their conviction was a breach of Article 9 of the Convention. The court's conclusions in the two cases were significantly different. According to Carolyn Evans "the wording used by the Court in *Kokkinakis,* to distinguish between permissible and unacceptable forms of proselytism, is indicative of the difficulty that the Court has when dealing with non-Christian religions." For a more detailed discussion of the ECHR's failure in *Dahlab* in relation to proselytizing, see 62–64.

20 Ibid., 60.

21 Rorive, "Religious Symbols," 2680.

22 ECHR, *Sahin v. Turkey,* App. No. 44774/98, June 29, 2004 (chamber), and Grand Chamber Judgment of November 10, 2005.

23 See *Sahin* 2004, para.12.

24 *Sahin* judgment 2004, paras. 14–28.

25 Sahin alleged that a headscarf ban violated her rights and freedoms under articles 8 (right to privacy), 9 (freedom of thought, conscience and religion), 10 (freedom of expression), and 14 (freedom from discrimination) of the Convention, and Article 2 of its Protocol No.1 (right to an education).

26 No separate question arose from the article in conjunction with articles 8, 10, or 14, or Article 2 of Protocol No 1. See *Sahin* 2004, para.117.

27 Rorive, "Religious Symbols," 2682.

28 "In those circumstances, it cannot be denied outright that the wearing of a headscarf might have some kind of proselytizing effect, seeing that it appears to be imposed on women by a precept which is laid down in the Koran and which, as the Federal Court noted, is hard to square with the principle of gender equality. It therefore appears difficult to reconcile the wearing of an Islamic scarf with the message of tolerance, respect for others and, above all, equality and non-discrimination that all teachers in a democratic society must convey to their pupils." See *Dahlab* judgment, 463.

29 In *Refah Party v. Turkey*, 2003, the Turkish government was challenged in the ECHR over the ban it imposed on an "Islamic extremist party" whose political aims, if elected, were alleged to include the imposition of Sharia law and the renunciation of the democratic process.

30 See para. 115 of the *Sahin* decision: "[as] the Turkish courts state…this religious symbol has taken on political significance in Turkey in recent years…The Court does not lose sight of the fact that there are extremist political movements in Turkey which seek to impose on society as a whole their religious symbols and conception of a society founded on religious precepts."

31 See para.136: "it is crucial importance that the Convention is interpreted and applied in a manner, which renders its rights practical and effective, not theoretical and illusory. Moreover, the convention is a living instrument which must be interpreted in the light of present-day conditions."

32 *Sahin*, para. 78.

33 Semih Gemalmaz, *Turk Kiyafet Hukuku ve Turban* [Turkish Dress Codes and Turban] (Istanbul: Legal yayincilik, 2005), 1214.

34 *Sahin*, para. 88.

35 In assessing the way in which internal university rules should be imposed, the ECHR states, "by reason of their direct and continuous contact with the education community, the university authorities are in principle better placed than an international court to evaluate local needs and conditions or the requirements of a particular course." See *Sahin* judgment, para. 121.

36 Ibid., paras. 89–98.

37 Ibid., paras. 100–123.

38 Ibid., paras. 104–108.

39 No provision of the Convention mandates this principle, but judges have characterized the ECHR's subsidiary jurisdiction as both a practical limitation as well as a philosophical preference. Therefore the margin is "variable in the sense that the closer you get to the core values of democracy, the narrower the margin will be." In this sense, the margin of appreciation doctrine resembles the American idea of a standard review; when the ECHR margin of appreciation is narrowed,

the effect is similar to the heightening of an American court's level of scrutiny. See Willi Fuhrmann, "Perspectives on Religious Freedom from the Vantage Point of the European Court of Human Rights," *Byrman Young University Law Review* 829 (2000).

40 Para. 109: "Where questions concerning the relationship between State and religions are at stake, on which opinion in a democratic society may reasonably differ widely, the role of the national-decision making body must be given special importance...As the comparative law materials illustrate in view of diversity of the approaches taken by national authorities on the issue, it is not possible to discern throughout Europe a uniform conception of the significance of religion in society, and the meaning or impact...Rules in this sphere will consequently vary from one country to another according to national traditions and the requirements imposed by the need to protect the rights and freedoms of others and to maintain public order."

41 *Sahin*, para. 110.

42 Ibid.

43 ECHR Chamber Judgment para. 108; and the Grand Chamber Judgment, para.115.

44 Jeremy Gunn, "Fearful Symbols: The Islamic Headscarf and the European Court of Human Rights," 18, http//www.strasbourgconference.org [webpage discontinued].

45 Sahin did not assert that she felt pressured to wear the headscarf, and indeed both chambers accepted her submission that her choice to wear a headscarf was completely voluntary. See *Sahin* judgment, para. 14.

46 According to Gunn, the court referred to proportionality only twice in its entire opinion, but both references simply state that this is an issue that should be analyzed. See Gunn, "Fearful Symbols," 26.

47 Para. 117.

48 In the United States, the Supreme Court has likewise indicated that courts should not take into account or decide whether or not a practice is "central" to an individual's religion. "It is not within the judicial ken to question the centrality of particular beliefs or practices to a faith, or the validity of particular litigants' interpretations of those creeds." See *Employment Div. v. Smith*, 494 U.S. 872, 887 (1990).

49 No consensus exists among Muslims about wearing the headscarf as a religious duty for women. The prime minister of Turkey criticized the ECHR for arriving at its decision in *Sahin* without relying on "theologians" to judge the relevance of Islamic religious duty. Turkish newspapers made it a big issue, interpreting the prime minister as having wanted a religious person (*ulema*) in the court. See *Milliyet Daily Newspaper*, December 13, 2005.

50 *Sahin* judgment, dissenting opinion, para. 12.

51 Ibid., para.120.

52 Gunn "Fearful Symbols,"; Jennifer Westerfield, "Behind the Veil: An American Legal Perspective on the European Headscarf Debate," *American Journal of Comparative Law* 54 (3): 641.

53 Benjamin D. Bleiberg, "Unveiling the Real Issue: Evaluating the European Court of Human Rights Decision to Enforce the Turkish Headscarf Ban in Leyla Sahin v. Turkey," *Cornell Law Review* 91 (2005): 129–162.

54 Talvikki Hooper, "The Leyla Sahin v. Turkey Case before the European Court of Human Rights," *Chinese Journal of International Law* 5, no.3 (2006): 719–722.

55 Ample writings about modern headscarf trends indicate that wearing the headscarf may well have emerged for reasons quite distinct from the veiling of traditional Turkey, but it is by no means a flag of religious fundamentalism. See Nilufer Gole, *Modern Mahrem* (Istanbul: Metis, 1996).

56 77.3 percent of the Turkish population favors the secular republic despite positively identifying themselves as Muslim, and 77 percent of households in Turkey include at least one woman who wears some form of headscarf. See: "Turkey: Headscarf Ban Stifles Academic Freedom," June 29, 2004, Human Rights Watch Report: http://www.setav.org/ups/dosya/24491.pdf.

57 "[A]ppears to be imposed on women by a precept which is laid down in the Quran." See *Dahlab*, para. 449.

58 Evans "The 'Islamic Scarf' in the European Court of Human Rights," 65.

59 Ibid., 52.

60 Ibid.

61 *Sahin*, Chamber judgment, para.107.

62 Jeremy Gunn, "Religious Freedom and *Laïcité*," *BYU Law Review*, no. 2 (2004): 422.

63 The court referred to the decision of the Turkish Constitutional Court of 1989: "This notion of secularism to be consistent with the values of underpinning the Convention. It finds that upholding that principle, which is undoubtedly one of the fundamental principles of the Turkish State which are in harmony with the rule of law and respect for human rights, may be considered necessary to protect the democratic system in Turkey." See para. 114.

64 Westerfield, Behind the Veil, 639; see also Carolyn Evans, Jeremy Gunn, Tore Lindholm, and many others. According to Gunn, the ECHR's unqualified assumption that Turkey's headscarf ban, as well as its constitutional principles of secularism and equality, arose as the result of a democratic process, at best "systematically misleads the reader." "Fearful Symbols," 610.

65 Elizabeth Chamblee, "Rhetoric or Rights? When Culture and Religion Bar Girls' Right to Education," *Virginia Journal of International Law* 44 (2004): 1072.

66 *Dogru v. France,* App. No. 27058/05; *Kervanci v. France,* App. No. 31645/04. See Registrar of the ECHR, press release, December 4, 2008.

67 It is interesting that the ECHR borrowed the word "ostentatious," which was largely used during the 1990s by the Conseil d'Etat and was replaced by "conspicuous" in official documents subsequent to the work of Stasi Commission on the question of *laïcité*. See Rorive, "Religious Symbols," 2686.

68 "Pupils wearing signs in schools by which they manifest their affiliation to a particular religion is not in itself incompatible with the principle of secularism...but

that this freedom should not allow pupils to display signs or religious affiliation, which inherently, in the circumstances in which they are worn, individually or collectively, or conspicuously or as a means of protest, might constitute a form of pressure, provocation, proselytism or propaganda, undermine the dignity of freedom of the pupil or other members of the educational community, compromise their health or safety, disrupt the conduct of teaching activities and the educational role of the teachers, or, lastly, interfere with order in the school or the normal functioning of the public service." *Conseil d'Etat*, no. 346.893, Nov. 27, 1989, http://www.counseil-etat.fr/ce/rappor/index_ra_cg03_shtml.

69 *Dogru*, para. 51.

70 Ibid., para. 21.

71 Ibid., paras. 23–32.

72 Ibid., para. 37.

73 Ibid., para. 37.

74 On the connection and complexities of the two cases, see Gabriel Moens, "The Action–Belief Dichotomy and Freedom of Religion," *Sydney Law Review* 12, no. 195 (1989).

75 *Dogru*, para.72.

76 *Fatima El Morsli v. France*, App. No.15585/06 (Eur. Ct. H.R. 2008) is available at http://cmiskp.echr.coe.int/tkp197/.

77 Rorive, "Religious Symbols," 2695.

78 Admissibility decision, *Mann Singh v. France*, App. No. 24479/07. See ECHR press release, November 27, 2008.

79 Rorive, 2687.

80 Ibid.

81 Some examples: In February 2008, Pepsi Co. launched a promotional campaign that invited its Turkish customers to send their photos to the company, which would select the best picture as the winner. However, they specifically asked participants not to send photos with headscarves, which would disqualify them. In July 2007, the local head of the Republican Peoples Party in the Avcilar district complained to the District Election Committee that three ballot-box observers were wearing headscarves. They were subsequently removed from their duties. In April 2006, a woman wearing a chador was not allowed to enter an official building to pay her estate tax. For details see "Turkey's Failure to Implement Its Responsibilities Towards Headscarved Women," (Islamic Human Rights Commission Report, October 2009), www.iConvention.org.

82 In another incident, in March 2006, Dr. Aysu Say, head of the Pediatrics Department in Zeynep Kamil Hospital, refused to admit a four-month-old baby to the hospital because her mother wore the headscarf, allegedly causing the child's death. She received only a warning for her action. Ibid.

83 In December 2007 at the Cerrahpasa Medical Faculty, the mother of a twenty-two-month-old baby Z.K. was forced to leave her baby alone while he was anesthetized

before an operation and also afterward. The doctors would not allow her to see her baby because she wore the headscarf. Her suggestion that she cover her head with surgical scrubs, thereby concealing her headscarf, was turned down. In December 2008, Saziye Gerede responded to a blood donation appeal by Hacettepe Hospital in Ankara. When she arrived at the hospital, duty Nurse Zubeyde insulted her headscarf, saying that "this place is not a mosque, don't come here like this," and refused to draw her blood. Ibid.

84 Although Turkey had ratified the Convention back in 1954, it accepted Article 25 of the Convention, which allows individuals to file complaints against the state, only in 1987, when it formally applied for EU membership. Toward the same end, Turkey recognized the jurisdiction of the ECHR on December 26, 1989. Since then, more than five thousand applications from Turkey have flooded the court's docket. Statistical information is available at http://www.echr.coe.int.

85 Turkey has responded in more cases involving in right to life (Article 2), torture (Article 3), liberty and security (Article 5), fair trials (Article 6), free expression (Article 10), free association (Article 11), and right to an effective remedy before a national authority (Article 13). According to statistics of the ECHR, between 1995–2004, there were only five judgments about Article 9, and there was only one adverse judgment. For more information on this matter see Thomas W. Smith, "Leveraging Norms: The ECHR and Turkey's Human Rights Reforms," in *Human Rights in Turkey*, ed. Zehra Arat (Philadelphia: University of Pennsylvania Press, 2007), 262–274.

86 In *Kalac v. Turkey* (App. No. 20704/92, judgment July 1, 1997) the court upheld the Supreme Military Council's decision to dismiss a judge in the Turkish Air Force who allegedly, "revealed that he had adopted unlawful fundamentalist opinions" through his conduct and attitude. The application was denied in *Tepeli v. Turkey* (App. No. 31876/96, September 11, 2001), in which forty-one former members of the armed forces claimed they had been purged for their religious beliefs. In *Erdem v. Turkey* (App. No. 26328/95, September 11, 2001), the court blocked approximately twenty petitions involving military personnel and their religious observance.

87 See the judgment, 09/04/1991, E. 1990/36, K. 1991/8, in AYMKD, 27, V.1 Ankara 1993, at 285–323; or RG, 31/07/1991, at 20946.

88 See *Karaduman* and *Refah* judgments.

89 See *Sahin* Chamber Judgment, paras. 31, 108, 109.

90 *The Refah Party and Others v. Turkey* (No. 41340/98, 41342/98, 13/02/2003).

91 Gemalmaz raises these three arguments, but he disagrees that the ECHR was right not to investigate the *Sahin* judgment under Article 10. See *Turk Kiyafet Hukuku ve*, 1303.

92 In *Dahlab*, which characterizes the headscarf as a "powerful external symbol...imposed on women by a religious precept," that is "hard to square with the principle of gender equality." Para. 10.

93 *Sahin*, dissenting opinion, para.17.

94 Skach, "Sahin v. Turkey," 193.

95 See "The Amendment to The Higher Education Law," No. 2547, article 44, *Official Gazette*, 20032, December 27, 1988.

96 See *Sahin* Chamber decision, para. 110.

97 *Sahin*, para. 93.

98 "Tekaya ve zevayanin seddine be ilmiye sinifi ile kisvesine ve bilimum Devlet memurlarinin kiyafetine dair Kararname." This 1925 decree, cited in Gemalmaz, *Turk Kiyafet Hukuku ve*, bans any religious dress worn on streets (open areas) and in common places.

99 Gemalmaz lists all newspaper articles in favor of and against the headscarf ban that specifically addressed the public space debate, asserting that among Turkish writers and academics there was no deep knowledge about what is meant by "public space." See *Turk Kiyafet Hukuku ve*, 1086–1124.

100 Susan B. Rottman and Myra Marx Ferree, "Citizenship and Intersectionality: German Feminist Debates about Headscarf and Antidiscrimination Laws," *Social Politics* 15, no. 4 (2008): 481–513.

101 *Sahin,* dissenting opinion, para. 2.

102 Ibid., para. 3.

103 Ibid.

104 In earlier judgments, e.g., *Serif v. Greece* (No. 38178/97. 14/12/1999) and *Hassan v. Bulgaria*, (30985/95. 26/10/2000), the ECHR protected a Muslim minority against a Christian majority.

105 *HRW Report*, 24.

106 See conclusion in chap. 9 of this book, 192-195.

107 *Senay Karaduman v. Turkey* (Commission decision, 03/05/1993); *Yanasik v. Turkey* (Commission decision, 06/01/1993); *Kalac v. Turkey* (ECHR inadmissibility decision, 23/06/1997); *Dal and Ozen v. Turkey* (ECHR inadmissibility decision, 03/10/2002); *Akbulut v. Turkey* (ECHR inadmissibility decision, 06/02/20030); *Dahlab v. Switzerland* (2004); *Dogru v. France* (December 2008).

108 Bakir Caglar, *Insan Haklari Avrupa Sozlesmesi Hukuknda Turkiye* [Turkey in European Human Rights Law] Turkiye Bilimler Akademisi Forumu, no.6 (Ankara: Tubitak Matbaasi, June 2002), 50.

CHAPTER 5

1 Yasemin Karakasoglu, "Anti-Islamic Discourses in Europe: Agents and Contents," (paper presented at the conference "Muslims in Europe and in the United States: A Transatlantic Comparison," Harvard University, December 15–16, 2006), http://www.ces.fas.harvard.edu/conferences/muslims/muslim_program.html.

2 Olivier Roy, *Secularism Confronts Islam* (New York: Columbia University Press, 2007), 3.

3 Joan Wallach Scott, *The Politics of the Veil* (Princeton, NJ: Princeton University Press, 2007), 60.

4 Ibid.

5 People like Hans Peter Raddats in Germany, Oriana Fallaci in Italy, or Caroline Fourest and Michel Houellebeq in France, or perhaps Poly Toynbee in Britain are among them. Cited in Karakasoglu, "Anti- Islamic Discourse," 5.

6 Ibid.

7 Ibid.

8 Ibid.

9 Ibid.

10 Ibid.

11 Ibid.

12 Ibid.

13 Ayaan Hirsi Ali, Necla Kelek, and Chardott Djavann. Ibid.

14 Ibid.

15 A recent article begins: "What do the controversies around the proposed mosque near Ground Zero, the eviction of American missionaries from Morocco earlier this year, the minaret ban in Switzerland last year, and the recent burqa ban in France have in common? All four are framed in the Western media as issues of religious tolerance. But that is not their essence. Fundamentally, they are all symptoms of what the late Harvard political scientist Samuel Huntington called the 'Clash of Civilizations,' particularly the clash between Islam and the West." Hirsi Ali goes on to attack President Obama's famous speech in Cairo as futile, because he hopes for a new understanding between the United States and the Muslim world. She blames Turkey because, jointly with Brazil, it tried to "dilute the American led effort to tighten sanctions against Iran," and for Prime Minister Erdogan's domestic politics. See "How to Win the Clash of Civilizations: The Key Advantage of Huntington's Famous Model Is That It Describes the World as It Is—Not as We Wish It to Be," *The Wall Street Journal,* August 18, 2010.

16 Karakasoglu, "Anti- Islamic Discourse."

17 Marcel Maussen, "Representing and Regulating Islam in France and in the Netherlands," (paper presented at the conference "Muslims in Europe and in the United States: Transatlantic Comparison," Harvard University, December 15–16, 2006), http://www.ces.fas.harvard.edu/conferences/muslims/muslim_program.html.

18 On April 30, 2010, Belgium's lower house voted to ban Muslim women from wearing veils that fully cover their faces. On June 30 in the UK, a member of Parliament introduced a Face Coverings (Regulation) Bill that would make it illegal for anyone to cover his or her face in public. And on July 6, the French Parliament began debating legislation that would outlaw the wearing of burqas and niqabs in public places. In July 2010, the Catalonia assembly narrowly rejected a proposed ban on the Muslim burqa in all public places, reversing a vote of the week before in Spain's upper house of Parliament supporting the ban.

19 Pew Research Center, "Widespread Support for Banning Full Islamic Veil in Western Europe," July 8, 2010. The opinion poll took place from April 7 to May 8, 2010, http://pewresearch.org/pubs/1658/widespread-support-for-banning-full-islamic-veil-western-europe-not-in-america?src=prc-latest&proj=forum.

20 Far-right politician Geert Wilders first made this proposition in the Netherlands in October 2005. Accepted by a majority in the Parliament, the proposal was addressed to the minister of Integration and Alien Affairs, political hardliner Rita Verdonk. See Maussen, "Representing and Regulating Islam," 4.

21 Standing Committee of Experts on International Immigration, Refugee and Criminal Law of the Netherlands. See also Dutch Equal Treatment Commission, Ibid., 6; "Niqabs and Headscarves in Schools," April 2003, http://www.cgb.nl/dowloadables-en.php.

22 See "Beyond a Planned Dutch Ban," *Economist*, November 25, 2006.

23 Ibid.

24 Roy, *Secularism Confronts Islam*, xi.

25 Ibid.

26 For a thorough analysis, see Ian Buruma's *Murder in Amsterdam* (New York: Penguin Press, 2006).

27 V. M. Bader, "Dutch Nightmare? The End of Multiculturalism?" *Canadian Diversity* 4, no. 1: 9–11.

28 "Muslim Headscarves: The Controversy That Will Not Die," *Economist*, Sept 10, 2009.

29 Ibid.

30 Ibid.

31 Wallach Scott, *Politics of the Veil*, 222.

32 Ibid.

33 See; Hilal Elver, "The Role of International Influences and Transnational Incentives in Constitution Making: The Cases of the EU v. Turkey and the EU v. CEE Countries," in *Haluk Konuralp Anisina Armagan* C. II (Ankara: Yetkin Yayinevi, 2009), 272–300.

CHAPTER 6

1 Law No. 2004–228, March 15, 2004, *Journal Officiel de la République Française* (O.J.) March 17, 2004, at 5190. Article 1: "In public elementary, middle and high schools, the wearing of signs or clothing which conspicuously manifest student's religious affiliations is prohibited. Disciplinary procedures to implement this rule will be preceded by a discussion with the student." There is also an explanation of what counts as "conspicuous": "The clothing and religious signs prohibited are conspicuous such as large cross, a veil, or a skullcap. Not regarded as signs indicating religious affiliation are discreet signs, which can be, for example, medallions, small crosses, stars of David, hands of Fatima, or small Korans." Cited in Joan Wallach Scott, *The Politics of the Veil* (Princeton, NJ: Princeton University Press, 2007), 1.

2 Stephanie Giry, "France and Its Muslims," *Foreign Affairs* 85, no. 5 (2005): 90.

3 Dr. Sonia Tebbakh, *Muslims in the EU: Cities Report, France: Preliminary Research Report and Literature Survey 2007*, EU Monitoring and Advocacy Program (Grenoble, France: Open Society Institute, 2007), http://www.soros.org/initiatives/home/articles_publications/publications/museucities_20080101/museucitiesfra_20080101.pdf. Final Report, *Muslims in Europe: A Report on 11 Cities*, Open Society Institute, 2010, http://www.soros.org/initiatives/home/articles_publications/publications/muslims-europe-20091215/a-muslims-europe-20110214.pdf.

4 After François Mitterrand became president in 1981, his government and his prime minister, Pierre Mauroy, helped to create a political climate more favorable to immigration and the rights of immigrants in France. Ibid., 91.

5 The most significant Muslim populations are in the following *régions* (counties): Île-de-France (where Muslims comprise up to 35 percent of the population), Provence-Alpes, Côte-d'Azur, PACA (20 percent), Rhône-Alpes (15 percent), Nord-Pas-de-Calais (10 percent) and Alsace. Ibid.

6 Ibid.

7 See "Behind the Furor, the Last Moments of Two Youths," *New York Times*, Nov 7, 2005.

8 For comprehensive arguments by various scholars on the French riots of 2005, see Social Science and Research Council (SSRC), "Riot in France Essay Forum," http://riotsfrance.ssrc.org.

9 Peter Sahlin, "Civil Unrest in French Suburbs," SSRC, October 24, 2006. Ibid.

10 For a deeper interpretation of the colonial roots of the French riots, see Paul Silverstein, "Urban Violence in France," *Middle East Report Online*, November 2005. http://www.merip.org/mero/interventions/silverstein_tetreault_interv.htm.

11 Giry, "France and Its Muslims," 90.

12 Ibid., 95.

13 Immigrants from sub-Saharan Africa are characterized by a higher level of educational achievement, while those from Turkey, Morocco, and Tunisia are much more likely to have no diploma or only a primary level of education. Cited in Tebbakh, *Muslims in the EU: Cities Report*, 36.

14 For evidence, the report relies on one study conducted by Sylvain Brouard and Vincent Tiberj claiming that, even while statistics on the number of girls or women wearing the *hijab* in France are not available, the majority of the French populations of African and Turkish origin are favorably disposed toward the prohibition of the headscarf in schools. Between 53 percent and 59 percent of this population support the prohibition, compared to 80 percent of the national population in support. This interpretation shows that EU officials are trying to justify the French headscarf law that caused an outcry among Muslim women in Europe.

15 Katrin Bennhold, "French Muslims Find Haven in Catholic Schools," *NY Times*, September 29, 2008, http://www.nytimes.com/2008/09/30/world/europe/30schools.html?pagewanted=all.

16 Opinion of the *Conseil d'Etat,* No. 346.893, November 27, 1989.

17 Tebbakh, *Muslims in the EU: Cities Report,* 37.

18 See Veil Project: Values, Equality and Differences in Liberal Democracies, http://www.univie.ac [website discontinued].

19 Ibid.

20 See the ECHR's most recent judgment, *Dogru v. France,* 2009, para. 19: "In France, the troubles have given rise to various forms of collective mobilization regarding the question of the place of Islam in Republican society."

21 *The International Herald Tribune,* December 18, 2003.

22 The 2004 survey was correlated with another survey, conducted by Caitlin Killian in 2003, which reported that 43 percent were in favor of preventing girls from wearing the headscarf to school, and fewer than 60 percent opposed the ban. The other 15 percent made more nuanced replies or had mixed feelings. See Caitlin Killian, "The Other Side of the Veil: Women in France Respond to the Headscarf Affairs," *Gender & Society* (August 2003): 567–590.

23 The commission suggested integrating the following statement into a text of French law concerning secularism: "Out of respect for the freedom of conscience, dress and symbols showing religious or political membership are forbidden in elementary schools, secondary schools and high schools. Any penalty is proportional and imposed after the pupil has been invited to conform to his/her obligation." The commission also makes clear that this new rule must be explained to the pupils and the school staff. The penalty should be applied only in the last resort. See "Report to President of the Republic," handed over on December 11th, 2003, http://www.ladocumentationfrancaise.fr/.

24 Vincent Geisser, *La Nouvelle Islamophobie* (Paris: Editions La Découverte, 2003), quoted in Caitlin Killian, "From Community of Believers to an Islam of the Heart: 'Conspicuous' Symbols, Muslim Practices, and Privatization of Religion in France," *Sociology of Religion* 68, no. 3 (2007): 308.

25 Ibid.

26 In France, as in Turkey, the word used to define the headscarf symbolizes the view of the users. For instance, proponents of the headscarf use the word "foulard," while opponents use "hijab." This is not a simply a choice of words. Hijab has foreign, Islamic (Arabic) connotations, while *foulard* is the French word for scarf. In Turkey, however, opponents of the headscarf call it a "turban," a special type of head-cover originally from France, which connotes that it is foreign to Turkish culture.

27 See chap. 4.

28 In 2004–2005, Hanifa Chérifi drafted a report for the minister of education Gilles de Robien concerning the law prohibiting religious symbols at school. She found a total of 639 religious symbols listed during 2004–2005, which represented "less than 50 percent of the symbols listed during the previous year." Out of 639 cases, 626 concerned headscarves, eleven Sikh turbans, and two Christian crosses. The *hijab* incidents are concentrated in six cities with important immigrant populations:

Strasbourg, Lille, Créteil, Montpelier, Versailles, and Lyon. Finally, 47 pupils (including 44 Muslim girls) were excluded. See Tebbakh, *Muslims in the EU: Cities Report*, 37.

29 Sophy Body-Gendrot, "France Upside Down over a Head Scarf?" *Journal of Sociology of Religion* 68, no. 3 (2007): 289–304.

30 However, in a book entitled *Les féministes et le garçon arabe*, Nacira Guénif-Souilamas and Eric Macé showed that this discourse stigmatized Arab men, by accusing them of oppressing girls and women in general. Ibid., 298.

31 Ibid.

32 Oddly enough, in the report, they mentioned that one was "beautiful." Ibid., 300.

33 *The Stasi Report, The Report of the Committee of Reflection on the Application of the Principle of Secularity in the Republic* [English] (William S. Hein & Company, December 2004) 46–47.

34 See "Speaking as a Muslim: Avoiding Religion in French Public Spaces," in *Politics of Visibility: Young Muslims in European Public Spaces,* eds., Jonker, Gerdien and Valerie Amiraux, (Bielefeld: Verlag, 2006), 26.

35 Françoise Gaspard and Farhad Khosrokhavar, *Le Foulard et la République* (Paris: La Découverte, 1995).

36 Anthony K. Appiah and Amy Gutmann, *Color Conscious* (Princeton, NJ: Princeton University Press, 1996).

37 Body-Gendrot, "France Upside Down over a Head Scarf?" 291.

38 Shifting from 2,000 girls per year, ten years ago, to a little over 1,000 girls in 2004, longtime Department of Education mediator Hanifa Cherif puts the figure for incidents requiring her intervention at only 150 in 2003 compared to 300 in 1994. Cited in Killian, "From Community of Believers," 309.

39 See chap. 4, 75.

40 VEIL Project.

41 Dounia Bouzar and Saida Kada, "One Wearing the Hijab, the Other Not," cited in Tebbakh, *Muslims in the EU: Cities Report*, 38

42 According to Killian, some participants responded, "religion is an affair of the heart," cited in Killian, "From Community of Believers," 313.

43 Leora Auslander, "Bavarian Crucifixes and French Headscarves: Religious Signs and the Postmodern European State," *Cultural Dynamics* 12, no.3 (Nov. 2000): 283–309, 2.

44 For more detailed discussion about generational differences among Muslim women in France. See: Killian, "From a Community of Believers."

45 "For Liberty? The Impact of the French Ban on the Islamic Headscarf and Other Religious Symbols in Schools," Islamic Human Rights Commission (2009), http://www.ihrc.org.uk/file/FRANCEHijabBookv6.pdf   [hereafter   IHRC Report].

46 The figures cited are from the ECHR's *Dogru v. France* judgment. The Court's claim is that before the 2004 law there were many cases, but after its passing, there

was a significant reduction in headscarf conflicts. For example, a report prepared for the Ministry for Education in July 2005 refers to three thousand cases in 1994. According to the governmental report, these figures have dropped tremendously since that time. The ECHR is using this data in order to justify its decision claim. See: *Dogru v. France*, para. 32.

47 "Headscarf Ban is Judged Success as Hostility Fades," *Times*, September 5, 2005.

48 CEDAW is one of the major international human rights agreements under United Nations auspices. The member states are responsible for submitting a yearly report on domestic policies and legal initiatives concerning women's rights. Based on the French report submitted to the 40th session of CEDAW, IHRC argued that the French government, by enacting the law of 2004 (and other, similar laws and policies), acted demonstrably and catastrophically in opposition to the Convention. The French government's own discourse surrounding the headscarf ban has hitherto been grounded mainly in a debate about integration, assimilation, and a very recent and particular interpretation of *laïcité*, having nothing to do with its commitment to the Convention. See http://www.un.org/womenwatch/daw/cedaw/.

49 IHRC Report, 15.

50 "One student told us that, after being left alone in an office for a very long time, she was joined by an adult who did not greet her and did not introduce herself, but who asked: 'What subject do you hate most?' The girl, said, 'But, Madam, I like all subjects!' 'What subject do you like the least?' I don't know...perhaps geography?' The adult left the room and after some time, she came back with a geography book and said: 'There you are! And now, work!'" [ibid.].

51 Ibid., 23.

52 Ibid.

53 In 2003 the inspector Nadjet ben Abdallah was sanctioned for wearing a headscarf to work, in a decision supported by the court in Lyon. In 2005, by the decision of the Court Administrative d'Appel de Lyon, a Muslim tax inspector as prevented from wearing her headscarf. Cited in Dominic McGoldrick, *Human Rights and Religion—The Islamic Headscarf Debate in Europe* (Oxford: Hart Publishing, 2006), 73–4.

54 In 2004, a woman was refused treatment by a local doctor because she was wearing a headscarf. The doctor later put up a sign asking women who wore the headscarf not to enter into the private medical practicing business. Cited in IHRC Report, 29.

55 "A security guard at a Paris branch of the French bank Societe General refused access to a woman wearing a headscarf. As a justification, he invoked the standard security measure forbidding scarves, caps, and other head coverings which could provide disguise for robbers." Saida Kada said: "She had been excluded from a human rights association run by Gerard Collomb, the mayor of Lyon, after another member, a feminist, insisted she resign." See "Woman Wearing Hijab Refused.

Entry into French Bank," August 27, 2009, http://www.nowpublic.com/world/
woman-wearing-hijab-refused-entry-french-bank.

56 IHRC Report, 43.

57 Ibid., 70.

58 Chaambi Bouteldja, "Integration, Discrimination and the Left in France; a
Roundtable Discussion," *Race and Class* 49, no. 3 (2008): 79.

59 Ibid.

60 "The ideologues and managers of the HALDE, and more generally, the policy makers, working on anti-discrimination prefer, with only few exceptions, to handle discrimination within a closed legal context, to ensure that it remains below the media
radar. Cases must remain unknown, and so a better option is to quietly negotiate
compensation payments for the victims." Ibid., 85.

61 "Some law firms specialize in conciliation with the victims of discrimination in
order to avoid politicization of the issue. It's the preferred choice of business and, to
a large extent, it is endorsed by the state." Ibid.

62 According to Abdelaziz Chaambi, who works with the Coalition of Muslims from
France, "In the beginning [HALDE] was granted an effective power of sanction,
but this was quickly removed, proving that the political authorities don't want
to fight against discrimination. The system accepts and even thrives on discrimination." Ibid.

63 Ibid.

64 Bouteldja, "Integration, Discrimination and the Left in France," 28.

65 Roy, *Secularism Confronts Islam*, 2.

66 Ibid., 22.

67 Ausslander, "Bavarian Crucifixes," 300.

68 Ibid.

69 In the 1980s, Sephardic Jews repatriated from Algeria injected more demon-
strative piety into French Judaism; evangelical Protestantism and charismatic
movements raised the question of Christian faith. See Roy, *Secularism Confronts
Islam*, 29.

70 Ibid., 30.

71 Wallach Scott, *Politics of the Veil*, 99–100.

72 Roy, *Secularism Confronts Islam*, xiii.

73 Charles Taylor, "The Politics of Recognition" in *Multiculturalism: Examining the
Politics of Recognition*, ed. A. Gutmann (Princeton, NJ: Princeton University Press,
1994), 25–74.

74 Quoted in Sophie Body-Gendrot, "France Upside Down over a Head Scarf?"
Sociology of Religion 2007 68 (3): 301.

75 Ibid.

76 Ibid., 303.

77 Ibid.

78 Ibid.

CHAPTER 7

1 Beverly Weber, "Cloth on Her Head, Constitution in Hand: Germany's Headscarf Debate and the Cultural Politics of Difference," *German Politics and Society* 72, no. 22/3 (2004): 33–64; Tekla Syszmanski, "Germany: Prejudices Unveiled," *World Press Review* 50, no. 12 (2003): 27.

2 Susan B. Rottman and Myra Marx Ferree, "Citizenship and Intersectionality: German Feminist Debates about Headscarf and Antidiscrimination Laws," *Social Politics* 15, no. 4 (2008):484.

3 Heide Oestreich, *Der Kopftuch-Streit* (Frankfurt am Main: Brandels und Apsel, 2004), cited in Christian Joppke, *Veil: Mirror of Identity* (Cambridge: Polity Press, 2009), 54.

4 Ibid.

5 Constitutional patriotism (*Verfassungspatriotismus*) has been influential in the development of the European Union and is considered a key quality of Europeanism: Citizenship often relies on a shared sense of values rather than a common history or ethnic origin.

6 Baden-Wurttemberg, Bavaria, Hesse, and North Rhine-Westphalia are the states with the largest populations of Turkish origin. Berlin and Lower Saxony also have a high number of Turkish immigrants.

7 Current exact statistics on religious affiliation do not exist in Germany. Statistical estimates usually attribute religious affiliation based on country of origin, which produces ambiguity. Cited in *Discrimination on the Name of Neutrality: Headscarf Bans for Teachers and Civil Servants in Germany*, Human Rights Watch Report, Feb. 26, 2009. [Hereafter HRW Report.]

8 Gokce Yurdakul and Y. Michal Bodemann, "We Don't Want to Be the Jews of Tomorrow," *German Politics and Society* 24, no. 2 (2006):44–67.

9 Joppke, *Veil*, 60.

10 Many evangelical churches; the Roman Catholic Church; a number of minority Christian churches, including Jehovah's Witnesses; the Central Council of Jews, and other Jewish organizations have received the status of publicly recognized legal bodies under German law. This status includes a number of privileges, such as the right to levy taxes on their members with the help of state agencies. See Sabine Berghahn and Petra Rostock, "Cross national comparison Germany," 2008, unpublished report produced for VEIL (Values, Equality & Differences in Liberal Democracies), a 6th Framework Project of the European Commission .[Website discontinued].

11 Joppke, *Veil*, 63.

12 Ibid.

13 Kleinmann (FDP/DVDP), *Landtag Baden-Wuerttenberg*, Feb. 4, 2005, 4397. Ibid.

14 Oliver Gerstenber, "Germany: Freedom of Conscience in Public Schools," *International Journal of Constitutional Law* 3, no. 1 (2005).

15 As was noted by Jutta Limbach, former president of the German Constitutional Court, "the Weimar Republic collapsed...from deep-rooted authoritarian state traditions. The Court's case law may be seen as one fruit of this insight, and the protection of religious freedom is no exception." Cindy Skach, "Sahin v. Turkey," *American Journal of International Law* 100, no. 196 (2006): 191.

16 Article 9 (2) of the European Convention on Human Rights.

17 After the decision, the state of Bavaria subsequently passed laws that enabled schools in this predominantly Catholic region to sidestep the Court's ruling. The Bavarian state government defended its decision by saying, "This is not just a question of religion. It is all about cultural traditions going back more than a thousand years, and the crucifix is one of our most cherished historical symbols...In a peaceful democracy, the minority must consent to go along with the majority view." See William Drozdiak, "Crucifix in Classroom Sparks German Debate," *Washington Post*, Aug.17, 1997, cited in *Comparative Constitutional Law*, ed. Vicki J. Jackson and Mark Tushnet (New York: Foundation Press, 2006), 1407.

18 Decision of the FCC on the *Kruzifix*, May 16, 1995 (1 BvR 1087/91).

19 Decision of the Federal Administrative Court (6th Senate), August 25, 1993 (6 C 8/91).

20 Ibid.

21 Hartmut Albers, "Glaubensfreiheit und schulishe Integration von Auslanderkindern," *Deutsches Verwaltungsblatt*, September 1, 2007, 984–90, cited in Joppke, *Veil*, 55.

22 For instance, the duty not to eat pork, or the duty to pray five times a day would be comparable to the "sickness indicating situation of a partially psychically handicapped who could travel only with another person accompanying her." See decision of the Upper Administrative Court of North Rhine Westphalia (19th Senate), January 17, 2002 (19 B 99/02).

23 Joppke, *Veil*, 55.

24 Ibid.

25 Ibid., 56.

26 Ludin - BVerfGE 10, 282.

27 One of the arguments of the Federal Administrative Court was that the decision "does not excessively affect the Islamic religious community [because] the prohibition is limited to teachers in public schools, and thus affects neither the rights of students in public schools, nor the right of teachers in private schools, to wear an Islamic headscarf." Decision of Federal Administrative Court (BverwG 2c2.4.01) July 4, 2002, at 7, cited in Ruben Seth Fogel, "Headscarves in German Public Schools: Religious Minorities are Welcome in Germany, Unless—God Forbid—They Are Religious," *New York Law School Law Review* 51, no. 3 (2006–2007): 618–653.

28 Joppke, *Veil*, 68.

29 *Bild am Sonntag* (Hamburg), Dec. 21, 2003, http://www.bpb.de/themen, cited in HRW Report, 9.

30 At first, Ms. Ludin claimed that the headscarf was constitutive to her personality, and that she would be robbed of her dignity without the covering. But later, she emphasized her religious motivations. This shift was not accidental. It allowed Ms. Ludin to avoid the unpleasant question of whether all Muslim women who do not wear a headscarf lack dignity. Cited in Hans Michael Heinig, "The Headscarf of a Muslim Teacher in German Public Schools," *Religion in the Public Sphere,* ed. Winfred Brugger and Michael Karayanni (Leiden: Springer, 2007), 184.

31 Millî Görüş is an organization that supports a Turkish-Islam synthesis as a political goal and is outlawed in Turkey.

32 HRW Report, 17.

33 Heinig, "The Headscarf of a Muslim Teacher," 188.

34 Ibid., 183.

35 A prominent representative of this position is Alice Schwarzer, editor of the feminist magazine *EMMA,* who cites veiling of the female body or hair as evidence of the incompatibility of Islam with German values of democracy and freedom. Heinig, "The Headscarf of a Muslim Teacher," 185; and HRW Report, 10.

36 See Intercultural Council, "Theses on the Headscarf," January 2004, http://www.interkultureller-rat.de/projekte/deutsches-islamforum-und-islamforen-in-den-laendern/, and Kirsten Wiese, *Teachers with Headscarf* (Berlin: Ducker and Humbold, 2008).

37 In December 2003, many prominent women from the political and artistic worlds signed the call "Religious diversity instead of forced emancipation. Call against a headscarf law," http://www.bpb.de/themen/XUDYWD,0,0,Religi%F6se_Vielfalt_statt_Zwangsemanzipation!.html, cited in HRW Report, 9.

38 Ibid., 9.

39 Because the majority of immigrants in Germany are from Turkey, the reference to Anatolia carries a special meaning. "Anatolia" refers to the rural, village populations of Turkey. The word has been used to emphasize the immigrants' background as nonurban, uneducated women and carries a strong undertone of racial and ethnic discrimination against Turks.

40 HRW Report, 11.

41 C. Hillgruber, Der deutsche Kulturstaat und der muslimishe Kulturimport, JZ 1999, 538, cited in Heinig, "The Headscarf of a Muslim Teacher," 186.

42 HRW Report, 13.

43 Berghahn and Rostock, "Cross National Comparison," 11.

44 TGD, "No Compromises in the Headscarf Discussion," and "14 Religion Policy Theses of the Turkish Community in Germany," September 26, 2006, http://www.tgd.de/index.php?name=News&file=article&sid=615.

45 Heinig, "The Headscarf of a Muslim Teacher," 187.

46 In the context of a military deployment, the German Federal Administrative Court has rescinded the disciplinary sentence for a refusal to follow orders for religious or conscientious reasons, since the soldier's freedom of conscience cannot be suppressed by the Army's protected interest of its functionality, ibid., 188.

47 BVerfGE 93, 1 (18); ibid.

48 Heinig, "The Headscarf of a Muslim Teacher," 189.

49 *Die Tageszeitung*, June 4, 2003, cited in Joppke, *Veil*, 69.

50 Heinig, "The Headscarf of a Muslim Teacher," 190.

51 Joppke, *Veil*, 68.

52 Annette Schavan, minister of education in Baden-Wurttemberg, justified her anti-headscarf bill before the *Landtag*: "The veil as a political symbol is also part of a history of oppressing women…so it is not reconcilable with a constitutional value that is anchored in our Basic Law." See *Landtag von Baden-Wurttemberg*, February 4, 2004, 43, 87, cited in Joppke, *Veil*, 68.

53 BVerfGE 108, 282 (303–304), cited in Heinig, "The Headscarf of a Muslim Teacher," 190.

54 Ibid.

55 Ibid., 191.

56 Joppke, *Veil*, 69.

57 Cited in Heinig, "The Headscarf of a Muslim Teacher," 192.

58 Ibid., 193.

59 Ibid., 192.

60 Ibid.

61 Ibid.

62 HRW Report, 8.

63 "Christian Western and European tradition is not a breach of the neutrality requirement if a teacher commits to this tradition…accordingly, the nun's habit and Jewish kippa remain therefore permissible." Cited in HRW Report, 28.

64 Ibid.

65 See "Not Without My Habit," *Der Spiegel*, Oct. 12, 2004.

66 Cited in HRW Report, 26–27.

67 Three of those states, Brandenburg, Rhineland-Palatinate, and Schleswig-Holstein considered, but ultimately rejected, such restrictions.

68 HRW Report, 28.

69 Gesetzentwurf der Fraktion der CDU and der Fraktion der FDP: Nordrhein-Westfalen, October, 31, 2005. [Ibid., 29]

70 HRW Report, 25.

71 Ibid., 30.

72 Dietmar Hipp, "Headscarf Decision: Nuns Rescue Islam," *Spiegel Online*, July 8, 2006, cited in HRW Report, 32.

73 Ibid., 33.

74 Ibid.

75 A headscarf wrapped around and tied at the back, instead of pinned at the front, as worn by the actress and Princess of Monaco Grace Kelly, ibid.

76 State Labor Court Judgment of April 10, 2008, Ref.5 Sa 1836/07, ibid.

77 Bavarian Constitutional Court on January 15, 2007, AZ:Vf.11–VII-05, ibid., 35.

78 Ibid.

79 HRW Report, 39.

80 Directive 78/2000/EC and Council Directive 2004/113/EC implementing the principle of equal treatment of men and women in the access and supply of goods and services.

81 For more detailed information and a hypothetical headscarf case, see Titia Loenen, "The Headscarf Debate: Approaching the Intersection of Sex, Religion and Race under the European Convention on Human Rights and EC Equality Law," in *European Union Non-Discrimination Law: Comparative Perspectives on Multidimensional Equality Law,* ed. Dagmar Schiek and Victoria Chege (U.K.: Routledge, 2008), 313–327. [Hereafter "Approaching the Intersection."]

82 Isabella Rorive, "Religious Symbols in the Public Space: In Search of a European Answer," *Cardozo Law Review* 30, no. 6 (2009): 2670..

83 Newspaper ads saying things such as "no Jews or disabled people" will be banned., Cited in *Loenen, Approaching the Intersection,* 315.

84 See Sigrid Kneist, "Religion Clash: Muslim Trainee Is Not Allowed into Courtroom with Headscarf," Cited in HRW Report, 50.

85 According to a May 2004 nonbinding recommendation of the Cologne council of judges, Muslim trainee lawyers with headscarves should sit among the witnesses and spectators, separated from judges, to prevent being "identified with the court." It includes a clear instruction that each judge is responsible for deciding individually whether trainees are permitted to wear headscarves during the court proceedings. See European Forum for Migration Studies (EFMS) Migration Report, May 2004. Ibid.

86 The position of lay judge in Germany is honorary. Ordinary citizens without legal training are elected to sit as judges.

87 HRW Report, 50.

88 Martina, a schoolteacher in Frankfurt, converted to Islam, who is trying to apply for a teaching position in a private school, told HRW, "I wear it because I deem it a religious duty to myself. I needed 10 years to decide on the headscarf. Through the law, they impute to me a sort of constant Islamic work, which I strongly reject. When I teach German, I teach German…Neutrality should have to apply everybody." Ibid.,40.

89 Maryam, an elementary schoolteacher who converted to Islam, had worn a headscarf in school for decades, explained to HRW, "one has the feeling 'we don't want you'…Where should I go? I belong here…I would never have thought that would be possible." [Ibid., ,41.]

90 A converted Muslim, a German-born woman said, "I suddenly felt like a stranger in Germany…I will never forget that." Another Muslim woman, a third-generation German, said, "I can imagine that one can come to this conclusion from the representation of Muslim women in the media. So what, I am not like this…Many women with headscarves are not like this and one cannot completely condemn a religion because of some being like this…I am an example of integration…going

out, striving for a job, finished my studies, did not marry young and I choose my husband freely...I was also not forced to wear a headscarf. I am practically a model of what they look for. They have now a promotional program for immigrant women to study to become a teacher. Hello? Here I am, take me!" [Ibid., 43]

91 Fahima, an elementary schoolteacher, told HRW, "Those who made these laws don't know us. They should ask our colleagues, directors, school inspectors, the parents, the pupil what kind of persons we are. All of them have experienced me and know me so well that I do not wear the scarf because of oppression...One cannot regard the headscarf as a symbol for that. There are certainly persons who neither wear headscarf nor are Muslim and are oppressed and where do you see it in their cases then? I don't understand how one can want to base this on a cloth." [Ibid., 42]

92 "I will not go and tell a 15-year-old pupil to wear it. If I would like to influence pupils I could do that also without a headscarf—it would make more sense...The headscarf is overestimated. One does not need a headscarf to manipulate, and there are other mechanisms to act against indoctrination." [Ibid.]

93 Emilie, an elementary schoolteacher who converted to Islam explained financial difficulties faced as a result of the ban because her husband was also unemployed and they needed her income from teaching: "Since my husband was looking for a job, we will go now for some time abroad, to Morocco, where he is from. I am leaving with mixed feelings, since even a part-time job would have enabled a frugal life here. Now I am waiting for other Muslim women to fight for the right of free practice of religion, and hope it will be successful." [Ibid., 46]

94 "I started to wear the headscarf when I was 15...There are no pictures with me and the wig, I avoid that. I feel uncomfortable. Do I give up on all my years of studies and completed education, or do I find a loophole to still work?...To leave my home-town would have been too much of a sacrifice. I also looked at wigs before, which are quite expensive. 'Like real' the saleswoman said at the end, and I thought, I might just as well show my own hair! To renounce the headscarf is very difficult. On the first day I disguised myself in the school toilet. When a colleague spoke to me, I broke down in tears." Rabia added, "My son asked me, 'what is more important—Allah or work?' I answered him that it is complicated, when he gets older." [Ibid.]

95 According to an elementary schoolteacher, "I would never go to court, I don't have the strength and nerves to deal with that. Even if maybe it would help others if many of us would go to court, I just can't. I was never someone who is politically or legally versed." Another elementary schoolteacher stated: "I cannot get into conflict with the law. I saw what other colleagues faced when they challenged the law: the press comes to the school, they receive inquiries and also sometimes hostility." [Ibid., 47]

96 In the words of one woman, "as long as we were cleaning in schools, nobody had a problem with the headscarf...In the schools most cleaning ladies wear headscarves, because these jobs belong to Muslim immigrants, and then you show the girls that with a headscarf they only let you take cleaning jobs." [Ibid., 51]

97 Intercultural Council is an umbrella group that includes civil society organizations, unions, employers' organizations, municipalities, state institutions, and media. See http://www.interkultureller-rat.de/.

98 HRW Report, 62.

99 Berghahn and Rostock, "Cross National Comparison," 13.

100 Ibid., 10.

101 Ibid.

102 Ibid., 11.

103 Ibid.

104 Ibid.

105 For instance, Alice Schwarzer, Necla Kelek, and Seyran Ates.

106 HRW, 14.

CHAPTER 8

1 Catherine J. Ross, "Children and Religious Expression in School: A Comparative Treatment of the Veil and Other Religious Symbols in Western Democracies," in *Children in the Discourses of Religion and International Human Rights*, ed. Marta Fineman and Karen Worthington (UK: Ashgate Press, 2008) [hereafter Ross, "Children and Religious Expression"].

2 In his dissenting opinion in *McCreary County v. ACLU* 125 S. Ct. 2722, 2748 (2005), Justice Scalia argued that the United States never adopted a "secularist" model. For a detailed analysis of the American and French *laïcité*/secularism debate, see T. Jeremy Gunn, "Religious Freedom and *Laïcité*: A Comparison of the United States and France," *BYU Law Journal*, no. 2 (2004).

3 Jennifer Westerfield, "Behind the Veil: An American Legal Perspective on the European Headscarf Debate," *American Journal of Comparative Law* 54 (2006): 637.

4 The Turkish constitutional order is a good example of comprehensiveness. Also, in German Basic Law (*Grundgezets*), not only is the free exercise of religion protected, but paragraph 1 and 2 of Article 4 ensure the freedom of faith and conscience, as well as the freedom to profess a religious or philosophical creed.

5 For more detailed statistics and an ethnic breakdown of Muslims who attend mosques in the United States, see http://www.cair-net.org.

6 According to the Hartford Institute for Religion Research, the ethnicity of Muslims are 33 percent South-Central Asian, 30 percent African American, 25 percent Arab, 2 percent European, 2 percent Southeast Asian, 2 percent African, and 5 percent other. "Fast Facts: How many Muslims are there in the United States?" http://hirr.hartsem.edu/research/fastfacts/fast_facts.html.#muslims

7 For the most recent and comprehensive book on American Muslims, see John Esposito and Dalia Mogahed, *Who Speaks for Islam? What a Billion Muslims Really Think* (Washington DC.: Gallup Press, 2008).

8 Cathleen M. Moore, *Al Mughtaribun: American Law and Transformation of Muslim Life in the United States* (Albany, NY: SUNY Press, 1995).

9 Oscar Handlin, *Race and Nationality in American Life* (New York: Doubleday Anchor Books, 1957); John Higham, *Send These to Me, Immigrants in Urban America* (Baltimore: John Hopkins University Press, 1984); Maldwyn Allen Jones, *American Immigration* (Chicago: University of Chicago Press, 1960); and Carl Wittke, *We Who Built America, The Saga of the Immigrant* (Cleveland, OH: Case Western University Press, 1964); ibid.

10 Edward W. Said, *Covering Islam: How the Media and the Experts Determine How We See the Rest of the World* (New York: Pantheon Books, 1981); and *Orientalism* (New York: Vintage Books, 1978).

11 John Tehranian, "Performing Whiteness: Naturalization Litigation and the Construction of Racial Identity in the United States," *Yale Law Journal* 109 (2000): 842.

12 Stephen Yale-Loehr, "America's Challenge: Domestic Security, Civil Liberties and National Unity After September 11," a report issued by the Migration Policy Institute in July 2003, http://www.migrationpolicy.org.

13 For comprehensive information about post-9/11 human rights violations against Muslims, Middle Easterners, and Arabs, see David Cole, *Enemy Aliens,* 2nd ed. (New York: The New Press, 2005), 25.

14 "The conversion of African Americans to Islam is a twentieth-century phenomenon and must be understood, at one level, as a reaction to American racism...many of the alternative belief systems which arose wholly negated the message of white supremacy that was seen as inherent to Christianity, and rendered their distinctiveness—i.e., their blackness—a virtue, rather than evidence of their inferiority." Quoted in Beverly Thomas McCloud, "African-American Muslim Women," in *The Muslims of America*, ed. Yvonne Haddad (New York: Oxford University Press, 1993), 177–187. [Hereafter, Haddad (1993).]

15 Wallace F. Caldwell, "A Survey of Attitudes Toward Black Muslims in Prison," *Journal of Human Relations* 16 (1968): 22.

16 Haddad (1993), 180.

17 Ibid., 37.

18 Aminah B. McCloud, "Racism in the Ummah" in *Islam: A Contemporary Perspective*, ed. Monhammad A. Siddiqi (Chicago: NAAMPS, 1991), 73–80.

19 Ibid.

20 On November 17, 2001, former First Lady Laura Bush claimed in her radio address that the fight against terrorism is also a fight for the rights and dignity of women. Available at http://www.whitehouse.gov/news/releases2001/11/20011117.html.

21 Kathleen M. Moore, "Visible through the Veil: The Regulation of Islam in American Law," *Sociology of Religion* 68, no. 3 (2007): 239.

22 Syed Ali, "Why Here Why Now? Young Muslim Women Wearing Hijab," *The Muslim World,* 95 (2005): 515–30; Nadine Naber, "Muslim First, Arab

Second: A Strategic Politics of Race and Gender," *The Muslim World* 95 (2005): 474–96; Maram Hallak and Kathryn Quina, "In the Shadow of the Twin Towers: Muslim Immigrant Women's Voice Emerge," *Sex Roles* 51 (2004): 329–338.

23 Moore, "Visible through the Veil," 248.

24 Ibid.

25 Yvonne Yazbeck Haddad, "The Post-9/11 Hijab as Icon," *Sociology of Religion* 68, no. 3 (2007): 253–267. [Hereafter Haddad (2007).]

26 For similar arguments see Haddad (1993); Yvonne Yazbeck Haddad, *Muslims in the West* (New York: Oxford University Press, 2002); Yvonne Yazbeck Haddad and Adair T. Lummis, *Islamic Values in the United States* (New York: Oxford University Press, 1987); Yvonne Yazbeck Haddad and Jane Idleman Smith, *Mission to America* (Gainesville, FL: University Press of Florida, 1993); Yvonne Yazbeck Haddad, ed., *Muslim Communities in North America* (Albany, NY: SUNY Press, 1994); Yvonne Yazbeck Haddad, ed., *Muslim Minorities in the West* (Lanham: Altamira Press, 2002); Yvonne Yazbeck Haddad and John Esposito, *Muslims on the Americanization Path?* (New York: Oxford University Press, 2000); Yvonne Yazbeck Haddad, ed., *Religion and Immigration* (Lanham: Altamira Press, 2003); Yvonne Yazbeck Haddad, Jane Idleman Smith, and Kathleen M. Moore, *Muslim Women in America* (New York: Oxford University Press, 2006).

27 As one young woman explained the meaning of her new headscarf, "Islam is beautiful! Deal with it!" Cited in Haddad (2007), 254.

28 Yvonne Yazbeck Haddad, "Islam and Gender Dilemmas in a Changing World," in *Islam, Gender and Social Change*, ed. Yvonne Yazbeck Haddad and John Esposito (New York: Oxford University Press, 1998), 2–29. [Hereafter Haddad and Esposito (1998).]

29 Lamia Ben Youssef Zayzafoon, *The Production of Muslim Woman: Negotiating Text, History and Ideology* (Lanham, MD: Lexington Books, 2005).

30 Some of the scholars in this line are Homa Hoodfar, Guity Nashat, and Zehra Arat. Cited in Haddad (2007), 255.

31 See Rana Kabbani, *Imperial Fiction s—Europe's Myths of the Orient* (Bloomington: University of Indiana Press, 1994).

32 Haddad and Esposito (1998), 259.

33 Maina Chawla Singh, *Gender, Religion, and "Heathen Lands"—American Missionary Women in South Asia (1860–1940)* (New York: Garland Publishing, 2000). Cited in Haddad (2007), 262.

34 Suraya Duval, "New Veils and New Voices: Islamists Women's Group in Egypt," *Women and Islamization: Contemporary Dimensions of Discourse on Gender Relations*, ed. K. Ask and M. Tjomstand (Oxford: Berg, 1998), 45–72. Ibid.

35 In an article published in *The Guardian* of London, six Muslim women discussed the irrelevance of Western social values to their lives. They affirmed that Islam had been a major liberating force for them and bolstered their arguments by reference to the Quran, which guarantees gender equality. See Madeleina Bunting, "Can

Islam Liberate Women? Muslim Women and Scholars Think It Does—Spiritually and Sexually," *The Guardian*, December 8, 2001, 16.

36 Haddad (2007), 263.

37 Ibid., 264.

38 Ibid.

39 Cited in Ross, "Children and Religious Expression ," 21.

40 The Supreme Court has only once considered the issue of religious garb, in a case involving an adult in the armed forces in *Goldman v. Weinberger* 474 U.S. 503 (1986) where the rational basis test was applied. The Court held that an Orthodox Jew serving as a psychologist in the armed forces was not entitled to an exception from the military dress code in order to wear his kippa. Ibid.

41 D. Carpenter, "Free Exercise and Dress Codes: Towards More Consistent Protection of a Fundamental Rights," *Indiana Law Journal* 63 (1987/88): 607–608.

42 Ross, "Children and Religious Expression" 16–17.

43 Ibid.

44 See: *Tinker v. Des Moines Independent Community Opinion* 393 U.S. 503 (1969).

45 *Stull v. School Board of Western Beaver Junior-Senior High School:* 459 F. 2d 339, 347 (3d. Cir. 1972), cited in Anita Allen, "Undressing Difference: The Hijab in the West" (book review: *The Politics of the Veil*, by Joan Vallach Scott) *Berkeley J. Gender L. & Just.* No. 23 (2008):208.

46 425 U.S. 238 (1976), cited in ibid.

47 Judgment of Nov 17, 1981, 527 F. Supp. 637. Cited in Dagmar Richter, "Religious Garments in Public Schools in Separation Systems: France and the United States of America," in *Religion and the Public Sphere*: *A Comparative Analysis of German, Israeli, American and International Law*, Winfried Brugger and Michael Karayanni, eds. (Germany: Springer, 2007) 199..

48 Oct. 12, 1995, 67 F.3d 883, 135 A.L.R. Fed. 675. Ibid.

49 Ibid.

50 March 30, 1999, 40n F.Supp. 2d 335. Ibid, 223.

51 Cited in Allen, "Undressing Difference," 210.

52 *Ala. & Coushatta Tribes v. Big Sandy School District,* 1993, at 1329, "Religion is not limited to the traditional faiths, but can be discerned whenever a belief system encompasses fundamental questions of the nature of reality and the relationship of human beings to reality." Cited in Ross, "Children and Religious Expression," 19.

53 See *Chalifoux v. New Caney Independent School District* 976 F. Supp 659 (1997), 665. Cited in Westerfield, Behind the Veil, 637.

54 *Tinker v. Des Moines Independent School District* 393 U.S. 503 (1969).

55 "Any departure from absolute regimentation may cause trouble. Any variation from the majority opinion may inspire fear…But our constitution says we must take this risk, and our history says that it is this sort of hazardous freedom—this kind of openness—that is the basis of our national strength and of the independence and

vigor of Americans who grow up and live in this relatively permissive, often disputative, society." Ibid., 508–509.

56 U.S. Department of Education, 2004, cited in Ross "Children and Religious Expression," 18.

57 Nashala "Tallah" Hearn was suspended from Muscogee School District's Benjamin Franklin Science Academy. See Brian Knowlton, "Bush Administration Intervenes to Allow Muslim Schoolgirl to Wear Scarf: U.S. Takes Opposite Tack from France," *International Herald Tribune,* April 2, 2004, www:iht.com/articles/2004/04/02/ islam ed3.php.

58 Ross, "Children and Religious Expression," 17.

59 United States' Memorandum of Law in Support of Its Cross-Motion for Summary Judgment and in Opposition to Defendants' Motion for Summary Judgment: *Hearn v. Muskogee Pub. Sch. Dist.,* No. Civ. 03–598-S (E.D. Okla. May 6, 2004), http://www.usdoj.gov/crt/religdisc/musk_memo.htm.

60 Ross, "Children and Religious Expression," 19.

61 See R. Nelson, "Scarf Grabbing Teacher Ejected Student, Accusing Him as Missing Court Twice," *New Orleans Times-Picayune,* Nov. 10, 2004.

62 Statistical evidence in the CAIR report shows that discrimination, harassment, and violence against Muslim Americans increased by 49 percent in just one year. There was a 52 percent increase in the number of reported cases of violent, anti-Muslim hate crimes, and ten states alone accounted for almost 80 percent of the incidents. See *The Status of Muslim Civil Rights in the United States: Unequal Protection,* 2005, http://www.cair-net.org/asp/2005CivilRightsReport.pdf.

63 Ibid., 50.

64 On April 24, 2004. a Muslim woman and her son were harassed and attacked by another woman while shopping in Pennsylvania. The woman shouted that American troops were fighting in Iraq and Afghanistan so women did not have dress like her and repeatedly hit her with a shopping cart. Employees of the store refused to assist the Muslim woman by calling the police or stopping the harassment. On June 26, 2004, another Muslim woman was stopped in her car by three individuals who demanded a lighter, which she did not have. They said "Stupid Muslims, f— Muslims," kicked her car, punched her in the face, and tore her headscarf. Ibid., 53–56.

65 Ibid., 56.

66 "City of Omaha and ACLU of Nebraska Announce Settlement in Lawsuit Over Muslim Woman Barred from Public Pool," cited in Moore, "Visible through the Veil," 243.

67 Ibid.

68 Michael Schneider, "Muslim Woman Was Denied Job for Wearing Headscarf, Suit Says," *Miami Herald,* June 23, 2005, cited in Moore, "Visible through the Veil," 245.

69 In *Goldman v. Weinberger,* the case for permitting the military to ban religious headgear was based on the same reasoning used to make the case for permitting

municipal police departments to prohibit long hairstyles: the importance of uniformity. Uniforms and uniformity communicate discipline, professionalism, and submission to a common authority.

70 Allen, "Undressing Difference," 217.

71 *Meyer v. Nebraska* (1923); *Pierce v. Society of Sisters* (1925); *Wisconsin v. Yoder* (1972), cited in Ross, "Children and Religious Expression," 13.

72 *Troxel v. Granville* (2000) 539 U.S. 57, cited in Ross, "Children and Religious Expression," 13.

73 S. L. Carter, *The Culture of Disbelief: How American Law and Politics Trivialize Religious Devotion* (New York: Basic Books, 1993); D. B. Tyack, "The Perils of Pluralism: The Background of the Pierce Case," *The American Historical Review* 74 (1968); B. B. Woodhouse, "Who Owns the Child? Meyer and Pierce and the Child as Property," *William and Mary Law Review* 33 (1992): 995–1122. Ibid.

74 *Fields v. Palmdale School District,* 2006; *Mozert v. Hawkins Co. Bd. Pf Educ.,* 1987. Ibid.

75 K. Greenwalt, *Does God Belong in Public Schools?* (Princeton, NJ: Princeton University Press, 2005).

76 National Center of Educational Statistics, 2006a, cited in Ross, "Children and Religious Expression," 22.

77 Ibid.

78 Ibid., 23.

79 Ibid.

80 S. L. Carter, *The Culture of Disbelief: How American Law and Politics Trivialize Religious Devotion* (New York: Basic Books, 1993); M. V. McConnell, "Equal Treatment and Religious Discrimination" in *Equal Treatment of Religion in a Pluralistic Society,* ed. S.V. Monsma and J. C. Soper (Grand Rapids, MI.: Eerdmans Pub. Co.1998).

81 For more comprehensive information, see C. J. Ross, "An Emerging Right for Mature Minors to Receive Information," *University of Pennsylvania Journal of Constitutional Law* 2 (1999): 223–275; Woodhouse, "Who Owns the Child?"

82 Ross, "Children and Religious Expression," 23.

83 Richter, "Religious Garments," 222.

84 A comprehensive survey on the jurisprudence was published in 1958. See L. Tellier, "Wearing of Religious Garb by Public -School Teachers," *American Law Report,* 2nd ed. 60 300 et seq. 90 164 Pa 629, ibid., 224.

85 The relevant provisions read: "No teacher in any public school shall wear any religious dress while engaged in performance of his duties as a teacher." The term "religious dress" connotes clothing that is associated with and symbolic of religion, that is, clothing that communicates the wearer's adherence to a particular religion. The term "while in performance of his duties as a teacher" only refers to those duties that systematically bring the teacher into contact with the students. Cited in 708 *Pacific Reporter,* 1161, Or. App. 1985, ibid.

86 March 30, 1987, 480 U.S. 942, 107 S. Ct. 1597, with Justices Brennan, Marshall and O'Connor dissenting.

87 This statute reads in its relevant parts: "(a). That no teacher in any public school shall wear in said school or while engaged in the performance of his duty as such teacher any dress, mark, emblem or insignia indicating that fact that such teacher is a member of adherent of any religious order, sect or denomination. (b). Any teacher…who violated the provisions of this section, shall be suspended…and in the case of a second offense shall be permanently disqualified from teaching in said school." Cited in Richter, "Religious Garments," 231.

88 The relevant part of the Title VII (a) is: "It shall be an unlawful employment practice for an employer (i) to fail or refuse to hire or discharge any individual with respect to his compensation, terms, conditions, or privileges of employment, because of such individual's…religion." Title VII also defines the term of "religion," thereby establishing an exception: "The term 'religion' includes all aspects of religious observance and practice, as well as belief, unless an employer demonstrates that he is unable to reasonably accommodate an employee's or prospective employee's religious observance or practice without undue hardship on the conduct of the employer's business."

89 432 U.S. 63, 97 S. Ct. 2264, cited in Richter, "Religious Garments," 222.

90 Ibid.

91 See H. Bastian, "Religious Garb Statutes and Title VII: An Uneasy Coexistence," *Georgetown Law Journal* No. 80 (1991–1992):211 "Court failed to address the most pressing issue" and "Inappropriately relying on summary dispositions of the U.S. Supreme Court."

92 Judgment of the U.S. District Court for the District of Mississippi of Nov 30, 1992, 829 F. Supp. 853. Cited in Richter, "Religious Garments," 230.

93 As quoted from the Supreme Court, a religious belief rather must have "an institutional quality about it"; that is, it must "concern a comprehensive religious theory, and be sincere." See *Brown v. Pena*, 441 F. Supp. 1382.

94 Richter, "Religious Garments," 235.

95 Kimberley Crenshaw first introduced the concept of intersectionality in American legal scholarship. See *Black Feminist Thought: Knowledge, Consciousness, and the Politics of Empowerment*, 2nd ed. (Routledge, 2001) Also see Paulette M. Caldwell, "Intersectional Bias and the Courts: The Story of Rogers v. American Airlines," in *Race Law Stories*, ed. Rachel F. Moran and Devon Carbado (New York: Foundation Press, 2008), 571–90.

96 A court ruling in 1977 relaxed this requirement in practice.

97 Moore, "Visible through the Veil," 245.

98 See Jeffrey Breinhold, "Muslim Employment Discrimination: A Legal Examination," http://strategycenter.net/research.

99 *Lewis v. North General Hosp.*, 2007 WL 2398077 (S.D.N.Y. 2007). Ibid.

100 The acceleration began in the 1990s. The year 2007 saw the largest number of Muslim discrimination opinions in history. Ibid.

101 Ibid.

102 *Saint Francis College v. Al-Khazraji*, 481 U.S. 604, 107 S.Ct. 2022, U.S. Pa., 1987.

103 Ibid.

104 Available at http://eeoc.gov/press/11–13-02.html, cited in Moore, "Visible through the Veil," 245.

105 *E.E.O.C. v. Alamo Rent-A-Car LLC*, 432 F. Supp.2d 1006 (D. Ariz. 2006).

106 Moore, "Visible through the Veil," 246.

107 For more information on this case, see Kimberly A. Sukunik, "Civil Liberties in the Face of 9–11: The Case of Sultaana Freeman," http://org.law.rutgers.edu/publications/law-religion/new_devs/RJLR_ND_68.pdf.

108 *Sultaana Lakiana Myke Freeman v. State of Florida, Department of Highway Safety and Motor Vehicles*, 9th Circuit, Orange County, Fl. 2002-CA-2828.

109 *Sultaana Lakiana Myke Freeman v. State of Florida, Department of Highway Safety and Motor Vehicles*, Court of Appeal, Fifth District (2005 Fal. App. LEXIS 13904, September 2, 2005), at 22.

110 UCLA law professor Khaled Abou El Fadl, a prominent expert in Islamic law called by the state, said he thought the rigorous code of Sharia allowed exceptions to the rule that Muslim women must cover their faces, including for driver's license photos. See http://www.courttv.com/trials/freeman/05283_ctv.html.

111 Moore, "Visible through the Veil," 248.

112 508 U.S. 520 (1993). In this case the church brought an action challenging the city ordinances dealing with the ritual slaughter of animals. The Supreme Court held that the government interest asserted to be advanced by the ordinances did not justify the targeting of religious activity.

113 494 U.S. 872 (1990). In this case, the religious use of peyote resulted in loss of employment and inability to obtain unemployment compensation. Justice Scalia held that the free exercise clause of the Constitution did not prohibit the application of Oregon drug laws to the ceremonial ingestion of peyote, and, therefore, the state could, consistent with the free exercise clause, deny claimants unemployment compensation for work-related misconduct due to the use of the drug.

114 Allen, "Undressing Difference," 217.

115 141 U.S. 250 (1891): The case held that a woman who filed a tort action alleging physical injuries need not submit to a medical exam at the request of defendant. This decision, however, has been overruled by modern rules; but what endures is the sentiment about the importance of privacy advanced in *Botsford*: "No right is held more sacred, or more carefully guarded, by the common law, that the right of every individual to the possession and control of his own person, free from restraint or interference of others, unless by clear and unquestionable authority of law." Ibid., 217.

116 Ibid., 218.

117 *Johnson v. Phelan* 69 F. 3d 144, 152 (7th Cir. 1995).

118 Allen, "Undressing Difference," 218.

119 Ibid., 219.

120 One American-born Muslim woman was strip-searched after refusing to remove her headscarf in a public passenger screening area of an airport. See *Kaukab v. Harris*, No. 02 C 0371, 2003 WL 21823752 (N.D. Aug.6 2003).

121 A Missouri law passed in 2005 states, "No employee of or volunteer in or school board member of or school district administrator of a public school or charter school shall direct a student to remove an emblem, insignia or garment as long as such emblem, insignia or garment is worn in a manner that does not promote disruptive behavior." MO. Rev. Stat. & 167.11 (2005), cited in Christina A. Baker, "French Headscarves and the U.S. Constitution: Parents, Children, and Free Exercise of Religion," *Cardozo Journal of Law & Gender* 13, no. 2 (2007): 354.

122 *Church of Lukumi Babalu Aye v. City of Hialeah* (508 U.S. 520, 546, 1993). The Supreme Court stated, "If the object of a law is to infringe upon or restrict practices because of their religious motivation, the law is not neutral."

123 *Sherbert v. Verner* (374 U.S. 398, 1963). Strict scrutiny requires: (i) The claimant to demonstrate a *substantive burden* on religiously motivated conduct; (ii) The state to demonstrate a *compelling interest* in enforcing the challenged rule; (iii) The state to demonstrate that this interest cannot be served by a less restrictive means that the rule is *narrowly tailored*.

124 *Employment Division, Oregon Department of Human Resources v. Smith* (494 U.S. 872, 1990).

125 John Mikhail, "The Free Exercise of Religion: An American Perspective," in *Ein Neuer Kampf der Religionen? Staat, Rech, un religiose Toleranz* 281 no. 41 (2006).

126 *Wisconsin v. Yoder* (406 U.S. 205, 1972). The two fundamental rights raised in this judgment were the right to free exercise of religion and the rights of parents to raise their children in the manner they choose. The First and Fourteenth amendments prohibited the state from compelling Amish children to attend formal high school until the age of sixteen.

127 Stephanie Walterick, "The Prohibition of Muslim Headscarves from French Public Schools and Controversies Surrounding the Hijab in the Western World," *Temp. Int'l & Comp. L.J.* 20, no. 251 (2006).

128 Baker, "French Headscarves," 358.

129 Ibid.

130 Allen, "Undressing Difference," 210; Ross, "Children and Religious Expression" 451.

131 *Reynolds v. United States,* 98 U.S. 145, 166 (1878). "Laws are made for the government of actions, and while they cannot interfere with mere religious beliefs and opinions, they may with practices."

132 "Plural marriages were 'odious' to the civilized West, and they were odious in part because of the shame they brought on women and children of such relationships, who were stained with an aura of illegitimacy." Ibid.

133 494 U.S. 872, 878–79 (1990)."We have never held that an individual's religious belief excuse him from compliance with an otherwise valid law prohibiting conduct that the state is free to regulate." Cited in Allen, "Undressing Difference," 212.

134 Ibid.

135 John Esposito, "Islamophobia: A Threat to American Values?" *The Huffington Post*, August 10, 2010, http://www.huffingtonpost.com/john-l-esposito/islamo-phobia-a-threat-to_b_676765.html.

136 "New York City Bus Ads Sponsored by Anti-Islam Extremists," *New York Times*, August 9, 2010.

137 In California, a Tea Party Rally to protest an Islamic Center in Temecula encouraged protesters to bring their dogs because Muslims allegedly hate Jews, Christians, women, and dogs. Christians from a right-wing church in Dallas, Texas traveled to a Bridgeport, Conn. Mosque to confront worshippers. They shouted "murderers" at the young children leaving the mosque. Carrying placards, they angrily declared "Islam is a lie," "Jesus hates Muslims," and "This is a war in America and we are taking it to the mosques around the country," cited in Esposito, "Islamophobia."

138 "Mosque Used by 9/11 Plotters is Closed," *New York Times*, August, 9, 2010.

139 Esposito, "Islamophobia."

140 "Dutch Opponent of Muslim Gains Ground," *The New York Times*, August 5, 2010.

141 In U.S., Religious Prejudice Stronger Against Muslims, January 21, 2010, http://www.gallup.com/poll/125312/religious-prejudice-stronger-against-muslims.aspx.

142 Esposito, "Islamophobia."

143 Ibid.

144 Ibid.

145 In all, just 47 percent of respondents believe Obama is a Christian; 24 percent declined to respond to the question or said they were unsure, and 5 percent believe he is neither Christian nor Muslim. According to a *Time* magazine survey, 28 percent of voters do not believe Muslims should be eligible to sit on the U.S. Supreme Court. Nearly one-third of the country thinks adherents of Islam should be barred from running for president. Read more at Alex Altman, " Time Poll: Voters like Obama, Not His Policies" August 19, 2010, http://www.time.com/time/nation/article/0,8599,2011799,00.html#ixzz1ICk7CTdc.

146 The full speech is available at http://whitehouse.gov/blog/New Beginning, last modified June 4, 2009.

147 Richard Wolin, "Veiled Intolerance," *The Nation*, April 9, 2007.

148 Erick Love, "Confronting Islamophobia in the United States: Framing Civil Rights Activism among Middle Eastern Americans," *Pattern of Prejudice* 43, nos. 3–4 (2009): 402.

149 Michael Ellison, "Sikh Shot Dead in US 'Retaliation' Attack" *Guardian*, September 17, 2001, 10.

150 Love, "Confronting Islamophobia," 402.

151 The relationships between Muslim immigrants, non-Muslim Middle Easterners, African American Muslims, and non-Muslim African Americans are complex and deserve independent research that goes beyond the scope of this book.

152 For more information about these see Nagwa Ibrahim, "The Origins of Muslim Racialization in U.S. Law," *UCLA Journal of Islamic and Near Eastern Law* 121 (2008):121–155.

CHAPTER 9

1 On this issue see a short piece by Asli Bali, "Turkey's Referendum: Creating Constitutional Checks and Balances," *Foreign Policy,* September 15, 2010, http://mideast.foreignpolicy.com/posts/2010/09/14/Turkey. For a more comprehensive version of this article, see Asli Bali, "Unpacking Turkey's 'Court-Packing' Referendum," *MERIP,* November 5, 2010, http://www.merip.org/mero/mero110510 .html.

2 "On Their Heads Be It," *Economist,* October 30, 2010, 56.

3 "Human Development Low in Turkey Despite Increase in Income," *Today's Zaman,* Nov. 6, 2010, http://www.todayszaman.com.

4 Ibid.

5 "Female Labor Force Participation in Turkey: Trends, Determinants and Policy Framework," Report No. 48508 TR, November 23, 2009, http://siteresources.worldbank.org/TURKEYEXTN/Resources/361711–1268839345767/Female_LFP-en.pdf.

6 *Basortusu Yasagi ve Ayrimcilik: Uzman Meslek Sahibi Basortulu Kadinlar* [Headscarf Ban and Discrimination: Professional Headscarved Women] (Istanbul: TESEV Yayinlari, October, 2010), available, in Turkish, at http://www.tesev.org.tr/default. asp?PG=DMK01TR11.

7 Muslim law students are very concerned that politicians targeted judges, who represent the top of the social hierarchy, with this bill. It appears very likely that the next step will address the lower levels of that hierarchy with the aim to ban the headscarf at all levels of the courts. See: Amani Hassani, "Hijab Ban in Danish Courts," Feb 9, 2009, www.islamonline.net.

8 *Lautsi v. Italy,* No. 30814/06, Nov. 3, 2009.

9 Article 2 on the "right to education" declares that "no person shall be denied the right to education. In the exercise of any functions which it assumes in relation to education and to teaching, the State shall respect to right of parents to ensure such education and teaching in conformity with their own religious and philosophical convictions."

10 For a strong criticism of the decision see *EJIL* 21, no. 1 (2010): 1–6. <author, title?>

11 Neil Addison, "Why This Ruling Should Make Us Cross," http://www.spiked-online.com/index.php/site/article/7839/.

12 Ibid., paras. 48 and 52.

13 Ibid.

14 Grand Chamber, *Lautsi and Others v. Italy*, 30814/06, March 18, 2011.

15 Ibid., paras. 71–72

16 Para 56.

17 It is remarkable that this harsh criticism of the court's decisions in headscarf cases only came up after the crucifix case. See Alessandro Amicarelli, "Two Weights and Two Measures: Comment on ECHR's *Lautsi v. Italy* Case Judgment," http://www.cesnur.org.

18 "*Lautsi v Italy*—A Lost Opportunity," European Humanist Federation, http://www.humanistfederation.eu/index.php?option=com_content&view=article&id=277.

19 Cited in Slavoj Zizek, *Living in the End Times* (London: Verso, 2010), 1.

20 Ibid., 1.

21 Elaine Sciolino, "The French, The Veil and the Look," *The New York Times*, April, 17, 2011.

22 Moreover, prominent Muslims, such as Fadela Amara, the founder of a women's rights group, have called the burqa "a coffin that kills individual liberties" and a sign of the "political exploitation of Islam." "No Cover Up," *Economist*, June 27, 2009.

23 For an excellent articulation of a political philosophy in relation to Muslim dress see Martha Nussbaum, "Veiled Threats?" *New York Times*, Opinionator, July 11, 2010.

24 Ibid.

25 Ibid.

26 A Muslim woman was not allowed to enter the French Embassy in Morocco and could not apply for a French visa because she was wearing a headscarf.

27 Nussbaum, "Veiled Threats?"

28 *Sahin*, paras. 160–162.

29 Nussbaum, "Veiled Threats?"

30 Cited in ibid.

31 Ibid.

32 "Irreconcilable Differences? Jacques Derrida and the Question of Religion," University of California, Santa Barbara, Oct. 23–25, 2003.

33 See investigative research on how anti-Islamic forces penetrate public servants and promote threats to rights and security in Thomas Cincotta, *Manufacturing the Muslim Menace: Private Firms, Public Servants, and the Threat to Rights and Security,* (Published by Political Research Associates, 2011), http://www.publiceye.org/liberty/training/Muslim_Menace_Complete.pdf. For the quote, see Report, p. i.

34 "U.N. Workers Killed by Afghan Mob," *New York Times*, April 1, 2011.

Selected Bibliography

Abdo, Geneive. *Mecca and Main Street: Muslims Life in America After 9/11*. New York: Oxford University Press, 2006.

Akbulut, Neslihan, ed. *Ortulemeyen Sorun Basortusu: Temel Boyutlari ile Turkiye'de Basortusu Yasagi Sorunu*. Istanbul: Akder, 2008.

———, Hilal Kaplan, and Havva Yilmaz, *Henuz Ozgur Olmadik*. Istanbul: Hayy Kitap, 2008.

Aktas, Cihan. *Bacidan Bayana; Islamci Kadinlarin Kamusal Alan Tecrubesi*. Istanbul: Pinar Yayinlari, 2001.

Aksin, Sina. *Turkey from Empire to Revolutionary Republic*. New York: New York University Press, 2007.

Allen, Anita. "Undressing Difference: The Hijab in the West. Book Review: Joan Wallach Scott, *The Politics of the Veil*." *Journal of Gender, Law and Justice*. 23, no. 208 (2008).

Amiraux, Valerie. "Speaking as a Muslim: Avoiding Religion in French Public Spaces." in *Politics of Visibility: Young Muslims in European Public Spaces*. Transaction Publishers, 2007.

An-Naim, Abdullahi Ahmed. *Islam and Secular State: Negotiating Future of Sharia*. Cambridge: Harvard University Press, 2008.

Anderson, Perry. "Kemalism." *The London Review of Books*, September 11, 2008.

Aras Bulent, and Sule Toktas. "War on Terror and Turkey." *Third World Quarterly* 28, no. 5 (2007):1033–1050.

Arat, Yesim. "Religion, Politics and Gender Equality in Turkey: Implications of a Democratic Paradox." Research report prepared for Heinrich Boll Stiftung, 2009.

Asad, Talal. *Formation of Secular: Christianity, Islam, Modernity*. Stanford, CA: Stanford University Press: 2003.

Baker, Christina A. "French Headscarves and the U.S. Constitution: Parents, Children, and Free Exercise of Religion." *Cardoza Journal of Law and Gender*, no. 13 (2007): 341–368

Bali, Asli. "Cultural Revolution as Nation Building: Turkish State formation and Its Enduring Pathologies." Unpublished essay, February, 2009.

Bauman, Zigmund. *Liquid Modernity.* Cambridge: Polity Press, 2000.

Bayoumi, Moustafa. *How Does It Feel to Be a Problem?* Penguin Press, 2008.

Benhabib, Seyla. "Models of Public Space: Hannah Arendt, the Liberal Tradition and Jurgen Habermas." In *Habermas and Public Sphere,* ed., Craig Calhoun. Cambridge: MIT Press, 1993.

———. *The Claims of Culture.* Princeton, NJ: Princeton University Press, 2002.

Belge, Ceren. "Friends of the Court: The Republican Alliance and Selective Activism of the Constitutional Court of Turkey." *Law and Society Review* 40 (2006): 652–92.

Berger, Peter L., ed. *The Desecularization of the World.* Washington, DC: Ethics and Public Policy Center, 1999.

Berghahn, Sabine, and Petra Rostock. *"Cross National Comparison Germany,"* Unpublished report produced for "Values, Equality and Differences in Liberal Democracies" (VEIL), a 6th Framework Project of the European Commission, 2008. www.veil.org.

———. "Cultural Diversity, Gender Equality—The German Case." Conference paper, Amsterdam, June 8–9, 2006. http://www.fsw.vu.nl/en/images/.

Berkes, Niyazi. *The Development of Secularism in Turkey.* New York: Routledge, 1998.

Bleiberg, Benjamin D. "Unveiling the Real Issue: Evaluating the European Court of Human Rights Decision to Enforce the Turkish Headscarf Ban in *Leyla Sahin v. Turkey." Cornell Law Review* 91 (2005): 129–162.

Bouteldja, Chaambi. "Integration, Discrimination and the Left in France: A Roundtable Discussion." *Race and Class* 49, no.3 (2008).

Bouzar, Dounia, and Kada Saida. "One Wearing the Hijab, the Other Not." IHRC Report, 2007. www.ihrc.org.

Bowen, John R. *Why the French Don't like Headscarves: Islam, the State and Public Space.* Princeton, NJ: Princeton University Press, 2007.

Bower, Bruce. *While Europe Slept: How Radical Islam is Destroying the West from Within.* New York: Doubleday, 2006.

Bozdogan, Sibel, and Kasaba Resat, eds. *Rethinking Modernity and National Identity in Turkey.* Seattle: University of Washington Press, 1997.

Bozkurt, Gulnihal. "The Reception of Western European Law in Turkey: From the Tanzimat to the Turkish Republic, 1839–1939." *Der Islam* 75 (1998): 295.

Brauch, Jeffry A. "The Margin of Appreciation and Jurisprudence of the European Court of Human Rights: Threat to Rule of Law." *Columbia Journal of European Law* 113, 116 (2004–5).

Brugger, Winfred, and Michael Karayanni, eds. *Religion in the Public Sphere: A Comparative Analysis of German, Israeli, American and International Law.* Germany: Springer: 2007.

Bursali, Orhan. *Turban Kadin Sorunu mu, Erkek Sorunu mu?* Ankara: Cumhuriyet Kitap, 2008.

Buruma, Ian. *Murder in Amsterdam: The Death of Theo Van Gogh and the Limits of Tolerance.* New York: Penguin Press, 2006.

Cagatay, Neset. *1923 the beri Turkiyede Islamci Hareketler.* Ankara: Ankara Universitesi Yayinlari, 1972.

Cagatay, Selin. *Kemalizm ya da Kadinlik: Cagdas Kadinin Basortusuyle Imtihani.* Master thesis, Istanbul Bilgi Universitesi, 2008.

Caglar Bakir. *Insan Haklari Avrupa Sozlesmesi Hukukunda Turkiye,* Turkiye Bilimler Akademisi Forumu, no.6. Ankara: Tubitak Matbaasi, 2002.

CAIR. *The Status of Muslim Civil Rights in the United States: Unequal Protection,* 2005.

Caldwell, Paulette M.. "Intersectional Bias and the Courts: The Story of *Rogers v. American Airlines.*" In *Race Law Stories,* eds. Rachel F. Moran and Devon W. Carbado. New York: Foundation Press, 2008.

Calmuk, Fehmi. *Merak Edilen Kizlar.* Istanbul: Merdiven Yayinevi, 2004.

Cangizbay, Kadir. *Cok-Hukukluluk, Laiklik ve Laikrasi.* Istanbul: Liberte, 2002.

Carkoglu, Ali, and Binnaz Toprak. *Degisen Turkiye'de Din, Toplum ve Siyaset,* Istanbul: TESEV Foundation, 2006.

Casanova, Jose. *Public Religion in the Modern World.* Chicago: University of Chicago Press, 1994.

Cesari, Jocelyn. *When Islam and Democracy Meet: Muslims in Europe and in the United States.* New York: Palgrave, 2004.

Cesari, Josely, and Sean McLoughlin, eds. *European Muslims and the Secular States.* London: Ashgate, 2005.

Chamblee, Elizabeth. "Rhetoric or Rights? When Culture and Religion Bar Girls' Right to Education." *Virginia Journal of International Law* 44 (2004).

Charlesworth, Hilary. "The Challenge of Human Rights Law for Religious Traditions." In *Religion and International Law,* eds. Mark W. Janis and Carolyn Evans, The Netherlands: Martinus Nijhoff, 2004.

Cinar, Alev. *Modernity, Islam and Secularism in Turkey.* Minneapolis: University of Minnesota Press, 2005.

Cindoglu, Dilek. *Basortusu Yasagi ve Ayrimcilik: Uzman Meslek Sahibi Basortulu Kadinlar* [Headscarf Ban and Discrimination: Professional Headscarved Women] Istanbul: TESEV Yayinlari, October, 2010.

Cohen, Howard, and Martha Nussbaum, eds. *Is Multiculturalism Bad for Women? Susan Moller Okin with Respondents.* Princeton, NJ: Princeton University Press, 1999.

Cole, David. *Enemy Aliens.* 2nd ed. The New Press: New York, 2005.

Connolly, William. *Why I am not Secularist.* University of Minnesota, 1999.

Crenshaw, Kimberly, Neil Gotanda, Gary Peller, and Kendall Thomas, eds. *Critical Race Theory: The Key Writings that Formed the Movement.* New York: The New Press, 1995.

Dallmyer, Fred. *Dialogue Among Civilizations.* New York: Palgrave, 2002.

Davison Andrew. *Secularism and Revivalism in Turkey.* New Haven, CT: Yale University Press 1998.

Davison, Andrew. "Turkey, a Secular State? A Challenge of Description." *South Atlantic Quarterly* 102, nos. 2–3 (2003): 333–350.

Deringil, Selim. *The Well Protected Domains: Ideology and the Legitimation of Power in the Ottoman Empire (1876–1909).* London: I.B. Taurus, 1998.

Dokupil, Susanna. "The Separation of Mosque and State: Islam and Democracy in Modern Turkey." 105 *West Virginia Law Review,* 53, 58 (2002).

Drzemczweski, Andrew. *European Human Rights Convention in Domestic Law: A Comparative Study.* Alderley: Clarendon Press, 1983.

Durham, W. Cole, Jr. "Perspectives on Religious Liberty: A Comparative Framework." *Religions Human Rights in Global Perspective.* Grand Rapids, MI: Eerdmans, 2000.

Duzdag Ertugrul, ed. *Mecliste Basortusu Mucadelesi.* Ankara: Sule Yayinlari, 1998.

Eck, Diana L. *A New Religious America.* New York: Harper Collins, 2001.

Eisenstadt, S. N. "The Reconstruction of Religious Arenas in the Framework of 'Multiple Modernities.'" *Millennium* 29, no. 3 (2000).

Elver, Hilal. "Gender Equality from a Constitutional Perspective: The Case of Turkey." In *The Gender of Constitutional Jurisprudence,* eds. Beverly Baines and Ruth Rubio-Marin. Cambridge: Cambridge University Press, 2005.

———. "Lawfare and Wearfare in Turkey." *Middle East Report Online,* April 2008. http://www.merip.org/mero/interventions/lawfare-wearfare-turkey.

———. "Religious Freedom and Women's Rights: Evaluating the Decision of European Human Rights Court of 2005." (Turkish) In *Turkiye'nin Ortulu Gercegi.* Istanbul: Hazar Foundation Press, 2007.

———. "Reluctant Partner." *Middle East Report,* May, 2005.

Erdogan, Mustafa. "Religious Freedom in the Turkish Constitution." *The Muslim World,* nos. 3–4 (July–Oct. 1999): 377–388.

Esposito, John, and Hakan Yavuz, eds. *Turkish Islam and the Secular State: The Gulen Movement.* Syracuse, NY: Syracuse University Press, 2003.

Esposito, John, and Dalia Mogahed. *Who Speaks for Islam? What a Billion Muslims Really Think.* Washington D.C.: Gallup Press, 2008.

Evans Carolyn. *Freedom of Religion Under the European Convention on Human Rights.* New York: Oxford University Press, 2001.

———. "The 'Islamic Scarf' in the European Court of Human Rights." *Melbourne Journal of International Law* 7, no. 52 (2006).

Evans, Malcolm D. *Religious Liberty and International Law in Europe.* Cambridge: Cambridge University Press, 1997.

Fogel, Ruben Seth. "Headscarves in German Public Schools: Religious Minorities are Welcome in Germany, Unless—God Forbid—They Are Religious." *New York Law School Law Review* 51, no. 3 (2006–2007): 618–653.

Fuhrmann, Willi. "Perspectives on Religious Freedom from the Vantage Point of the European Court of Human Rights." *Brigham Young University Law Review* no.3, (2000): 933.

Gemalmaz, Semih. *Turk Kiyafet Hukuku ve Tuban.* Istanbul: Legal Yayincilik, 2005.

Gerstenber, Oliver. "Germany: Freedom of Conscience in Public Schools." *International and Constitutional Law Journal* 3, no. 94 (2005).

Giry, Stephenie. "France and Its Muslims." *Foreign Affairs* 85, no. 5 (2005): 90.

Gole, Nilufer. *Modern Mahrem.* Istanbul: Metis Yayinevei, 1996.

———. "Secularism and Islamism in Turkey: the Making of Elites and Counter-elites." *Middle East Journal* 51, no. 1 (1997): 46–58.

———. *Melez Desenler: Islam ve Modernlik Uzerine.* Istanbul: Metis Yayincilik, 2002.

———. *Islamin Yeni Kamusal Yuzleri.* Istanbul: Metis Yayincilik, 2000.

Greenwalt, K. *Does God Belong in Public Schools?.* Princeton University Press, 2005.

Gunn, T. Jeremy. "Fearful Symbols: The Islamic Headscarf and the European Court of Human Rights." http://www.strasbourgconsortium.org/document. php?DocumentID=3846.

———. "Religious Freedom and Laicite: A Comparison of the United States and France." *Brigham Young University Law Review* (Summer 2004): 421.

Habermas, Jurgen. *Structural Transformation of Public Sphere.* MIT Press, 1991.

——— and Joseph Ratzinger. *The Dialectic of Secularization.* San Fransisco: Ignatius Press, 2005.

Haddad, Yvonne, ed. *The Muslims of America.* New York: Oxford University Press, 1993.

———. "The Post 9/11 Hijab as Icon" *Sociology of Religion* 2007.

Haddad, Yvonne Yazbeck, and John Esposito, eds. *Islam, Gender and Social Change.* New York: Oxford University Press, 1998.

Haddad, Yvonne Yazbeck, and Adair Lummis. *Islamic Values in the United States: A Comparative Study.* New York: Oxford University Press, 1987.

Haddad, Yvonne Yazbeck, Kathleen M. Moore, and Jane I. Smith, eds. *Muslim Women in America.* New York: Oxford University Press, 2006.

Hallward, Maia Carter. "Situating 'Secular': Negotiating the Boundary between Religion and Politics." *International Political Sociology* (2008): 1–16.

Heinig, Hans Michael. "The Headscarf of a Muslim Teacher in German Public Schools." In *Religion in the Public Sphere.*

Hooper, Talvikki. "The Leyla Sahin v. Turkey Case before the European Court of Human Rights." *Chinese Journal of International Law* 5, no. 3 (2006): 719–722.

Human Rights Watch. *Discrimination in the Name of Neutrality: Headscarf Bans for Teachers and Civil Servants in Germany.* Human Rights Watch Report, 2009.

Hunt Krista, and Kim Rygiel, eds. *(En)Gendering the War on Terror.* London: Ashgate Press, 2006.

Hurd, Elizabet Shakman. *The Politics of Secularism in International Relations.* Princeton, NJ: Princeton University Press, 2008.

Jackson Vicki J., and Mark Tushnet, eds. *Comparative Constitutional Law*. New York: Foundation Press, 2006.

Jonker, Gerdien, and Valerie Amiraux, eds. *Politics of Visibility: Young Muslims in European Public Spaces*. New Jersey: Transaction Publishers, 2006.

Joppke, Christian. *Veil: Mirror of Identity*. Cambridge, UK: Polity, 2009.

Kaboglu, Ibrahim, ed. *Laiklik ve Demokrasi*. Ankara: Imge Kitabevi, 2001.

Karpat, Kemal. *The Ottoman States and its Place in World History*. Leiden: Brill, 1974.

———, ed. *Osmanli Gecmisi ve Bugunun Turkiyesi*. Istanbul: Bilgi Universitesi Yayinlari, 2004.

Keaton, Trica Danielle. *Muslim Girls and the Other France*. Bloomington: Indiana University Press, 2006.

Keyman, Fuat. "Modernity, Secularism and Islam: The Case of Turkey." *Theory, Culture and Society* 24, no. 2 (2007): 215–234.

———, ed. *Remaking Turkey: Globalization, Alternative Modernities, and Democracy*. Boulder, CO: Rowman and Littlefield, 2007.

Kili, Suna. *Ataturk Devrimi, Bir Cagdaslasma Modeli*. Kultur Yayinlari, 8. Baski, 2007.

Kirik, Hikmet. *Turban Sorunu? Kamusal Alan ve Demokrasi*. Istanbul: Salyangoz Yayainlari, 2007.

Klausen, Jytte. *The Islamic Challenge: Politics and Religion in Western Europe*. New York: Oxford University Press, 2005.

Koenig, Matthias. "Religion and Public Order in Modern Nation States: Institutional Varieties and Contemporary Transformation." In *Religion in the Public Sphere*.

Koker, Levent. *Modernlesme Kemalizm ve Demokrasi*. Istanbul: Iletisim Yayinlari, 8. Baski, 2004.

Kologlu, Orhan. *Cilbabtan Turbana: Turkiyede Ortunmenin Seruveni*. Istanbul: Pozitif Yayinlari, 2008.

Kucukcan, Talip. "State, Islam, and Religious Liberty in Modern Turkey: Reconfiguration of Religion in the Public Sphere." *Brigham Young University Law Review*, no. 2 (2003): 475–507.

Kymlica, Will. *Multicultural Odysseys: Navigating the New International Politics of Diversity*. New York: Oxford University Press, 2007.

Lopez, Ian Haney. *White by Law: The Legal Construction of Race*. New York: New York University Press, 1996.

Mahmood, Saba. *Politics of Piety: The Islamic Revival and the Feminist Subject*. Princeton, NJ: Princeton University Press, 2005.

Malik, Jamal, ed. *Muslims in Europe: From Margin to Center*. New Jersey: Transaction Publishers, 2004.

Mardin, Serif. "Projects as Methodology: Some Thoughts on Modern Turkish Social Science." In *Rethinking Modernity and National Identity in Turkey*, eds., Bozdogan Sibel and Resat Kasaba 64–80, Seattle: University of Washington Press, 2000.

———. *Religion and Social Change in Modern Turkey*. New York: Oxford University Press, 1989.

Mazlumder. *Basortusu Sorunu: Olaylar/Belgeler/Anilar,* 2inci Basim, Insan Haklari ve Mazlumlar icin Dayanisma Dernegi. Ankara: Mazlumder Yayini 1998.

———. *Basortusu Raporu,* Insan Haklari ve Mazlumlar icin Dayanisma Dernegi. Ankara, 2007.

McCrudden, Christopher. "Human Rights and Judicial Use of Comparative Law." In *Judicial Comparativism in Human Rights Cases,* ed. Orucu, UK: Esin British Institute of International and Comparative Law, 2003.

McGoldrick, Dominic. *Human Rights and Religion: The Islamic Headscarf Debate in Europe.* Oxford, UK: Hart Publishing, 2006.

Modood Tariq. *Multicultural Politics: Racism, Ethnicity, and Muslims in Britain.* Minneapolis: University of Minnesota Press, 2005.

———. *Multiculturalism.* Cambridge, UK: Polity, 2007.

Moghissi Haideh. *Muslim Diaspora: Gender, Culture and Identity.* London: Routledge, 2006.

Moore, M. Cathleen. *Al Mughtaribun: American Law and Tranformation of Muslim Life in the United States.* Albany, NY: SUNY Press, 1995.

———. "Visible though the Veil: The Regulation of Islam in American Law." *Sociology of Religion* 68, no. 3 (2007).

Motha, Steward. "Veiled Women and the Affect of Religion in Democracy." *Journal of Law and Society* 34, no.1 (March 2007): 139–62.

Mecham, R. Q. "From the Ashes of Virtue, a Promise of Light: The Transformation of Political Islam in Turkey." *Third World Quarterly* 25, no. 2 (2004): 339–358.

Modood, Tariq. "Anti Essentialism, Multiculturalism, and the 'Recognition' of Religious Groups." *Journal of Political Philosophy* 6 (1998): 378–399.

Modood, Tariq, Anna Triandafyllidou, and Richard Zapata-Barrero, eds. *Multiculturalism, Muslims and Citizenship: A European Approach.* London: Routledge, 2006.

Navarro-Yashin, Yael. *Faces of the State: Secularism and Public Life in Turkey.* Princeton, NJ: Princeton University Press, 2002.

Norris, Pippa, and Ronald Inglehart. *Sacred and Secular: Religion and Politics Worldwide.* Cambridge: Cambridge University Press, 2004.

Nussbaum, Martha. "Veiled Threats?" *New York Times,* July 11, 2010.

Oguzhan, Zekiye. *Bir Basortusu Gunlugu.* Istanbul: Iz Yayincilik, 1998.

Onis, Ziya. "Political Islam at the Crossroads: From Hegemony to Co-existence." *Contemporary Politics* 7, no. 4 (2001): 281–298.

Open Society Institute. *Muslims in the EU Cities Report: France, 2007.* EU monitoring and Advocacy Program.

Orucu, Esin. *Critical Comparative Law: Considering Paradoxes for Legal Systems in Transition.* Deventer: Kluwer, 1999.

———. "The Impact of European Law on the Ottoman Empire and Turkey." *European Expansion and Law,* eds. Wolfgang. J. Mommsen and Jaap De Moore, London: Berg Publishers, (2003).

———. "Law, Colonial Systems of, Ottoman Empire." *Macmillian Reference USA*, vol. 3, 717–719.

Ozbudun,Ergun. "Turk Anayasa Mahkemesinde Yargisal Aktivizm ve Politik Elitler." *Ankara Universitesi Siyasal Biligiler Fakultesi Dergisi,*Temmuz-Agustos 62 3 (2007): 257–268.

Ozsunay,Ergun. "A Model of Modernization through 'Reception of Foreign Law': Some Remarks and Evaluation of Ataturk's Legal Revolution." In *Ataturks' Legal Revolution*. Istanbul: Comparative Law Institute, 1983.

Pultar, Gonul, ed. *Islam ve Modernite*. Istanbul : Remzi Kitabevi, 2007.

Ramazanoglu, Yildiz, ed. *Osmanlidan Cumhuriyete Kadinin Tarihi Donusumu*. Istanbul: Pinar Yayinlari, 2nci Baski, 2000.

Razack, Sherene H. *Casting Out: The Eviction of Muslims from Western Law and Politics*. Toronto: University of Toronto Press, 2008.

Rorive, Isabella. "Religious Symbols in the Public Space: In Search of a European Answer." *Cardozo Law Review* 30, no. 6 (2009).

Ross, Catherine J. "Children and Religious Expression in School: A Comparative Treatment of the Veil and Other Religious Symbols in Western Democracies." In *Children in the Discourses of Religion and International Human Rights*, ed. Marta Fineman and Karen Worthingtton. UK: Asghate Press, 2008.

Rottman, Susan B., and Myra Marx Ferree. "Citizenship and Intersectionality: German Feminist Debates about Headscarf and Antidiscrimination Laws." *Social Politics* 15, no. 4 (2008):481–513.

Roy, Olivier. *Secularism Confronts Islam*. New York: Columbia University Press, 2007.

Sachsenmaier, Dominic, and Jens Riedel, with Shmuel Noah Eisenstadt, eds. *Reflections on Multiple Modernities: European, Chinese and Other Interpretations*. Leiden: Brill, 2002.

Said, Edward. *Covering Islam, How the Media and the Experts Determine How We See the Rest of the World*. New York: Pantheon Books, 1981.

———. *Orientalism*. New York: Vintage, 1979.

Schahter, Ayalet. *Multicultural Jurisdictions: Cultural Differences and Women's Rights*. Cambridge: Cambridge University Press, 2001.

Hurd, Elizabeth Shakman. "Political Islam and Foreign Policy in Europe and the United States." *Foreign Policy Analysis* 3 (2007): 345–367.

Sentop Mustafa. "The Headscarf Ban: A Quest for Solutions." SETA Foundation Policy Brief no.8., March 2008. http://www.setav.org.

Sisman, Nazife. *Kamusal Alanda Basortululer*. Istanbul: Iz Yayincilik, 2005.

———. *Basortusu Magdurlarindan Anlatilmamis Oykuleri*. Istanbul: Iz Yayincilik, 2004.

Skach, Cindy. "Sahin v. Turkey," *American Journal of International Law* 100, no. 196 (2006).

Shakland, David. *Islam and Society in Turkey*. U.K.: Eothen Press, 2000.

Spoth, Wilfried. "Multiple Modernity, Nationalism and Religion: A Global Perspective." *Current Sociology* 51, nos. 3/4 (May–July 2003): 265–286.

Star, June. "Islam and the Struggle over State Law in Turkey." In *Law and Islam in the Middle East*, ed. Daisy Hilse Dwyer. New York: Bergin and Garvey, 1990.

———. *Law as Metaphor: From Islamic Courts to the Palace of Justice*. Albany, NY: SUNY Press, 1992.

Taspinar, Omer. "The Old Turks' Revolt: When Radical Secularism Endangers Democracy." *Foreign Affairs*, November–December 2007.

TBMM Komisyonu. *Guneydogu ve Turban Tartismasi*. Istanbul: Gorus Yayinlari, 1992.

Tehranian, John. "Performing Whiteness: Naturalization Litigation and the Construction of Racial Identity in the United States." *Yale Law Journal* 109 (2000): 842.

Toprak, Binnaz, Irfan Bozan, Tan Morgul, and Nedim Sener. *Being Different in Turkey: Religion, Conservatism and Otherization*. Research Report on Neighborhood Pressure. Istanbul: Bogazici University and Open Society Foundation, 2009.

Tunaya, Tarik Zafer. *Turk Politik Yasaminda Batililasma Hareketleri*. Yedigun Matbaasi, 1960.

Turam, Berna. *Between Islam and the State: The Politics of Engagement*. Stanford, CA: Stanford University Press, 2007.

Turkiyenin Ortulu Gercegi: Basortusu Yasagi Alan Arastirmasi. Hazar Vakfi, 2007.

Turkone, Mumtaz. *Turk Modernlesmasi*. Lotus Yayinlari, 2003.

Ubicini, M. A. (Ceviren Cemal Aydin) *Osmanli'da Modernlesme Sancisi*. Istanbul: Timas Yayinlari, 1998.

Van der Vyver, Johan D., and John Witte, Jr., eds. *Religious Human Rights in Global Perspective: Legal Perspective*. The Hague, The Netherlands: Martinus Nijhoff, 1996.

VEIL Project. *French Team Executive Report*. Available at www.veil.org.

Wallach-Scott, Joan. *Politics of the Veil*. Princeton, NJ: Princeton University Press, 2007.

Walterick, Stephanie. "The Prohibition of Muslim Headscarves from French Public Schools and Controversies Surrounding the Hijab in the Western World." *Temple International Law and Comparative Law Journal* 20, no. 251 (2006).

Westerfield, Jennifer. "Behind the Veil: An American Legal Perspective on the European Headscarf Debate." *American Journal of Comparative Law* 54, no. 3: 637–678.

White, Jenny B. *Islamist Mobilization in Turkey*. Seattle: University of Washington Press, 2002.

Wing Adrien, and Ozan Varol. "Is Secularism Possible in a Majority-Muslim Country? The Turkish Example." *Texas International Law Journal* 42, no. 1 (2006).

Wiles, Ellen. "Headscarves, Human Rights, and Harmonious Multicultural Society: Implications of the French Ban for Interpretation of Equality." *Law and Society Review* 41 (2007): 699.

Winter, Browyn. *Hijab and the Republic: Uncovering the French Headscarf Debate.* Syracuse, NY: Syracuse University Press, 2008.

Yavuz, Hakan M. *The Emergence of New Turkey: Democracy and the AK Party.* University of Utah Press, 2006.

Yilmaz, Halim. "AIHM Ictihadlarinda Din Ozgurlugu ve Leyla Sahin Karari." *Toplum ve Hukuk* year 3, no. 11 (Fall 2004):122–131.

Yilmaz, Ihsan. "Non-recognition of Post-modern Turkish Socio-legal Reality and the Predicament of Women." *British Journal of Middle Eastern Studies* 30, no. 1 (2003).

Index

$5 \cdot 3 \cdot 5 : 17.5$

$3 \cdot 3 = 9$ $3 \cdot 3.5 = 10.5$

$4 \cdot 4 = 16$

12

Made in the USA
Middletown, DE
07 January 2016